BEYOND IDEOLOGY

BEYOND IDEOLOGY

Religion and
the Future of Western Civilization

GIFFORD LECTURES DELIVERED IN
THE UNIVERSITY OF EDINBURGH, 1979–1980

NINIAN SMART

COLLINS
St James's Place, London
1981

William Collins Sons & Co Ltd
London · Glasgow · Sydney · Auckland
Toronto · Johannesburg

Smart, Ninian
   Beyond Ideology: Religion and the future of Western civilization.
   1. Christianity and other religions –
Buddhism
   2. Buddhism
   I. Title
   200   BR128.B8

First published in 1981
©Ninian Smart 1981

ISBN 0 00 215846 9

Printed in the United States of America

FOR MY BROTHER ALASTAIR
AND HIS FAMILY

Contents

Acknowledgements

I am grateful to the University of Edinburgh for the honour it did me in inviting me to deliver Gifford Lectures during the academic year 1979–1980. My wife and I received much hospitality from friends and members of the University, summed up in the kindly reception by the Principal and Mrs Burnet. Particularly too I should thank Miss Margaret Ewing, who organized our visits, Peter Malakoff who helped with the preparation of the manuscript, and Michiko Yusa who did much valuable work in assisting with the bibliography and also in preparing the manuscript. I am grateful too for support from the University of California, Santa Barbara, and from the University of Lancaster. My wife Libushka motorized my pilgrimages to Edinburgh, and made much of all this writing possible. I dedicate the book to my brother Alastair and his family: though he was raised, like me, partly in Glasgow, Edinburgh was also a city of inspiration for him.

NINIAN SMART

Santa Barbara, California
26 June 1980

Introduction

Western civilization finds itself in a new scene, and in troubled times. But though there are conflicts within its soul, it can look forward to a brilliant future, if only it can exploit the resources, both spiritual and secular, which lie both within and beyond the Western mind. This book, which has grown out of the Gifford Lectures which I delivered in the University of Edinburgh in the winter of 1979 to 1980, is an attempt to bring certain insights drawn from the history of religions to bear on the task of framing a worldview which synthesizes important ingredients both from East and West and from individual experience and secular politics. We live in a planetary place now, a kind of global city, in which communications have bound the world into a tight ball, and in which the great cultures of the past, and the differing cultures and political systems of the present, are in continuing and intimate interplay.

To the end of weaving together a worldview, I first survey the situation of the religions and ideologies of the contemporary planet. I make use of history-of-religions ideas, such as the analysis of myth, in order to illuminate the nature of the secular ideologies, notably varieties of nationalism and of Marxism. They are like the traditional religious symbol-systems and philosophies of action. It is true that their style is more 'modern' – but modernity itself is part of the contemporary Western symbol-system. It is true too that they do not typically have that transcendental reference – that pointing to the sacred Beyond – which typifies traditional faiths. But that itself invites us to consider what the critique from the Beyond means in our world. My view is that the critique from the regions of the divine or ultimate light (which shines both through Christian and Buddhist thoughts) is important for the secular ideologies – liberalism needs the concept of the sanctity of the person and the notion that politics is in the end about happiness (but why is the person sacred? and what is ultimate happiness?); while Marxist collectivism needs a theory of history to justify the sacrifice of individualism (but what faith beyond reason does this involve? and what after all is the nature of human history?). I see therefore the transcendental stance as one which continues the questioning which is such an integral part of modern experience, since science itself has flourished out of the critical questioning searching spirit.

Thus also in our global city traditional religions and modern ideologies all need to consider how they relate to science: it is not that religion reduces to science or that politics is exhausted by scientific knowledge of human behaviour. But rather the human being has to put her heart where her mind is, and her mind where her heart is. Existential questions cannot be answered in a void as though science has not produced its own magic, both in its mysterious unravelling of nature into tiny threads and squirts of energy and fantastical evolutions of living forms, and in its applications which mean that we now no longer sacrifice hecatombs to Poseidon or plead cheerfully with the Earth Mother, but instead do deference to electrical energy. Thus another theme which I treat is the relation of religion East and West to the scientific outlook. Briefly I see Christianity and Buddhism, here reinterpreted as complementary, combining with a critical personalism as being highly congruous with the spirit of science; while Marxism and some forms of traditional religion have in differing ways a severe difficulty in adjusting to the open world of scientific humanism. This is one reason why a new world-view, more planetary than just Western but drawing heavily upon Western ideas, has a more brilliant future than the tired forms of Marxism which are currently still so politically powerful and than the spiritually vital but intellectually problematic authoritarianism of some older religions.

Of all the secular ideologies in the modern world nation-alism in its varied forms has been the most compelling. Out of the nation and the state human beings have fashioned a sense of identity. Marxism and Islam – both international in scope – have, especially the former, served as wider ideologies which can yet help to recreate national pride. Thus Maoism in China, Ho's Marxism in Vietnam, the Marxisms of Cuba, Angola and Mozambique, Titoism – these have been used in the service of nation building and nation rebuilding. But once such liberation has occurred, that is liberation from foreign rule, other questions begin to emerge, about individual destiny and meaning. And the transcendental religions raise too a question mark over the new collectivism of the national idea, especially when reinforced by the dogmatic solidarity of the socialist sys-tem. The desire to maintain cultural identity is itself the engine often through which older values are subverted.

In a way, what I here describe and reflect on is the varieties of religious and symbolic identity. Partly out of piety towards William James, whose *The Varieties of Religious Experience* must be the most famous presentation in the Gifford Lectures series, I originally called this book *The Varieties of Religious Identity*. For if we take religion in its widest sense to mean the response to our cosmic and personal environment, then indeed at the heart of religion lies a kind of quest for identity: and so too at the heart of secular worldviews there lies a reflection about what the identity of the human being consists in. For it is for such

worldviews that people are often summoned to sacrifice
their lives and their happiness.

The liberal West has its own identity problems. Glory-
ing in self-criticism it yet sometimes seems to wallow in
confusion and doubt. But there is sense which can be made
out of the West's tradition and its modernity. Both its
religious past – its once existence as Christendom – and its
critical spirit can be brought together: and its modest
creation the history of religions can provide a basis for
reflecting upon a new synthesis of East and West.

The spiritual ideology which I here outline is already
implicit in much of the West's thinking and experience; and
some of it derives from the new encounter with Asia. It is I
believe a vital alternative to (though it need not always
remain hostile towards) the other main universalisms of the
planet, namely Marxism and Islam. It also is something
which with its power and pluralism can find a place for the
many small traditions scattered through the Third World
which have to struggle against the vast threats, sometimes
too the great cruelties, of the forces from the North. If I
had to find a brief name for the ideology here described it
would be 'transcendental pluralism': transcendental
because the sorrows and happinesses of humans, the quest
for identity in individual and in group, are illuminated by
what lies Beyond, whether looked at from the angle of the
Christian tradition or from the Eastern and Buddhist
tradition. It is a kind of pluralism because the desires of
persons are respected, the creativity which comes from
many different flavours of thought and feeling is prized,
and the security which comes from tolerant acknowledgement of different ethnic, national and spiritual traditions
conserves vital resources from the past in the outward
adventure of the future.

In California, it is easy to think of such a transcendental
humanism as something which overleaps the great ocean:
what we need after all is that which can be dubbed 'the

Pacific mind'. With luck it might even embrace tamed versions of the hard line monodoxies which act as alternatives and challenges to the Western and the Asian outlooks. For those who are not authoritarian have to find a place in their world for those who are, and that is the strength of the Pacific mind.

1

The World's Religions
and Ideologies in Interaction

The Views across the Pacific and the North Sea

When you stand on a tumbling grey cliff and look out from California onto the ocean the golden light bathes not only the blue swell but also the shadow of something unseen. You can sense Japan and the distant East, and the many islands of the South Pacific. Because this is California where the streets of San Francisco and Berkeley often show the sights and symbols of Japan and old China, and sometimes even the images of Mao and radicalism from the sixties, and where too the Eastern cults beg for cash and promise new journeys inwards and new gurus, you cannot help thinking about how the truths and values of the different civilizations will in the end live together. How in this new meeting of East and West can truth be grasped and sorted out? Does the planet hold some promise of a new way of understanding our life?

Because it is California you cannot either forget the swarms of ships that sailed out of San Diego and the Bay, heirs to Perry and Teddy Roosevelt, and went to do battle with Japan. You might even recall the great planes which took cargoes of drafted men to fight that late, somewhat bitter, fruit of Pacific destiny, the Vietnam War. But often the cruelty of war brings cultures together in the aftermath

17

to what we call the Eastern world (going West to get East, as we also often find) you sense the strange promises held by the encounter of civilizations lying on either side of the great Pacific rim. How can their relationships be judged?

The views from Europe are, and this is no surprise, more complex and are more loaded with questions from the past. If you stand on the cliffs of Kent you may feel the wind that scuds across the great northern European plain, from Kuibyshev and the Vistula to Heligoland and Hull; and you will see tankers passing empty down the Channel on their tangled way through Suez or round the Cape. In either case there is much for the mind to digest before it reaches the shores of Asia. To the East are the vast battlefields of Europe's great internecine conflicts – Flanders, Tannenberg, Kursk, Arnhem, Bastogne; and also the places of cold horror and ideological madness – the death camps of the Nazis, the Warsaw Ghetto, Dresden, the Gulag Archipelago. And if further south we follow the tracks of the fossil-bearing ships, we may pass to the Levant and Egypt or to the Persian Gulf, and before we ever reach South Asia proper we are reminded of Europe's strange feelings towards Islam, brother of Christianity yet often its deathly enemy, and now despite all its inner quarrels mostly united in its outrage at the planting of a Jewish state in Israel and Palestine.

Although it has been the fashion for us in the West, or at least in the modern West, and especially in America, to make a divide between religion and politics, and perhaps to think of the former as lacking the zealous power of its past and as having lost its intellectual grip, displaced by science and a rational ethic, the divide and the judgement miss the mark. The so-called secular ideologies – Nazism, Marxism, Maoism, humanism – may lack a sense of the transcendent or of spirituality in the traditional sense. Their purgatories and heavens lie on earth (the heavens being not above but in the future). But they too feed on myth and doctrine, and mobilize people's feelings with a sense of purpose and sacrifice, commitment and identity. Moreover, the cult of modernity, so gripping in our 'modern' world, bristling with economic theory, aeroplanes, equality, fertilizers, contraception, telecommunications and other excellences, is itself beyond science and reason, inhabiting still the regions of value and feeling. Modern is (we think) good: we wish to be 'with it' – and so we have the heavy symbolism of the new technology: sleek planes, mighty motorbikes, glass-wrapped architecture, silent (but alas now cracked) white nuclear domes. The subtle clash between modernity and older religion is something of which the Shah was rather roughly reminded. So secular ideologies themselves are replete with symbols and half-articulated values, and play in the same league (as we might say) as the traditional religions. The questions then which we might ponder, looking outwards across the wonders and terrors of recent European history, are questions which cross the frontier between religion and politics.

Religion and Ideology: an Ideological Distinction

The idea that there is such a frontier is often itself part of a modern ideology. Religion, it is said, is a private matter. It is for the individual and his conscience, and deals with what is 'existential', that is, what has to do with personal feelings and choice, and not with what is public and objective. This privatization of religion has as a main root the distinction between church and state which flowed from the desire to ensure religious tolerance and to defuse religious conflict. As I shall argue later, this stance is of the greatest importance for the dignity and freedom of human beings; but in the first place the principle has to apply beyond religions to secular worldviews. A major flaw in totalitarian systems is precisely that no distinction is made between church and state, only that now the Party stands for the church. And in the second place, the distinction between Church and State does not affect the question of how we should scientifically analyse worldviews. If a worldview such as Maoism has many of the formal properties of what hitherto has been treated as a religion, namely Confucianism or Buddhism, then it is important that scientifically they should be investigated and compared together. We should not be inhibited by a distinction which is becoming entrenched mainly in our language.

Thus an important part of the study of religion, which is the analysis of worldviews providing an interpretation for individual and collective experience, applies to the understanding of secular attitudes. Thus I regard it as an important part of my task to undertake an analysis of those systems of belief and symbolism which are most relevant to our contemporary condition in our global city, and especially in the West. I shall be delineating the various major worldviews of the planet as they exist in interaction today. But of special interest are those which promise to give us a new outlook which will be both Western and yet go beyond the West, and so will be truly a possible *world* worldview. But this is not to say that all beliefs can merge and come together.

As West and East and North and South intermingle and present to one another their various faiths and values, we may seek for some reconciliations perhaps; but there is also, acutely, the question of truth. Worldviews, as the name implies, relate both to us (our outlook) and to the world. They are the bridge between truth and action, and between reality and feeling; and they have to be judged at both levels. So the task which we have before us, if we wish to explore religions and ideologies, is a double one. On the one hand there is the analysis of the various structures of belief and feeling; and beyond that on the other hand is their evaluation. On the one hand we need to see how the various beliefs of men inter-relate and interact, and to see their points of compatibility and incompatibility. This is a descriptive task. On the other hand there is the reflection about them which may issue in a new way of seeing our world. On the one hand there is what used to be called the comparative study of religion and which now more broadly can be called the comparative study of worldviews. On the other there is what used to be called the philosophy of religion, which aimed to explore among other things the criteria of truth in religion, and which now we may more broadly extend to be the philosophy of worldviews. This is the more urgent today because we live in a global city, where ideas and powers jostle one another in its many thoroughfares.

The Global City

The earth has become in our time more or less a planet, a single globe: lonely perhaps as it wanders blue in space, but on its surface a loose human unity. The ancients, with their idea of the *oikumene* or inhabited world, may have had a similar sensation of unity in diversity; but it was partly based on an illusion, for quite other worlds lay beyond their world. When Jesus walked with his comrades beside the hot blue shore of the lake, the Buddha's message was already centuries old in the minds of the shaven monks of Sri Lanka. And men who went for a change of soul to the dramas of Eleusis or to the shining mysteries of Isis knew nothing of Confucius and the Tao. But now there is no world beyond our world. Our *oikumene* is spherical, closed, and there is no new frontier. True, we may hop grandly and with breathtaking ingenuity into space, but hardly further than the moon. That is almost nowhere amid the light years. And who can tell whether we shall ever communicate with other living beings beyond the solar system? It seems doubtful; and at best deep in the future. For our times and the times of our children and their children, the planet is now a single place, a kind of city, the geopolis. It is as if America were Manhattan, Russia the New Jersey side, Europe Queens, Asia the Bronx, Africa Brooklyn and Oceania Staten Island.

Thus it is that no culture or system of ideas can ignore others. The Christian is necessarily confronted by Buddhism and the Hindu mind. The Muslim cannot ignore Marx and the 'modernizing' West. The Polish Marxist cannot ignore Catholicism. Africa cannot ignore Islam. The Polynesian is in contact with Hindus. Our era then is one of planetary connectedness. In the last twenty years the ubiquity of the jet, the instantaneous availability of telecommunication, the migrations of peoples and guest workers – such factors have bound the city together very closely. Moreover it has done so as the culmination of a period of unprecedented change.

I call our planet a global city, rather than village. Villages are more homogeneous. They are less given to mayhem and riot than cities. And a city has quarters, and all sorts of graduations of power and wealth. It is industrialized and bureaucratized, as our world increasingly is. So I prefer the metaphor of the global city, which, as I say, like cities of the modern period, has grown and flourished, yet also bred squalor, amid great human changes. Let us briefly recite some of these changes.

The Mad and Brilliant Changes of the Last Half Century

For sentimental reasons I start in the year 1927, the year when I was born. In that year Chiang Kai-shek purged the Kuomintang of its red connection and prepared the way for Mao to switch the revolution into the mountains, the Long March and the sea of peasants. Stalin finally consolidated his hold on the Soviet Communist Party and got rid of Trotsky, thus opening the way towards his ruthless drive for steel and tanks, and the permanent change of Russia and

its colonies into a new ideologically controlled industrialized power. That year Hindenburg, hero of World
War I, and President of Germany's weakening democracy,
publicly denied German responsibility for the earlier
bloodbath, and helped to confirm thereby the feelings of
millions who were to turn to Hitler. Heisenberg announced
his principle of indeterminacy and so the ultimate decay of
the old physics: the new physics was almost ready to
conceive and to fashion the nuclear bomb.

Since then we have seen the Holocaust, which must
forever change people's views of the interface between
Christianity and Judaism. We have seen the heroism of the
Great Patriotic War and the terrible sufferings thereafter in
the last mad decade of Stalin's rule; and this must permanently alter our consciousness of practical Marxism. We
have seen the collapse of Germany and Japan, and their
resurrection; and this already changes the rules both of
European and Asian politics. We have seen the overwhelming victory of Mao and this must for the future mean a
different China, however much the ideology may be sof-
tened and adapted. We have seen the foundation of Israel
and the emergence of a new Islamic nationalism, which,
with oil, must greatly alter the balance of religious power.
We have seen the Indo-Chinese wars, which are potent to
disillusion all who contemplate them and which soiled the
reputations of Marxists, liberals and traditionalists alike,
and yet which also contributed to a new phase of American
consciousness. We have also seen the bombers turned into
civilian jets, and radar into new methods of communication: so that now intercontinental travel is more and more a
commonplace, and this may lead us to wonder what a
hundred years or five hundred of the jet will do for the
world, seeing it has done so much in thirty. We have also
seen Hiroshima, and that has forever altered the equations
of international conflict. Aggrandisements may in the end
fry us in the twinkling of an eye.

But of all the changes, the most significant, in relation at least to politics and to human identity, has been the spread of nationalism across the globe. Had World War II not already spoken so potently about the force of nationalism in its good and bad forms, we might have been blinded by ideology into thinking that the divisions of the world are essentially economic and ideological. Instead economics and worldviews are everywhere modified by the demands of ethnic identity and the struggles of the world are more often than anything to do with nationhood and ethnicity – the Basques, the Irish, the Cypriots, the Palestinians, the Kurds, the Bengalis, the Vietnamese, the Somalis, the Algerians: all these and many other groups have been fighting in order to establish some vision of national independence.

So we have a certain dialectic of change in the last fifty years. The world has seen a kind of tribal fighting, nation against nation, empire versus empire: but in the name of freedom to establish separateness. But the very conflicts have helped to accelerate the technologies which have drawn the planet into a close bound whole. The lesson is clear, and I shall come to it later. But we need to see these divisive and binding forces at work together. So now because of the mutation which has occurred in the means of transport and communication over the last three decades (jets, supertankers, container ships, satellites, television) there has been decisively created a world economy, whose parts, though different in design, interact in a holistic manner.

The price of wool in Australia has early effects in Helsinki. Drought in Kazakhstan affects the Iowan farmer. A riot on the Persian Gulf sends tremors through Wall Street. New blueprints in Osaka will cut car prices in Ireland. Research in silicon circuits stores up changes in the whole industrial world. So we now exist in a 'world system', which I call the global city. Since the arrival of this new order has been in great part due to the clash and inspiration of a variety of worldviews, one may also note another paradox. Very often the rapid change itself helps to amplify the effect of that primordial search for security and aggrandisement that so often lives behind the sophisticated ideas with which we interpret the world to ourselves.

The Relationship of Worldviews: a Matter of Flesh and Blood

Though it is profoundly important to take a calm and scientific view of the actual worldviews which humans hold, and though it is unwise to rush to judgement before grasping the nature of the religious and secular traditions and ideologies with which the various peoples and groups in the world express their values, it is also important to recognize that the issues transcend mere scholarship and philosophy: or perhaps I should turn that statement around and say that in regard to these living, often bitter, interactions between commitments and identities, scholarship and philosophy begin to clothe themselves in flesh and blood. For the question of how Buddhism and Marxism relate to one another within the material world is not just a philosophical topic. It is not something which, serious as it may be, is resolved only at the level of thought and insight. The shocks of change in Tibet and the flight of the Dalai Lama were the results of action driving against the grain of the Buddhist quest. The militancy of Marxist atheism can find expression in camps and shot priests. The agnosticism of the Western liberal can also issue in arrogances of power, as in the bombing of Cambodia. So the problems of worldview in our divided planet are practical ones, and have to do with human happiness and suffering. Those questions cross, as I have stated, the borders between religion and politics, and between the transcendent and the secular. But my exploration of the problem of worldviews will start with the religions, and then move to the ideologies. But whether we speak of religions or ideologies, we speak of identity and location: for human beings are restless without placement and a sure feeling of who and where they are.

Thus a worldview can be seen as to do with a triangle. One corner is the individual; another is his or her fellows; another is the cosmos. The fully satisfying myth or doctrine tells a person where he is in relation to society and the universe, and what the true constitution of his self is. Thus the old myth of *Genesis* worked as a resonant triangle. It shows forth the divine origin of the cosmos, something of mankind's origin and nature, and starts the linked story which relates people here and now to the ancestral Adam. It is true that the story of Adam's temptation and fall may be interpreted as showing that there is something deeply wrong in our nature and in my own being: but that too can be satisfying, for in stating the disease already the story may hint at the remedy. That there is evil in my life is alas obvious: its diagnosis however permits hope. But because the way in which modern ideologies function is more likely to be opaque to us, given the sharp divide between religion and the secular which we (ideologically as I have said) make, it is useful to begin our analysis of the spiritual and mythic aspects of worldviews, and of the way they relate to a sense of identity, with the religions. So the first part of my exploration will concern itself with Christianity and Buddhism. The reason for my choosing these two traditions to compare will come out shortly. But before we begin on that phase of our analytic and reflective voyage, it is useful to chart the state of belief-systems in the world today. For it is in the ambience of that real world that the process of philosophizing must occur.

Eastern Worldviews Today

The Eastern religions, and in particular Buddhism, have had considerable success since World War II in making a mark in the Western world. When I was learning Chinese in 1945 it was indeed a strange and surprising thing to do, and well in line with what friends expected of the mysteries of the Intelligence Corps. When ten years later I embarked on Sanskrit and Pali it was still something only a tiny minority would think of doing. Now it is almost easier to find a student of Sanskrit than of Latin. This impact of Eastern religions has various causes which need not now be uncovered. But it masks a fact on the other side. For while Buddhism may be fashionable in California and even on the wilder shores of Kent, it has undergone great traumas in some of its more traditional lands. It has been overlaid, though not entirely eliminated, in China and Tibet. It has no freedom in Vietnam and North Korea. It has been decimated in Kampuchea and its Laotian future is obscure. In Japan, Thailand, Burma and Sri Lanka it retains vigour, to be sure; but it has all the same suffered greater catastrophes than any other religion in the modern world, other than Judaism. Its dependence on the monastery exposes it to ready control and destruction, as the story both of Islam in North India and Marxism in East Asia shows. So we find here a paradox. This noble and subtle system of ideas and complex religious organism which represents perhaps the most vital force within Asian culture capable of responding to, and standing up to, the seductive and forceful secular philosophies of the West, is under assault through much of its Asian territory. The reasons we shall explore, but for the time being can be reduced to this fact – that Buddhism had not the brutal energy to reshape society in the face of the Western incursions which undermined the fabric of the old order in so much of Asia. It was the West's militant counter-ideology, Marxism, which was used by Chinese and Vietnamese nationalism to reconstruct mainland Asian power.

The case of Hinduism was somewhat different. That ancient and plural mass of often contradictory ideas and customs, kept in some kind of equilibrium by the fabric of caste, responded creatively to the British challenge. In a sense Hinduism is a new religion formed in the 19th and early 20th centuries. It had elements in its past – its chaotic inclusiveness, its subtle philosophies, its contemplative expertise, its prizing of learning, its fervent devotion, its ever fresh supply of holy men, its love of, and its scepticism about, images, its mysterious scriptures, its respect for power – which could be taken up and used in a great new synthesis. It was the great achievement of men such as Ramakrishna, Vivekananda, Tagore, Gandhi and Radhakrishnan to shape a mood and a pluralistic outlook which gave Hinduism both a positive world message and a role to play in the struggle for national freedom. All religions are true but the most true is that which recognizes (and has always recognized) this truth. If Christ is divine so also is Krishna and so in the last resort are all human beings. All images are useful and are all false. Such sentiments became part of the flesh of the new Hinduism. Its yoga and its *bhakti* have also come West, though perhaps with less lucidity and influence than have the like motifs of Buddhism.

Of lesser Indian religions Sikhism has dignity and some outward dynamic, even if it has become largely closed socially. Jainism, a sublime and subtle austerity, has no optimism about the conversion of the world. The Parsees keep alive the flame of Zoroaster, and form a modernizing part of the fabric of modern India. Such faiths become important footnotes within the greater text of the Hindu environment. Perhaps their situation will have much to teach us in the plural planet: for many such separately identified religious groups are likely to remain. But can their beliefs continue without being modified by some more embracing theory of religious truth?

To a great extent Confucianism and Taoism are sources of sustenance rather than real living organisms. Where in Taiwan and Hong Kong and elsewhere the old China persists after a fashion, the Taoist priest continues, and Confucian values are respected. But largely the Chinese, whether of the mainland or of the diaspora, are post-Confucian, post-Taoist. Both the old rituals and the old magic are in decay. This is not to say that there are not vast things to be learned from these ancient traditions. But they stand to modern Chinese civilization more as the classics did to modern Europe – sources from which something of value could be learned rather than a living, controlling culture and ideology. Confucianism is not on the modern ideological agenda as a living choice. It should be in our minds as a potent source of value, but that is a different matter. The dominant worldview, of course, of mainland China is Mao Zedong Thought. We shall later consider its roots. As a variety of Marxism it has (naturally) a Chinese shape: naturally, I say, because it was and is the great engine and expression of modern Chinese nationalism, resurgent in the face of the rampaging West and the erstwhile predatory Japanese. Not surprisingly it has as neighbours different varieties: the Vietnamese Marxism of Ho, and the grandiose Marxism of Kim. The history of the modern world tells us again and again that if you are in doubt as to the relative importance of ideological orthodoxy or national spirit, you should back the latter. The Soviets quarrel with the Chinese, who quarrel with the Vietnamese. The Jugoslavs quarrel with Albania and Moscow. Romania tries to keep its distance. If Czechs and Poles and East Germans are solid with Moscow it is because of the tanks.

Western Asia

Western Asia, in so far as it is not occupied by the USSR, is chiefly the scene of a reviving Islam. True, as within Marxism, there are ethnic tensions. The splitting of Pakistan was a critical example of the dominance of national groups over transnational religion as a constitutive basis of a state. The Kurds and Arabs of the new Iran likewise have proved restive minorities. Nevertheless the reviving vision of the Islamic State is manifest in a number of countries, and there is little doubt that Islam remains the single most vital reason why Marxism has little appeal in the Middle Eastern world. Like a great swathe Islam lies athwart the middle world, from the Western Pacific through Indonesia and Malaysia and into north India, Western Asia and North Africa, as far as Dakar: only Hindu India intervenes, and indigestible parts of Palestine and the Lebanon. It makes progress still in Africa. But it is interesting that somehow Christianity and Islam have exhausted their powers of mutual encroachment. Rather rarely does the Westerner become a Muslim, save for marriage or among blacks; still more rarely does the Muslim become a Christian: though the Muslim often enough becomes Westernized, leaving his old faith behind for a kind of utilitarianism. It is as if the three religions claiming descent from Abraham are destined to live together in a wary symbiosis (save where Islam sees in Judaism a form of Zionism and seeks therefore to wipe it out).

Judaism has, as a consequence of the Holocaust and of other tragic events, found its chief home in the Western democracies, and in the United States above all, of course. But the establishment of Israel has given it a different dynamic. Both the secularized Jew and the religious one must feel a special tie to the new State. Next year in Jerusalem is not next year anywhere else. But the Holocaust has given a special urgency to the reconsideration of Jewish-Christian relations. Many of the roots of anti-Semitism were Christian. But it should also be seen that violent nationalism was almost bound to be anti-Jewish: the logic of nationalism pointed towards the hounding of minorities, but whereas Armenians, Hungarians in Transylvania, Germans in Czeckoslavakia and so on had a majority place as well as a minority outreach, the Jews were in the national sense rootless, everywhere a minority in the heady upspringing of the nationalisms of Central and Eastern Europe.

Christianity at Large

It is convenient to see Christianity in five forms. There is the Christianity of Protestantism which has played such a large part in the formation of modern Western democracy. This success in bringing forth modernity has given it a puzzling relationship to liberalism and scientific humanism, its somewhat unexpected children. There is the Catholicism of Europe and a wider world, which embraces various conflicting incarnations: in the democracies Catholicism adopts more and more the style of Protestantism; in Poland and Hungary it is more conservative in its struggles with the State; in Latin America it is strongly caught up with revolution and redicalism, though institutionalized also in the older repressive forms of the post-colonial Church. Thirdly, there is Eastern Orthodoxy, greatly under the oppressive canopy of Marxist government, in disarray in Russia, revived in Romania tremendously, more influential through its various contacts with ecumenism. Fourth, there are the numerous new Christian movements in Africa, a great laboratory of the spirit in which old ethnicities and the Gosple are in creative interaction. Fifth, there is the non-European Christianity of ancient times – Copts, Nestorians and others, reminders of other heritages than that of the Roman Empire and the European matrix of the domin-

ant types of the faith. Both for historical and for logical
reasons, the main question on the agenda of modern Christianity is its relation to the secular ideologies: to liberalism,
to science, to Marxism. Much of the technical philosophy
of religion (whether out of linguistic philosophy or out of
Existentialism) is secretly or openly about the interface
between older faith and the worldview of scientific humanism. Liberation theology which relates to the torments of
Latin American poverty and exploitation is a debate about
Christianity and the Marxist analysis of capitalism. Yet, as
we shall see, the question of Christianity is a wider one: for
more clearly we need to see how Christianity can have a
theory of history relevant to the now global city, the blue
plural sphere of the planet.

Outside of the traditional religions and the ideologies of
Marxism, nationalism and liberal democracy there lie the
ideas and practices of the many smaller peoples, two
hundred and fifty million or so souls, who dwell in tribal
groups and have to face the great impact of modernity.
Such smaller peoples do not have much chance of surviving
with their old beliefs intact. It is noticeable how throughout
this smaller world there are new religious movements –
Peyotism, Cargo cults, independent churches. These are
new solutions to the problem of identity under threat.
Really the older ideas do not have much chance. They may
turn out to be resources of a kind, like Confucianism or like
the classical culture of Europe (as we have noted); but as
systems they can hardly stand up to the acid power of
modernity or even the evangelical, universal zeal of the
proselytizing great religions. What was proper and effective
in a small, nature-bound world can no longer serve in the
rich wide life opened up often so tragically to the tribal
mind. The secret lore of the Aboriginal, the shamanism of
the Eskimo, the lore of the Navajo, the myths of the
Gikuyu – these motifs must be transformed if they are to
stay alive. Remaining the same, they die. Many world-

views thus are in process of dying across this smaller world. We may see the new cults which replace them as attempts to mediate across the cosmic triangle – to adapt identity to truth, and truth to the new conditions of society.

Each Worldview Needs a View of the Others

Yet the arrival of the planetary city, that loose unity of human-kind in a finite, though unbounded, world, means that each religion, each ideology, must have a theory about the others. A mindless coexistence cannot be stable. If the Christian faith claims to be ultimate, surely it must have something to say about Buddhism and modern atheism; if Islam is what it seems to be then it proclaims a view of the religions of the Book and by implication has to theorize about the place of other faiths in Allah's dispensation; Marxism has its theories of the genesis and meaning of religions. All such views imply a perspective on the modern history of the planet. Whether any such view is coherent and persuasive then itself becomes a criterion of truth in worldview. Incidentally it should be noticed that the comparative or scientific study of religion – the history of religions and such attendant approaches as sociology and anthropology of religion – would play a strong part in the evaluative process. For the misfortune of many older views, including those of Marx and many of his successors, is that they diagnose religion without having a true or full grasp of the facts. Often they could not: the facts are only lately known, say in the last fifty years with the growth of study of the great religions backed by a rounded knowledge both of the texts and practices. (Muslims who chopped off the noses of Buddhas at some of the great shrines of Northern India were mistaken in thinking them to be idolatrous: how can you have idolatry when there is no God?)

But as is clear enough the question of the Beyond is not a

single one. Islam, Christianity and Buddhism (for instance) may point to that which lies beyond this universe, to depths within it which somehow are beyond even the subtleties of the atom and the quark. In a word they may be transcendental, not secular. But they differ severely, it seems. There are Sufis who may speak profoundly and sincerely about the transcendental unity of all religions, and that somehow in the speechless night of the soul even the emptiness of the Buddha is to be found. There may be those who quote the alleged writings of Dionysius the Areopagite and see in their noble negations a reflection of the *neti neti* of the Hindu. There are those who may seek to outline to us a Perennial Philosophy in which at their most profound level all the faiths are one. But is it indeed the profoundest level? And do we not see at the same time that Mecca is not Banaras, and Rome is not Kyoto, and that the crucified Christ is blasphemy beside the curving script of the Qur'an and that the enlightened Buddha asleep it seems on his side as he passes into the final emptiness of the Beyond is a person of greatly different character from the shrewd statesman and warrior Muhammad, creator of a new state and a new forceful empire upon earth? The great God of the Jews, the Christians and the Muslims speaks sometimes imperiously, sometimes in love and compassion, to those who have ears to hear. But nirvana does not speak. There is no 'Thus saith the Tao'. At times the great faiths seem to converge, their fingers as it were to signal the same moon. At other times they seem in radical conflict. Were they just a misunderstanding, these old divisions? And so we come back to the hard reality, that as far as we can see in this world of men, there are different Beyonds: or at least different maps of that other world. The problem of the plurality of religions cannot be evaded.

Buddhism and Christianity: Widespread and Mirroring

As for the first part of this programme, in principle the task of diagnosing the varieties of religion and of seeing how far some kind of complementarity might be found is one which should relate to all the great traditions. I am here being selective. I am going chiefly to consider, in the context of the global city, what is to be made of the relationship between the Christian and the Buddhist traditions, in some of their major forms. It is partly space; partly competence; partly sympathy; partly a judgement about value – it is such factors that have caused me to light upon these two. To explain why I must first be slightly autobiographical. But as I shall try to show there are also more 'objective' reasons for this choice. These two faiths are clearly of astounding significance for the history of the planet, the one being the matrix of Western culture and science, the other the chief spiritual force in the majority of Asian countries at one time or another. But first let me be slightly autobiographical.

My first interest in Buddhism arose from two things. First, I was put to learn Chinese at the School of Oriental and African Studies in London as part of my army service, just after the end of World War II. But instead of ending up in China I was sent to Ceylon (Sri Lanka). Both countries began with C, enough perhaps for the War Office in London. But more important, Buddhism flourished in both. My later determination to learn Pali and Sanskrit arose not only from these encounters but also from a sense of the deep importance of Theravada Buddhism as a radical alternative to, not necessarily though as a challenge to, the theism of my somewhat Catholic Anglican background. An alternative, I say, rather than a challenge: by this I mean something which is personal but which I believe has a more 'objective' validity. In a period of rather dreary disillusion with the Christian tradition, and at a time when I was surrounded by rationalists of a sort, I found a new spirit blowing through the marvellous discourses of *The Questions of Milinda* and the poetry of the *Theragāthā*, and through the extraordinary parables and similes of the Suttas and the complex serenities of Buddhist thinking. I was a bit afflicted too by a sense of the tribalism of some of the religious debates of those days. The circumambient rationalism found its chief expression in the way Oxford philosophy was interpreted, which for all its many enjoyable glories and achievements was infected with a dogmatism and even authoritarianism not quite fitting the rational temper to which it often laid claim: there were Ryle, brusque; Austin, daunting; Waismann, wistful; Wittgenstein, unseen. So Buddhism came as a different wind. How could it be so different from Christianity and yet somehow, obscurely, show its affinity? It seems to me still that the greatest philosophical and religious question to be raised about the traditional cultures of the globe is that concerning these two religions, both multiple, so vastly different in origin, overtly conflicting in many concepts and practices. But are they perhaps in some way complementary?

Moreover, important as other faiths have been and other systems of thought, Christianity and Buddhism have had the most far-reaching influence on planetary history. There has been scarcely a country in Asia which has not felt the lasting imprint of the Buddha. Buddhism proved the major cultural ingredient in the histories of Sri Lanka, Burma, Thailand, Laos, Cambodia, Japan, Mongolia, Tibet and Nepal; it was a major force in India, and likewise in China, Vietnam and Korea. It was important too in Indonesia. It penetrated Central Asia. In brief, it was the single most vital spiritual force in South and East Asia. Even though Hinduism may have come to displace it in much of India, it yet left its mark on Hindu life and thinking. Not for nothing did the Buddha become an avatar of Vishnu; nor was it entirely wrong that Shankara was accused of being a secret Buddhist. With its strong philosophical fabric Buddhism retains the vitality to stand up to the forces of Western cultures; while its style of psychotherapy, its astonishing cosmology, its compassionate ethic, its theories of adaptation, its spirit of self-cultivation and its balance between realism and idealism make it seem subtly modern, ready to relate to modern science and to keep a sympathetic distance from rationalism. This modernity of Buddhism is sometimes quite striking in contrast to the crudities about the world which have often been inferred from the mythic cosmology of the bible. The analytic character of Buddhism is very different from the rushing spirit of the Bible. Yet for all the 'scientific' temper of Buddhism it was in fact, for various reasons, the Christian civilization of the West which gave birth to modern science and the industrial revolution. It is this fact, together with Christianity's astonishing spread over so many regions of the earth which gives Christianity its vast importance in the history of the global city. Christianity and Buddhism are, in short, two giants and greater in their influence and meaning even than the dynamic theocracy of Islam or even than the practical doctrines of Marxism.

Apart from the importance of the two traditions as giants of East and West, their enigmatic relationship, which has not been explored with a full systematic eye hitherto, presents to us some of the most sublime and challenging problems in the methods through which we should come to terms with descriptive comparisons. I shall describe some of these briefly in the next chapter, for they help us to see some of the fruits which our enterprise of comparison may yield.

Nationalism and other Identities

I have already spoken of Nationalism as an ideology. Actually it is a set of ideologies, or if you like a prescription for forming ideologies. A nation is a substance composed of matter and form. The matter is a language, a religion, a territory – the ingredients vary (and often the matter has to be brought together in the process of nation-building). The form is the consciousness of nationhood. That consciousness is reinforced and fed by myth and ritual. The myth, typically, is a special history, incorporating perchance a sense of destiny; the rituals are flag, anthem, battle, memorials of martyrs, presidential motorcades, poets and composers, ancestors celebrated. The nation state has become the dominant political form of our day, and though religion may help to furnish the matter of the nation it also often is subordinated to the demands of national substance and identity. If you have an uncle or great-uncle who died violently, the likelihood is that he did so for his country, not for Presbyterianism. Often too the nation is strengthened by worldviews claiming to be universal. Christianity is an ingredient in the civil religion of America. But it is Marxism which, because of its collectivism, helps most powerfully to unify the nation-state. The People easily becomes identified with (say) the Hungarian people; while the concentration of economic power through socialism makes for a centralism which while it may be tyrannical over individuals can give a strong sense of national identity.

Liberal democracy or democratic liberalism can, of course, take various forms; but it is by and large the ideology which shapes the thinking of the Western European countries and the nations of North American and Australasia derivative therefrom; it also informs certain Asian countries, such as India, Sri Lanka and Japan, and one or two South American nations. Theoretically its presence is much more widespread. Perhaps its thinking can be summed up as emphasizing individualism, human rights, an open society in which free expression of views is good for politics, science and the arts, and institutions whereby some control of those in power is exercised by the people at large. It is in this last area that its chief weaknesses lie: for instance, majority rule can mean tyranny over the minority if there are strong ethnic divisions in a society – for this reason liberal democracy on the British or European model is hard to implement in most artificially constructed Third World countries. Generally such countries as practise liberal democracy have evolved mixed capitalist-socialist systems and a welfare machinery. The relationship between liberalism and traditional religion is ambiguous, for on the one hand the idea of the sacred individual is in part a derivative from old notions of an immortal soul or of man being made in the image of God; on the other hand, liberalism has an iconoclastic temper and is critical of dogmatism and authority, and is often scandalously open in its legitimation of new sexual experiments and the like which do not jibe well with conservative religion and older rituals of human interaction.

In this panorama of worldviews and elements therein, there are also to be seen the many new groups: the cults as they are often called. The fact that the Western world harbours these so freely is both a tribute to and a criticism of its individualism. The forces of new industrial mobility, the solvents of youthful consumerism, the experimentation born of the desire for novelty and from the habits of criticism, the atomization of the family structure – these processes are an accompaniment of a kind of freedom; but they also bring great anguishes of insecurity. Individualism can place great loads upon the individual. The father and the guru are new popes to give security to individuals; the commune supplies a milieu in which responsibilities, because shared, are taken away. The load is thus lifted. Also, the cults can dramatize life, in a way that traditional religion often has ceased to do. Indeed to a great degree serious interpretation of history as having a significant pattern has been abandoned, in the West, to the Marxists.

Many liberal historians take such patterning as unscientific, while Christianity's salvation-history is somehow regarded as petering out (a well-chosen expression perhaps) at the end of biblical times.

The Understanding between Worldviews and a New View of the Planet

How then so far does my argument stand? The cliffs of California and Kent are places where we sense both the future and terrors from the immediate past. The very conception of a World War has heralded today's planet: a single, global city. In that city all the great religions and ideologies are in processes of interaction, some of them constructive, some of them violent. At the religious level some major traditions retain vigour: Christianity, shaper of the Western world; Judaism, noble and mysterious survivor of so many tragedies, none greater than the Holocaust; Islam, resurgent in that great swathe of lands from Dakar to the coasts of New Guinea; Hinduism, a new religion with the most ancient roots and maker of the modern Indian spirit; Buddhism subtle and profound Asian force, battered in some of its Eastern lands, finding new life in the Western world. And there are smaller faiths retaining old continuities, and new cults expressing new quests for identity. But most small-scale societies, and a number of ancient traditions, such as those of the Tao and of Confucius, have now become, by and large, 'classical' – resources to draw on rather than living organisms with life before them independently. Throughout the 'smaller world' of cultures whose strength is not enough to stand up head on to the huge forces of modernization (itself containing within it a set of values drawn from a technologically-suffused ideology) new religious movements grow, mediating the old worlds to the new. The traditional religions which retain real power pose the question of how far the modern world needs the transcendent. Though liberal democracy has been tolerant of that 'other world,' and rightly, for Protestant Christianity was one of its parents, Marxism has been on the whole aggressive in its attack upon religion; while for many folk, whether they have deep insight into scientific knowledge or only intuitive feelings about it and respect for its magic powers, a kind of scientific humanism has made the traditional faiths obsolete. Ikons are then, we may ask, destined to be collectors' pieces, and Buddha statues to be admired for their serenity and poise but not for their signalling of nirvana and the transcendent aspect of existence? Is the Gītā to be read only for its poetry and philology, and the bible to remain simply part of literature? Is human craving for the spiritual to be satisfied in music and paint, and men's mythic impulses illuminated only through drama and the film? So one major item on our agenda of exploration must be, in the new planetary world, the continued significance of those who point to the Beyond.

After all, there are some strange thoughts that rise to the mind of those who stand upon the cliffs and remember those wars and terrors which have helped to bring the globe into its blue unity. The new vision we have of our beautiful planet seen from outer space comes from the scintillating technology of the moon race. But this itself was born of two desires: one for an assertion of *machismo* – anything the Soviets can do we can do better. Another was the military use of rockets, inertial guidance systems, all the telemetry: the techniques could be used to cause Novossibirsk or Krasnoyarsk to disappear accurately in the frying of an eye. It is not a credit to secular ideologies that they should in our supposedly more enlightened age still act with cruelty and fear. Scientific humanism has not prevented the crime of the bombing of German cities. Nationalism has not prevented, but indeed encouraged, the Holocaust. Scientific Marxism has not sheltered men and women from the freezing terrors of the Gulag. Maybe we remember Rasputin too, and the bishops blessing war. We may remember more distantly the stakes of the Inquisition. Yet though there seems no way by taking thought that we can utterly protect ourselves from our cruel, stupid childishness, our ignorance and sin, we may yet pause to ask whether there are not spiritual resources in the great faiths which may help, like burning monks and nursing nuns, to moderate and challenge our evils. Certainly modern secularism has a mixed record, to put it too sweetly.

And another thing. The traditional religions refuse to face away. In Bucharest and Warsaw the churches glitter with a myriad candles. It may be in part a way of saying something to the great Bear, and it has much to do with national identity. But it happens. Conversely, where the pressures are not there, where life is in principle (one would think) very sweet, where food abounds and the good things of the planet, where technology and the car have solved so many of the problems of ordinary living – in such a place, the golden sun of the West is not quite enough. Nowhere more vigorously than in the globe's still most advanced and scientific nation, land of Nobel prizes and cyclotrons, of silicon and sociology – nowhere more vigorously than there do the new quests for Jesus, Krishna, the Buddha, abound. Sometimes those who live in Northern Europe forget the vigour of traditional religion and the siren sounds of new voices from the Beyond. A certain post-Protestant sangfroid, a feeling of working class alienation from the high traditions of the past, a certain smugness perhaps – these conduce to a sense that religion is somewhat of the past. Perhaps it is easy to think this in Gothenburg and Hull, in Bremen or Lille. But it is a special feeling, untypical of the spiritual passions of the world. Nothing perhaps stirs the blood greatly in these places, and one should be grateful for tranquillities and the harmless pursuit of a daily, quite prosperous, living. But as I say such a feeling does not reflect the genuine magic which the Transcendent still retains, whether in Cracow or San Luis Obispo, in Banaras or Qom, in Croatia or Fiji, in Osaka or Valparaiso, in brief: the idea of the Transcendent or perhaps I should say better the practice of the Transcendent is something which both can serve as a challenge to those whose heavens and purgatories are on this earth alone, and can say something about the quest for identity, once the material problems have for the most part been rubbed away.

And as we have seen, it is not possible simply to put the religions in a kind of superior ghetto as though they do not affect and are not affected by the new secular symbol-systems of the modern planet. Thus our exploration is into a range of pictures and a range of identities. The traditional religions must too have a view about these secular ideologies, and the latter about the traditional religions, and about each other. Even those societies, less concerned with the ideologies, but more tragically involved in fighting for ethnic traditions threatened by the tidal waves of Western and modern culture and technology, must place themselves and place their heritage somehow: and this means constructing at least a sketch of a general theory of their and others' existence.

In brief the global city is a place where each group must possess a map. There are no ghettoes left in that city, only enclaves.

Two Kinds of East and West

For various reasons, the major problems which the Western world has to face, of a spiritual kind, are to do with the relationship between the Christian (or post-Christian) West and the Asian East on the one hand, and between that West and Marxisms on the other hand. Sometimes it happens the phrase 'East and West' suggests the former polarity and sometimes the latter polarity. The first issue has to do ultimately with the relationship between the great Asian traditions and the Christian-cum-Jewish track of religion; the second has to do with the relationship between personalism and class collectivism. Both polarities are entangled with the forces of nationalism. And in turn all three are related to the North-South interaction: the way in which the more powerful industrial northern countries have inevitable effects upon the smaller-scale societies of the South.

Thus I wish to reflect upon these matters first from the perspective of the former polarity: to contemplate these two great transcendental religions, Christianity and Buddhism. The exploration will be quite a complex one. What I hope for is not that somehow the deliverances of the two traditions can be made identical or that they can be shown to have a secret single essence. But I would hope to show some of the dynamic reasons why they differ, and to show how aspects of the different dynamisms are like mirror images. There is no unknown Christianity of Buddhism or unknown Buddhism of Christianity. But there are convergences of experience and alternative ways of representing the Transcendent. Whether this will open up the possibility for Christianity of a new kind of natural theology, that is a new use of the cultural resources of the planet, in which Buddhist motifs are woven into the collage of a Western worldview; and whether by contrast it may be possible for Buddhists in their use of skilfulness in means – their capacity that is to adapt the teaching to the psychic condition of the hearers and the cultures as they develop – to attain a new synthesis. These questions belong to the further and philosophical phase of our exploration. But in the meantime let us address ourselves to the remarkable differences that the two great faiths display and to those echoes too which we hear mysteriously in Rome and Banaras, in Constantinople and Nara, and in Bible and Sutra.

If we look at the skies of Kent or California, or peer into the waves forming on the sea, is there anything we sense which lies so to speak behind or within them? When we gaze at one another in love or hate do we see anything beyond the body and the mind? We remain haunted by the sacred and cannot but reflect on the ways in which men have sustained and disturbed themselves by their intuitions of what lies beyond the strange veil of matter and experience. Should we forget those sacred echoes from great civilizations? Should we turn our gaze to solidarities here and now, techniques, fertilizers, the arts, sports, the glories of this world? Has the age of philosophical materialism truly arrived? Or are we still to learn something from the symbols and disciplines of the numinous and the mystical? It is in this quest that we are engaged. But it is a quest which is nothing if it does not engage with flesh and blood and bread and stone: unless, that is, it meets men's intuitions of the Beyond clothed in life and complexity, which is how they always have been clothed, for naked they are almost nothing, like a nude Emperor.

Our search is to try and discern better the facts. But it may also yield us, like other explorations, a map. And that may help us to live more easily in the labyrinths of the new global city.

That discernment of facts is not easy. The new shape of religion as a field of exploration is not clear to all. So before I directly pursue my gaze beyond the ocean I shall look in a mirror first, to see how seeing is and to delineate the methods of delineation.

2

Towards a Theory of the Configurations of Religion

Histories and Patterns

One of the great achievements of the modern mind has been the development of historical ways of unravelling the religious past. It has meant a certain distancing, a struggle even. Religions are ideologies; they call for commitments; they underpin security; they speak of certainty but often tremble; they are seen as treasures, and the guard dogs growl. The idea of looking more dispassionately at the sacred past, of deciphering the ingredients of what counts as revelation, of digging through hallowed ground – such an idea must arouse some hostilities. But the writing of the histories of civilizations and of religions serves the purposes of truth and clarity. But it could be all too dry if it were to cleave close to texts alone, and stones, and other documents, without trying to enter into the experience and attitudes of those whom it delineates. The history of religions is not just a set of chronicles, but chronicles with a soul. Facts are not just outer facts but inner ones too.

Sometimes the mode of apprehending religious facts which involves looking at and through the eyes of the believer is called the phenomenological method (though the term *phenomenology* also means much besides: sometimes it is shorthand for a particular philosophical slant on existence; sometimes it means the quest for a typology of religion, that is the classification of religious phenomena

46

into types). Bede Kristensen said that the believer is always right. This means that whatever I think of a believer's belief – be it good and true in my view or false and harmful or crazy or boring – I should as a historian, as a depicter of the human condition, try to bring out what the belief means to him. The rush to judgement breeds many errors: we think and act as if other folk believe what we believe, for we think we have the truth and are sensible, so that they (if they are sensible) will have the truth too. Or we think that they are simply not sensible if we detect that they do not in fact believe what we believe. We mistake them thus, too often, or despise them. The root of many foreign policy errors lies in this fallacious lack of empathy, this disastrous neglect of phenomenology.

The history of religions, then, involves depicting histories, but in a manner which involves empathy. It also – but more of this anon – involves a kind of structural delicacy, for religious acts and feelings occur in organic contexts, webs and skeins of beliefs, memories, associations. The history of religions is delicate and has a sensitive soul; and as such it represents a great achievement – a distancing, and yet a warmth; objectivity and yet subjectivity of spirit; description, but also evocation; method, but also imagination. It is one aspect of the nobility of the best of the humanities and the social sciences – a nobility which expresses itself in a willingness to enter into the experiences of others, and to go from a self-centred sense of what is the norm. It is because the science of religion has this warm inwardness and eschews the rush to judgement that I believe most passionately in its moral and intellectual claims upon us. It is not that we may in the last resort on these matters wish to suspend judgement. As academics, the historians of religion may wish indefinitely to do so. But we may also wish to be philosophers and reflect about the worldviews that we help to unfold and comprehend. But we must keep the two tasks separate in our minds.

But religious histories generate comparisons. For one thing the very transition in the imagination from one's own culture to that of another tradition involves the comparative method. For we use terms, categories, nuances from our own world in describing the other world. Often in the past great mistakes have been made by bringing Western concepts to bear on Eastern faiths, so it is important to bring comparison to the surface. By being aware of contrasts in assumptions and symbolisms and social values, a better method of empathy and structural description can be attained. It is when we think we are not being comparative that we are liable to make distortions.

But there is a second reason why comparisons sprout up through the tangles of history. It is because we detect or think we detect patterns, similarities. The love exuding from Krishna in the *Gītā*, the awesome power of the manifestation of the Divine Being in that same poem, the spirit of devotion and grace therein – such things suggest the question of their likeness to major elements in the Christian tradition. Are the similarities real? Do they arise from some diffusion, some borrowing? Are they independent manifestations of themes lying deep in the human spirit and its world? Histories thus move towards patterns.

Types and Organisms

The move through comparison to the discovery of patterns in religion promises us something philosophically, by the way. For as has been observed there appear to be certain patterns in religious experience which help to explain some developments in independent cultural traditions: the mystic finds an inner light in East and West, the shaman a wrestling with demonic forces in North and South, the prophet an apprehension of the numinous Other in desert and countryside, the saint the imprint of love in cloister and lamasery. If such comparisons hold up, they suggest some universal themes in religion and the possibilities of a cross-cultural approach to the question of spiritual truth. The transcendent finds operational meaning in the varieties of religious experience. But all that is, for the moment, by the way.

The first major problem of method which we meet as we move towards the discovery of patterns in religion lies in the fact of the organic nature of religious systems. This is so both at the level of ideas and at the level of practices and in the interaction between them.

Thus at the level of ideas, a given concept has to be understood in the context of a whole collage. In Christianity, consequently, the idea of sin or of grace is not there by itself: it is connected with the problem of men's alienation from God, and the history of the way this alienation has been remedied, by God's guidance to Israel, by his incarnation in Christ, by his continuing work through the Spirit in the Church. Think already how many key ideas are connected up: sin, grace, history, Israel, incarnation, redemption, Spirit, Church. Consider the Buddhist idea of *dukkha* – suffering as it is sometimes called, though 'dissatisfaction', 'illfare', 'unhappiness' are better ways of putting it. To understand it one has to see how craving and ignorance bring it about – ignorance of the true nature of the world, which is impermanent, and of the true nature of the living being, who is without soul or self. And this ignorance is only truly known by contrast with insight or wisdom which rids humans of craving, and follows from treading the Buddha's Path through virtue and meditation to the perception of emptiness. Consider here how many key ideas are linked up: *dukkha*, craving, impermanence, non-self, insight, Buddha, eightfold path, virtue, meditation, emptiness, and by implication liberation: *dukkha, tanhā, avijjā, anicca, anattā, paññā, bodhi, aṭṭhangika magga, sīla, jhāna, suññatā, nibbāna*.

Also, as it happens, there vary greatly the interpretations

of some of the key ideas: especially so in Christianity with the coming of the Reformation. There is no Christianity as a system, but rather systems. *Christianity* itself becomes a typological category, rather than the name of a single tradition, a pigeonhole rather than a name-tag.

The skein-like web of ideas in a system are related along a different plane to practices. One cannot understand what Buddhists mean by emptiness or insight without attending to the practice of meditation and reflection which typically form the process through which the liberated state is known in experience. Nor can one understand the idea of the creator in the monotheisms simply by thinking of a cause of the world: the creator is numinous, awe-inspiring, replete with special, sacred power. He is to be acknowledged through worship. Can one worship a bare First Cause, or prostrate oneself before a mere Prime Mover? By thinking there is an ultimate reality, can one experience the divine love shining through the sun, the willows by the edge of the brook, the hot sand under foot, the scent of the sage bushes?.

Thus doctrines are to be seen through the lens of practice, the optic of feeling, the glass of experience. They are to be seen too through the rites and sacraments through which the mythic dimension of religion is reenacted and made real in the souls of human beings and in the experience of the community. Christ, it is said, died for our sins, and being risen we may rise with him. This makes his death a thing of Good Friday: not something just to be chronicled but to be lived through again. And the resurrection is not mere corpse-revival, but something which is present at Easter and every time the Christian experiences the risen Christ. 'Jesus Christ is risen today' (not two thousand years ago, just: though *then* they too who felt it could use the present tense in the way the Christian does now).

Conversely, it is partly through the doctrines and myth

that the life and rites of the believer can be deciphered. The Christian at Mass holds in his head his own living web of beliefs; and he sees this Mass as a reenactment of *the* Mass. He places his actions now in the organic context of the Church as he understands it. The Buddhist in laying a flower before the statue of the Buddha does so because of a living web of the Dhamma in his brain.

So though we may make comparisons we have to respect too the contextuality. And often superficially similar organs may have quite different functions in different organisms.

Culture, Interpretation and Intra-religious Explanation

There have been those who have tried to centre religion upon a core experience: most obviously, the experience of the Holy, the numinous experience. Crudely, the argument has been something like this. If science has as its basis empirical experience, outer perception; and if morals rests upon moral experience, some special insight or feeling; then religion, if it has a separate basis, should have a basis in a special mode of experience. Now an examination of the data from the history of religions suggests that the numinous experience is vital and central, and can be found in different cultures and great traditions. Ergo we locate the basis of religion in the numinous. That one should take religious experience in the formation of religions and in their ongoing development and sustaining is, I think, correct, unavoidable. But to reduce it to a single type is wrong.

It does not, for one thing, explain the great differences between religion – the gulf between Emptiness and Yahweh. You do not find Emptiness or Nirvana speaking out of burning bushes, leading people in war, creating the world in seven days. The Buddha does not explain differences, and if we load those differences of interpretation on to varying cultures, different modes of interpretation, then

it cannot even explain what otherwise it might. For instance the awesomeness of God in the numinous experience
explains the response and propriety of worship, and it
explains why doctrine may stress the duality between God
and man, the great Otherness. But if doctrines of oneness
(say Advaita) essentially rest on the same core experience
the latter cannot after all be held to explain the Otherness,
etc.

It is hard to accept Otto's judgement. The numinous is
pervasive, important; but it is not, as he describes it,
everything. One at least has to add as important a quieter,
mystical, contemplative motif: the experience of the Cloud
of Unknowing, the dazzling obscurity of which Ruys-
broeck wrote, the Void of Buddhism, the stage beyond
perception and non-perception (as Buddhism also has it).
Now there is some controversy about mysticism and the
contemplative experience. Is it everywhere the same essentially (whatever that may mean)? Or is theistic mysticism
essentially different from non-theistic? At the moment I do
not wish to enter this controversy, though it will be
necessary to evaluate the position later. There is a tricky
nest of methodological problems to be faced, for how do
we, not having gained Enlightenment and being at best not
far along the way trodden by many saints, presume to
judge the glittering dark language which they allusively
use? Yet whether we say there are one or many mysticisms
they do seem different in style from much of numinous,
prophetic religion. A plural typology of religious experience allows us a certain rhythm in the explanation of
religions.

It could be a kind of chemistry. Take a strong numinous
ingredient into your tradition and certain effects are to be
expected. Combine the numinous with the mystical and
you get a variety of possibilities. Take mysticism more
purely and you have another trend.

You have the Theravada, the Tao, Neoplatonism,

perhaps; and these live in some tension and contrast to the explosive theism of Yahweh, Allah, Vishnu, Kali.

What I am suggesting is that we can look to a dynamic in religious experience which helps to explain something of the shape of religions. This is what may be called 'intra-religious explanation', moving from one ingredient of religion to another, not explaining religion by what lies outside it. Both kinds of explanation are called for as we explore the interaction between religious traditions and their environment. Of course, the distinction between inside and outside is only a rough one (for one thing, there is the definition of what religion is to consider, a thorny enough matter).

The problem of the classification of religious experiences may to many people seem a remote topic. But its cultural importance is vast. Thus the very power of the numinous experience of Yahweh as renewed in differing periods of Israel's prophetic history, and the distancing thus of Jewish religion from the polymorphous luxuriance of agricultural religion led to a dualism between God and creatures, God and the cosmos, such that the many gods were banished from nature. The combination of such a rigorous monotheism with Greek rationality was potent in bringing about a flowering of the scientific spirit, first in medieval Islam, then through the Renaissance and finally in Newton and what lay beyond.

I propose, then, a theory of religion which goes beyond Otto, and seeks plurality of patterns of basic religious experience. As a preliminary distinction there is the polarity between the numinous and the mystical. This helps to foreshadow a theory of how it is the radical monotheisms of the Western triad differ in emphasis from the non-theistic, mystical Buddhist phenomenon.

How do such experiences, though, differ from 'ordinary' ones? Why is it that they are taken somehow as pointing to, or emanating from, that which lies beyond the world – is in some way transcendent? The question arises precisely because in making the distinction between religious and secular worldviews we have made appeal to the idea of the transcendent. Moreover, part of what is meant by a secular attitude is the unwillingness to take seriously spiritual experiences as sources of knowledge. The numinous and the mystical lose their force amid the bright lights and turmoil of the secular city.

The reason why the numinous and the mystical have a transcendental meaning is that in either case there is a sense of going beyond what is conditioned. The numinous at its most powerful does not just dwell secretly in groves and streams and mountains, and in arks and images and sacraments. Its Otherness suggests an otherness from the created order: it is unconditioned, in that what it evokes is a sense of what lies behind the stream of events available to perception and material probing. At its deepest, the mystical shines in a timeless void, empty, that is, of the images and events of 'this world'. Thus there is a tendency for religious experience to incorporate a kind of intuition of what is transcendent.

Bracketing the Transcendent: Standing Back from God

But this does not mean that we have to believe in the transcendent in order to conduct the history of religions, or in order to construct a theory of the way religion works. Some people have written as though because religious experience, and with it much of religious practice, presupposes the transcendent (in the sense of interpreting itself through the idea of a transcendent source of object or experience) the study of religion must presuppose the transcendent. We do not have to believe in the Holy out there as an existing Being in order to explore religion. The question of whether there is truly a God or an Unconditioned – an Allah or nirvana – is a question of theology, buddhology, philosophy, value judgement, faith. The question of how humans have reacted to the numinous experience, to prophetic visions, to theophanies, to the appearance of the Divine – such a question belongs to the history of religion and such adjunct disciplines as the sociology of religion.

Some have conversely supposed that the social sciences in dealing with religion must presuppose the non-existence of the divine. How can the sociologist presuppose there is a God? This is not a scientific assumption. We have no need of that hypothesis. Truly. But it does not follow that we have to think that there is or is not a transcendent Being. We can surely examine the way religious experience operates in human history and in human society without rushing to judgement as to whether it does or does not rest on a fallacy. We put the transcendent in brackets. But we do not neglect it.

The former wrong path leads to prejudgement in one direction, the latter to reductionism. Reductionism is harmful because it devalues the force of religion, whether or not it is a human creation. It is a secret way of imposing a secular ideology on the facts, and in doing so it neglects the way it is in part because of spiritual outlooks that human society shapes itself. Reductionism tends towards the fallacy that what we do not believe in can have no independent power, for other people.

From the point of view of the science of religion, then, the Focus of experience is to be put in brackets. As explorers of faith we are neither (so far) believers or disbelievers, neither committed nor not committed. As it were we are neutral, and yet the very term may suggest the wrong things. Not neutral, like Switzerland, between the contenders. Not agnostic at the level of faith, for we are not at the level of faith. As users of the historical, scientific method, agnostics. By bracketing the Beyond we affirm a kind of methodological agnosticism, a way of approaching the phenomena of religious experience without any unnecessary slant, and trying to reveal the categories the believer uses rather than imposing our own categories on him.

It is like meteorology. One can study clouds and rainfall and the genesis of storms, jetstream, trade winds, monsoons: one does not need so far to decide whether rain is good or bad. And yet in one way it is not like meteorology, for (it will be said) you do not bracket off, in the study of the weather, the possible influence of sun spots. And isn't that what is here happening about religion – bracketing off the influence of God? Neutrality is either fatuous or a fraud (it will be said).

The *influence* of God? The concept leads to some dark and exciting questions of a philosophical kind.

If we postulate a God 'beyond', who has an influence, an effect, on events in this world; and if we suppose these effects to be particular, for instance the occurrence of certain religious experiences; then is God as cause independently somehow accessible to us? If I see smoke curling up from a hillside I can infer a fire, because experience has shown, and can continue to show, the connection between smoke and fire. I may not see fire now, but only infer it; but I can see fire (I could see it, if I were close by on that hillside). Is there an analogy with God? Can I correctly infer that God is cause of some religious experience because it is possible to see the fire of God as well as the smoke of experience? But there is a paradox here. The only way known to us of having an experience of God is by having an experience of him in this world, and it is the question of whether that experience in this world is caused by God with which we started. We seem to be in a cosmic Catch-22. Our best knowledge of a Beyond is through experience of it, but we cannot state that it *is* an experience of the Beyond independently of experience of the Beyond. Or to put it another way: If there is a Beyond we can know something of it through the relevant transcendental experiences; if there is not then those experiences lose their force – they are simply peculiar experiences on the surface of the universe. If we believe in the Beyond we have warrant in experience for the belief – the best possible. If we do not so believe in the Beyond there could in principle be nothing to cause us to change our mind. Belief in God is in a way verifiable; disbelief is unfalsifiable. Belief in the Beyond seems to be a matter of choice.

But we are still left with the fact of the power of religious experience. The influence of that which is ascribed to the transcendent is not affected by these philosophical arguments. The question of faith is a question of where to locate significance, whether in the numinous, the mystical or the secular world, whether in transcendental myth or not. This perhaps makes the task of bracketing the Beyond an easier one. Even if we believe in the Beyond as operative, it is so only as the secret Focus which lies beyond experience in this world.

In the theistic framework the situation of religious experience even more clearly shows itself. For according to theism everything is an effect of the divine Being: as Creator and Sustainer of the whole universe he has an unseen hand in every event. It is not as though my experience now of the blue sky and the Californian mountains which I see in the near distance is exempt from that unseen hand – the divine Being sustains the mountains and the sky, and they impinge on me. It is as much caused by the divine Being as some more extraordinary revelatory experience (and looked at in the right way is it not itself revelatory?). What makes the numinous and the mystical experiences of special significance is (we might say) a certain transparency to the ultimate. Even a naturalistic explanation of them does not affect their transparency. The fact that a numinous experience has natural causes or conditions does not by itself mean that it is not an experience brought about by the divine Being since his unseen hand is, as we have said, everywhere, and so in the natural causes of the supernatural experience.

But the judgement that there is a Beyond, that seminal experience of the Beyond is to be located in Sinai or at Mecca, or in the life of Christ or the theophany of Krishna – such a judgement is a religious, theological judgement. It is one of the things to be described in the exploration of religion. It has to be bracketed, if we are looking at religion and faith in a scientific manner (but I repeat, such science is warm science, evocative).

In brief, then, the real existence of the Beyond is to be bracketed, together with other beliefs in the realm of religion which are essentially open to debate and choice. Yet the power of religious factors as an ingredient in human history, society and psychology has to be acknowledged, and the question left open as to whether or not it is to be seen as some consequence of human projection. The danger of a projection theory is that it empirically undervalues the inherent powers of religion. The process of bracketing is designed to protect them. But the question of the power of religion has much wider scope than our examination of religious experience would suggest.

The Relationship of Power and Performance

I made use above of the idea of the location of significance (in certain events or experiences). The notion of significance is a complex one, but it includes the notion of being charged whether positively or negatively with value. Thus in a pre-scientific age an eclipse of the moon carries special significance because it may presage a disaster. 1066 is considered a significant year in English history because it brought a new rule into being continuous with the modern nation, and so in a sense is a founding event. As such it carries positive value for Englishmen in reflection about their identity.

Now for various reasons, religious experience carries a charge. It has an intrinsic significance. And yet how is that significance to be conveyed from one person to another? This is part of the wider question of the analysis of ritual and performance in the sphere of religion and more generally in human existence.

Very roughly and crudely we may consider religion as concerned with the powers within humanity and its environment – powers having both positive and negative charge. If we are used to the idea of objects of perception, we should perhaps take equally seriously objects of feeling, i.e., states of affairs, events, etc., 'out there' which 'naturally' bring about certain positive or negative feelings and moods in us. 'Naturally' means: given both how human beings are built and, more importantly, given those cultural assumptions which deeply implanted mean that people react in certain ways 'naturally' to things and events, the latter come invested with positive or negative charges. Thus for most Westerners snakes seem dangerous. This may have depth-psychological or ancient evolutionary roots, but it has something too to do with cultural attitudes. The sight of a snake does not typically give rise to an inference, such as 'Here is a thing which can emit poison dangerous, even fatal to human beings, so I had better back away'. Already the snake bears this message on its mien. Again: a sunset has a certain positive charge: for most people it evokes admiration. True, it may presage inconvenient weather and the normally positive charge may be over-ridden by reflections of this kind.

In brief: the world around us is not neutral, but soaked in feelings. It may be that 'scientifically' sometimes we may wish to bracket out the feelings, to train ourselves at a kind of anaesthetic objectivity. But in ordinary life perception has its feelings as well as its information. Things, people and events typically have their charges, and they are things and people of substance.

Much has been made in the history of anthropology and the study of religion of *mana*, that sacred power inhering in things and persons – for instance in a chief or a sacred rock. But we can generalize: such magical substance is met in even the most secular and modern environment. A President is endowed with a kind of *mana*: he has a socially and historically conditioned complex charged substance. The beloved has a magic substance, made available to the lover through reciprocated love. A forbidden action emanates a kind of dangerousness (it can be a sign of one's own powerful substance that this can be overcome: forbidden fruits thus seem to be sweetest).

Such substance is connected intimately with behaviour and language. It is to put it simply, conveyed through ritual, through performative acts. But first let me make a small terminological proposal. The capacity of things, etc., to arouse certain feelings and so certain kinds of behaviour in human beings I shall call their 'powers'. These can have positive, negative or neutral charge (a neutral charge is the case of no power). Regarding persons, I shall use the term 'substance', for the powers to alter others' behaviour and feeling is now attributable to a conscious being, who through his own behaviour may wish to increase his substance, since his powers to impress themselves become positively a sign of his or her own status, importance, etc. Thus I partly trade here on the sense of the expression 'a person of substance'. Moreover, substance suggests a quasi-material something which allows us to subsume under a person's substance his possessions – his clothes, house, etc. For a man's power to impress negatively or positively is bound up with the various extensions of his ego which are located in what he has, rules over, participates in. Moreover, one can extend this notion of substance to quasi-persons such as corporate groups, such as nations (which are liable to feel insulted, flattered, secure, fearful, etc. – in an analogical sense; but which is very real in feeling – for what German did not feel humilitated by Versailles in that Germany was humiliated?). Phenomenologically such quasi-persons exist, even if ideologically we may perchance wish to oppose such 'primitive' thinking, or philosophically wish to be nominalists and boil nations down to organized collections of individuals. The point is: a nation is defined in part by national self-consciousness, and this implies a notion of participation and mutual inherence.

Consider revenge. Someone has done me harm, or so I think. I 'naturally' wish to get even, as we say: in other words to inflict some humiliation upon him to make up for or more than make up for the harm he has done me. Exercising my power to harm the other person involves some kind of symbolic and ritual or performative act. Performative: for even when I kick someone back who has kicked me, it is with the thought of 'paying him back'. It is a meaningful movement of my foot, directed at him as a focus. It is to show the power which I have, and here power is exercised through a performative act. Performative speech is the most magical way of exercising power since it involves scarcely any material energy or force, but can have profound effects in changing the feelings and behaviour of other people. But often performative acts are speechless (though they may presuppose speech and reason as a basis for the direction of intentions and the identifying of the focus of acts).

Thus the history of religions, which among other things concerns itself with ritual, has a wider interest in performative acts and language. Once this widening of scope has taken place, it becomes once again inappropriate to draw any sharp line between ways in which the transcendental foci have their power and other persons or quasi-persons exercise their substance.

Ritual and Performative Acts as Paths of Power

The inner logic of performative acts is that something is being conveyed, but not primarily of course by way of information. Rather configurations of a person's substance are conveyed to another: his substance as loving or hating, menacing or consoling and so forth. Ritual or performative gestures open up a pathway so to speak between two persons or entities, so that influences can pass across. Thus if two persons pass each other daily in the street sooner or later the 'ice will be broken': they will not be able to ignore one another (i.e., ignore one another in a neutral kind of way, so no good or bad influences pass either way, for no contact is made). But once the ice is broken gestures are made: most typically, though not necessarily friendly, ones. Thus my substance under its friendly configuration is in part conveyed, and in exchange his to me.

Thus we can see most ritual as a form of non-informational communication. Thus rituals of worship enhance the substance of the divine Being, and open up a pathway through which hopefully benign divine power (grace) will be channelled to the worshipper. More generally, one can look to a wider history of religions approach as both divine-human and other-human interactions (e.g., State-individual, collective-individual interactions).

Thus not only is there the seminal study of religious experiences, in which power is conveyed or generated non-ritually, and in a psychic manner, but also there is the performative communication and generation of power. Thus we might define the central thrust of the history of religions as being the analysis and estimating of the powers transmitted through the experiential and ritual dimensions of religion (and analogies to religion). But since the Foci of experience and ritual are themselves delineated and defined mythically and doctrinally, it is not possible just to prise loose the experiential and ritual powers of religion from the mental and intellectual factors surrounding them.

Powers come as positive, negative and neutral. But it is worth remarking that there is a kind of earned neutrality, and a detachment which is striven for. Thus in Buddhism and elsewhere one sees the attempt made with great effort and detailed analysis to achieve a kind of transcendental calm: the experience of nirvana is itself that of a kind of ineffable peace. Here the positive and negative powers of the world of ritual and dynamic experience are somehow transcended. So one also needs to consider within the field of religion and worldview analysis the neutralization of powers. The secular analogy is the kind of calm, contemplative objectivity which science can demand.

If ritual and performative acts can be seen as pathways of power, they also confer certain shapes or configurations on the substances which are communicated along those paths. Thus most generally substance can be seen as positive or negative, benign or malign, as we have noted. But benignity can take a more particular form, as in love, or solemnity. And more particularly again, the shape of the Being or Person from whom the power ritually emanates can be depicted as having as very special mythic and doctrinal character. Thus in the Eucharist it is the essence of Christ which is conveyed – his body and blood. Not only to the very ideas of body and blood have particular echoes and resonances: but also Christ's own example and nature is somehow embedded in the life which is communicated in the Eucharist. To absorb Christ's substance truly is through grace to obtain the willingness to sacrifice oneself, to show love or *agape* to others, to rely lovingly upon God as he did, and so on. Thus the power has a configuration.

This is how too we can understand iconography. The holy picture or other symbolic representation of the divine or transcendental Being is a kind of congealed performative. It itself is a pathway of power. Not magically: for there is a certain sort of performative response in the face of the picture or statue which is necessary (typically) for the appropriation of the power, the unlocking as it were of the gate which the picture constitutes. Give the holy pictures a totally new performative setting – as in a museum of art in the modern world, and you call forth different responses – not divine power, but esthetic transformation, not holiness but beauty, not myth but story.

Although secularization does make an important difference to performative and symbolic styles (for one thing sacred ritual is no longer given a transcendental focus, so that spiritual power from the Beyond is not, so to speak, tapped), the same general principles apply. Thus instead of myth of the old sort we may have charged history – for instance the story of the Revolution. The celebrations of that story not only recreate the existential power of the primary events of the 'new era': they also help to give shape to action through the configurations of the Revolution itself, or at least as it has become depicted in official history and doctrinal interpretation. For this reason the scientific study of religion and worldview-analysis are important ingredients in the understanding of modern as well as ancient times.

The Science of Religion as an Interpreter of History

As we see then the history or science of religion, including within this the symbolic analysis of existential worldviews even if 'secular' in character, needs empathy, evocation, sensitivity as well as structural awareness. It is not descriptive in a merely external sense, for the facts are both inner and outer. But it does tend towards some generalization and some theorizing. It is at this level that it is useful now to discuss briefly some ways in which it is relevant to reflection about modern history. It is possible here to learn from and to advance beyond such theorists as diverse as Max Weber and Mircea Eliade.

What special contribution can the religionist make to the understanding of modern history? It is largely a matter of emphasis. There has been an unduly technical approach, itself not thoroughly scientific, because subjectively and symbolically loaded, to human affairs in so far as economics and political science (taken in a rather technical and 'scientific' way) have dominated thinking about modern history. On the other hand historians – 'pure' historians – have been more oriented towards the past (19th century history being very modern) and have rather inclined towards the nitty-gritty and the eschewing of wider-ranging hypotheses. Even now Toynbee is a dirty word among many professional historians. (Of course one might want to criticize him for being a bad generalizer, but the nisus is towards objecting to the very task of generalizing.)

Let me enter a disclaimer. I do not want in any way to minimize the importance of political institutions and economic forces in the shaping of history. It is only that we have to perceive them as playing a part in and partly being shaped by a wider world of human experience where the analysis of symbolic and meaning elements is often of crucial importance. Let us look to a few examples.

Modern economists are increasingly interested in returning to Weberian reflections but in a new key. Thus consider the role of post-Confucian mental factors in the extraordinary recent history of economic development in Singapore, Hong Kong, Taiwan and Korea.

Consider too the way in which economic and technological changes bring about the dissolution of certain kinds of ritual and performative behaviour. Modernization is not just (or even perhaps) a rational component in historical change, but rather has its own symbolic weight in relation to traditional identities. Thus modernization itself requires an intelligible symbolic mediation. This was for various reasons wanting in the Shah's drive towards modernization in Iran. Economist, especially developmental economists, must pay close attention to the relation between traditional values and those less consciously perhaps conveyed by the technologies and economic transactions and structures.

As I shall show later in my treatment of Mao, it is necessary to analyse ideologies not merely from the point of view of exhibiting their apparently rational content but also with a view to unfolding their existential or, if you like, spiritual function. Thus Maoism's success in reorganizing Chinese experience is due not to the supposedly scientific nature of Marxism but more to the way it was mediated both emotionally and intellectually to a major human predicament, namely that of the Chinese intelligentsia and peasant classes confronted by the disintegration of the old China in the face of foreign incursions and values. Its supposedly scientific character has however an attraction, since science itself comes to us charged with the symbolisms of power and modernity, because of its actual capacities to unlock secrets of the world and methods of manipulating it. In other words: the scientific air of Marxism itself needs symbolic analysis.

The contribution of the history of religions in the upshot can be said to be threefold. But the emphasis is after all only an emphasis. It is not unique to the science of religion to emphasize the three elements of empathy, organic analysis and awareness of the symbolic. But because the science of religion does stress these things it is well suited to a certain understanding of how historical processes operate. Thus that enigma of modern times, the Nazi period, is unintelligible without empathy, that is a recognition of what the world looked like through the eyes of German supporters of the Nazis; and that world itself has to be unfolded as a kind of organism, involving various interrelated elements of perception. Moreover it needs to be seen in symbolic and performative terms. The humiliation of Versailles after the tragic and long war of the trenches and the Eastern front, the devastation of the Depression – these generated a thirst for explanations of a myth-laden kind, and for a New Order, a kind of collective rite or passage into a new German identity. Who better to symbolize and focus than the leader who is betwixt and between, not associated (because Austrian and of humble origins) with the old ruling class, and yet deeply identified with the sufferings of Germany because of his four years in the trenches? Hitler was the Unknown Soldier, the anonymous hero, and at the same time at the Nuremberg rally he was the apotheosis of the humiliated, harsh for revenge and power.

Again the emphasis on mental and symbolic factors happens more generally to explain the course, or courses, which Marxism has taken in its interplay with nationalism. Thus the science of religion helps to redress certain balances. It seeks worldview analysis as important in the explanatory process. The existential and mental life of human beings is seen as no mere epiphenomenon. It thus redresses the balance against an over 'materialist' view of history. It suggests self-analysis and the uncovering of the symbolic forces which themselves can underlie fashions in academe and government. Moreover, the science of religion naturally enough does not tend to understimate the power of traditional religions, whereas rationalist historians and social scientists naturally bend in a different direction.

The fact is of course: religious and symbolic ideological factors are neither more nor less important than they are. Our job is to come to a just appraisal of their actual 'causative' force. Thus the emphasis in the science of religion is important as a counter-balance, but ultimately the sciences of humanity should not need such balancing acts. There is a seamless web connecting the various kinds and levels of explanation we use in trying to understand human history, experience and society.

And because we are concerned with change, a desideratum for a new perspective on universal history, now that the histories of cultures have flowed into a single global history, is a theory of the factors involved in symbolic change. Perhaps part of the answer is a kind of internal syncretism. As new forces arise, e.g. the scientific establish, academic history, etc., or new forms of art, so symbolism has somewhat to conform and adapt. New transformations attempt to relate old mythic functions to new forms of knowledge.

Another way all this can be described is as follows. Each conscious being is his own universe, and part of that universe is the world as he sees it: the constellation of values and entities that he relates to – his past, his friends and family, the nation, his god or other schematization of the cosmos. These foci of his feeling and imagination act dynamically: his actions relate to them and to the particularities with which he is confronted. It is that world of his foci which is what the science of religion is about, in its broadest sense. At the microscopic level then we are concerned with the delineation of the individual conscious universe. But macroscopically the science of religion concerns universes that overlap – the worlds of great groups and traditions. If the historian of religions sees the importance of the imaginative and mental inhabitants of these worlds (inhabitants both abstract and personal), it is because he thinks of them not just as vapours given off by social and economic forces, but themselves as engines of change, in continuous dynamic interplay with men's other levels of transaction.

Whether such gods exist, whether such abstract or other inhabitants have any truth, is beside the point. It is their power which is important to us.

It is in the first instance from this perspective that I embark upon the following comparisons and analyses, before getting round to reflections and evaluations concerning them.

3

Christianity Seen from Adam's Peak

Buddhism Ancient and Modern in Sri Lanka

Sri Lanka is cosmopolitan, but it is also deeply traditional. For all the changes which the island has undergone as a consequence of the arrival of Portuguese sailing ships, and after them the warships and merchantmen of the Dutch and the British; for all the transformations brought about by the growing of tea and rubber in great up-country gardens and low-country estates during the last hundred years; for all the modernizations implicit in its high standard of education – it yet retains its Buddhist ethos in a manner harking back to the great civilizations of the island in the past. The monks who walk in meditation, the mountain and forest hermitages, the winding pilgrimage to see the Buddha's footprint on Adam's Peak, the great stupas, the processions of the Perahera when the marvellous potent tooth-relic of the Buddha is taken in elephant procession, the various means of gaining merit, the begging for alms – such are reminders of a Buddhist past that is not too distant from the world of the Pali canon itself.

There Buddhism centres on the monastic life, but is surrounded by the gods and magic of the agricultural world, adapting itself, as usual, to the exigencies of ordinary men as well as to the demands of the Eightfold Way. But in one way the modern world is not the same as the old. In the scriptures themselves the temple cult had not arisen. Already it is true there is the custom, probably going back to pre-Buddhist times, of raising mounds to house the relics of the saints (the Buddha in particular); and it was out of this custom that the cult of the stupa and later of the pagoda arose. From that stemmed the tradition finding its visible Sri Lankan expression in the beautiful gleaming white dagobas rising like snow-white hard breasts out of the green of the surrounding country. But the cult of the buddha image was something relatively late in the island, influenced by the great Vehicle which once had a strong presence here. It is that cult which might provide the context of the first question posed to Christ by the Buddha.

A Question from Christianity

Visually, for instance, there are various notable contrasts. Were the Sri Lankan Buddhist to visit a Roman Catholic cathedral he would doubtless be struck by the directionality of it, the straightness with which the eye is directed onwards towards the altar, upwards to it to. Hanging above it the great Crucifix would show a young, very human figure, dying in that position we know so well, head drooping down, arms outstretched, feet nailed. The Buddha is a very different figure and comes in a very different ambience. The image room of a temple brings one very close to the great looming figure. If perhaps at first the figure of Christ seems absorbed in his own death, the Buddha seems to be massively confident of his own insight. In the cathedral the rhythm of space suggests an approach to the powerhouse of God, oddly expressed as such power may be by the dying figure on the Cross; the temple suggests a walking-past place, a filing-through place, a place where one indeed gets in contact somehow with merit and gains by the visit, but finds in it not so much a house of power as a solemn place of reminders, a calm interior of inspiration, with the Buddha there absorbed in his own transcendental vision, unable to enter into further contact with the faithful, gone out, in his own essence, like a flame. Or as the statues, enormous, of him lying in a sort of blissful sleep (but it is not really sleep) express it: he has gained nibbana, nirvana, the extinction of desire and with that the extinction of life, no more to be reborn. He is gone, ineffable, leaving behind him relics, memories, teachings. And these statues. Though Christ on the Cross may be by contrast a strange way of saying something about the power of God, there is nothing so ambiguous in those grave golden ikons of Christ Pantokrator, ruler of all, majestic and numinous; or of those swirling paintings of Christ comes to judge the living and the dead, the cracking thunderous divider of the world in the last fiery and golden days. Nor is there mistaking the intent of the soaring chants and fervent hymns to God and Christ. He seems to be a strange interplay of power and sacrifice, of the majestic and the meek, the overpowering and the unsuccessful. The combination is oddly disturbing beside the serenity of the Buddha. Who, it may be recalled, died at eighty of a digestive complaint, worn out rather peacefully after his many wanderings and preachings. He was not done to death in his prime of life after a brief and dangerous public career.

Western Civilization and the Eastern World-Picture.

It may be remarked in passing that the divine-human character of Christ gave a special dynamic to European civilization, in that it was a factor in the synthesis between Greek humanism and Semitic theism. This in turn pre- pared the way for that 'this-worldly' asceticism, that ambi- valent attitude to earthly goods, which is commonly held to be a reason for the development of European capitalism. It substituted a figure of deified humanity for ancient anthropomorphic gods. But the sacrificial aspect of Jesus' death remains disturbing, so that Europe has never seemed satisfied with humanism, however admirable: something stormier has been called for.

The Buddhist, looking at Christ, and seeing beyond him, is most likely to be struck by the very different world-picture into which Jesus fits compared with that of the Buddha, especially perhaps if we are remaining within the strict milieu of the Theravada. At the immediate ritual level there is the question of god, the gods and worship. At the metaphysical level there is the question of the eternity and substantiality of the divine which Jesus' fragile humanity masks. Thus on the first front there is a subtle but vital difference between the action of the pious Buddhist before the Buddha statue and the actions of the Christian as he presents himself in the cathedral or church before the symbols of his faith. The Buddhist may lay a temple flower before the great painted Buddha statue; but he or she does not strictly worship the Buddha. Who is there to worship? He is not a god. The gods in fact are next door, or further away at a quite different place. The Buddhist makes a distinction between worldly goods and services which with luck and suitable piety he can gain from the gods such as the great Kataragama (the Sinhala version of the South Indian god Skanda) and the spiritual blessing that he can gain by going for refuge to the Buddha. And so one who wears the saffron robe and whose existence thus is by definition given over to the higher life should not go to the gods. But the lay person, more compromised with the world and in any case not perhaps ripe for that higher existence in which the deeper search within occurs, that grasping for the higher insight, such a person can relevantly treat with supernatural powers. So though the Buddha is sometimes spoken of in the scriptures as being 'a god above gods', this is only a manner of speaking: he is not himself in their league. He belongs in the higher spiritual realm, and having given up the world he has vanished ultimately from mundane or even supramundane life. There will be no more transactions between his followers and him. So the flower laid before his statue is more in the way of a pledge and a memorial and an act of self-dedication from which some merit for the future may accrue than it is a positive personal here and now act of relationship with a living being. But Christ for the Christian worshipper lives still. He is moreover, eternal.

For of course for orthodox Christianity Christ is God and God is creator of the cosmos, a divine all-powerful being who works within and behind the universe. Buddhism does not see the world as created and it therefore has no place for the creator. The god Brahmā, who was rumoured in the Buddha's time to be the maker of the world, is no more than a superior denizen of the impermanent universe. That cosmos is according to Buddhism liable to fluctuation, for it ebbs and expands in a vast succession of ages. But it is in principle ever-lasting. To give some idea of ancient statistics on this front: the Buddha is supposed to have said

> With the mind thus composed . . . I directed it to the knowledge and recollection of former lives. I remembered a variety of them: one birth, two or fifty or a hundred or a thousand or a hundred thousand births; or many a kalpa of integration, disintegration and so on . . .

And each kalpa is itself part of a cycle in which each great kalpa contains eighty small ones; and the whole cycle goes on repetitiously without limit. It is not just this extraordinary scale of the universe, repeated in space for our world system is one of millions, each with its own Brahmā, which causes the Buddhism of the Theravada to reject the idea of a creator. For after all the great cosmology of early Buddhism found its modified way into the Hindu world picture, and was regarded not only as compatible with the idea of a supreme Creator, but much rebounding to his credit, staggering power and general creativity. Still, the huge cosmos is treated as having a place for even the most imposing gods, who are as a result of this treatment merely rather superior denizens of the perishable world. So from this perspective the old cosmology of the Old and New Testaments, carried forward with Greek changes into the Middle Ages, does seem rather small, rather unimpressive, perhaps even naive. But that small cosmos had its effects which are vital for the understanding of Christianity.

The Cultural Effects of the Small Cosmos

The small cosmos arose rather directly from the myth of creation and its strange addenda which the culture of ancient Israel formed out of various materials in a quite original way. For that myth means that the history of Israel is directly preceded by the first history of mankind which itself grows out of the very narrative of creation. It set the stage for an historical drama of suffering and redemption, of rebellion, guidance and hope, or glory and judgement bounds to the events of the earth. It was out of that small cosmos, then, that there arose the special concern for the historical process which became characteristic both of the Jewish and Christian traditions.

Sometimes it is said in this connection that there is a gulf fixed between the Eastern, and in particular Indian, conception of time which is cyclical, because of the rolling repetition of the kalpas and so on, and that of the West, with its linear sense of history. The contrast is too simple, and is wrongly stated. It is better stated as a preference in the one case for a picture of patterns of change in the cosmos which recur regularly, like the seasons, and a preference on the other for a picture of linear change. But the Buddhist does not just stress repetition in change, but also vastness. The picture too is one of relative pessimism, since things in our age are getting worse. Even if things may have been improved by the intervention of a Buddha, degeneration sets in after his time. By contrast the small world of the Christian sets the scene for an impressive but perhaps rather intimate cosmic drama, which is to end in hope, for whatever the dire predictions of the fire and chaos of the last days it is also the time of the Second Coming and God's ultimate triumph in time and history. And now it is better than it was, in that since the coming of Christ we are living in a new age.

The Buddhist may have absorbed his gods in the cosmos in part because of its very vastness. But there are other reasons why he looks upon the universal creative Christ, the Logos and Creator, as alien. God as creator and judge is also the God who shines numinously and mysteriously out of the ikon: he is also the great Being who spoke out of a whirlwind so thunderously to Job. He is the Christ who caused fear and divine consternation to Peter at Caesarea Philippi and on the lake. He is the shining sword-decked brilliance of the judgement throne in the Book of Revelation. This is where the Theravadin, as he shifts his gaze from the quiet self-contained Buddha to the more turbulent and unnerving figure of Christ, may find it hard to feel the full force of Christ's Godhead.

Christ, that is to say, is not worshipped for nothing. If the Buddhist in laying his flower before the statue feels a certain reverence and solemnity, he might in a sense be said to be at the fringes of the numinous, of the terrifying mystery of God. But his concern is not directed towards this facet of religion. On the other hand, the Christian is heir to the theism of Israel, in which the one God has risen in majesty over all the other gods so that they do not merely flee. They never were. That the Buddhist is not really concerned with the one God follows from the cheering laxity with which he allows the gods to insert themselves into the life of the laity. It is better to tame the gods, to see through them, than to meet them head on and to annihilate them. It is part of the skill of the Buddha that his religion makes these adjustments with the small traditions of his followers. But Christ the Pantokrator, the numinous Judge of the world (and not just that suffering human figure upon the Cross) is ovewhelming in strength and love and terror too for those who are separated from him. So the Theravadin shifting his gaze from the Buddha-image to the ikon; and listening perhaps to the Psalms as they are chanted and great hymns like the *Te Deum*; – he may then see something which we often forget, so familiar is it to us: that the Christian God is worshipped not just from gratitude or out of love, but from cosmic fear, from the sense of his shattering and creative Power. Christ is then to be compared more easily to Vishnu and Shiva and Kali than to the Buddha, so far as his transcendental majesty and fearfulness go.

These things can have long repercussions. The numinosity of Christ can easily be interpreted as a kind of militancy. It is strange that one who died on the Cross and did not resist arrest should have become also the hero of the warrior. It partly has to do with the somewhat undisciplined turbulence and power which the sense of divinity can inspire. There is something of the tragedy of both Buddhism and Christianity in the images of the Vietnam war. The crusading spirit of America owes much to its feeling of religious mission; its technology owes much too to the thought that men are on earth to change it and to be co-workers with God in the creative process. The flamethrower was the evil result of these two forces. Those monks who burned themselves, more nobly, represented something too – a kind of mutely horrifying withdrawal and protest, a hot flaming plague on both houses. But a dead end too as it happened.

Divine Power and Buddhist Knowledge

So, then, the Christ is worshipped because he is the Lord and God. The Buddha is not worshipped, because though he too is the Lord, he can be no longer perceived and no longer thought properly to exist, and he surely is not thought to be Creator or Ruler of the Universe. One might put the contrast too in another way. If the motif of Creation in the theistic tradition is one of transcendental power – of the power which existing independently of the universe as we know it yet at the same time gave birth to this world and continues to work in and through it, the motif of Buddhism is change and analysis of change. If the Buddha somehow conquers the forces of death and suffering, summed up in Buddhist writings and art as the devilish Mara, the Death-dealer, the Tempter, it is because he has true insight. He analyses the very notion of change; he analyses the constituents of the world which bring about illfare and unhappiness. The sword with which he smites Mara is the sword of insight. So his ultimate power is not power of the forceful kind; in a sense it is not power at all. It is knowledge. If only we have that transcendental knowledge which the teachings of the Buddha can impart then we may gain a riddance of those bad things which plague us and cloud our feelings and our vision.

This is brought out well in the statues. Often the Buddha holds up his hand in the gesture of analysis and preaching, the forefinger and the thumb making a circle, echoing the wheel of the Law which he set in motion in his first sermon and which rolls on for the welfare of all living things. That analytic gesture indicates that somehow the essence of Buddhahood is teaching. He is the Teacher. Well, Christ too was a teacher was he not? Did he not give us the two great Commandments? Did he not expound many parables? Was he not sometimes referred to as Rabbi? Has the Christian Church not through the ages carried on with the teaching function of Christ? It is part of the Christian's ministry as it was part of his ministry. True: but it is as crucified and risen that Christ showed most luminously the way in which men are saved. His teachings are subsidiary to his actions. Though we do not precisely know what the teachings of the Buddha were there is no mistaking, especially in the Theravadin tradition, the analytic cast of the early Buddhist mind. It would be very surprising if this did not go back to the Buddha himself. We have four truths, an eightfold path, five constituents of living beings, twelve fields, the twelvefold chain of causation, the various dharmas or elements, and so on. Maybe such lists were boosted by the needs of memory, for number groupings are good for the mnemonic art. But there is more to the lists than that. The root idea of the analytic – that is 'breaks things up' (or down) – is very pertinent to the mediative procedures of the Buddhist tradition. By seeing what the world is made of, down to its fine and shifting detail, and by breaking the individual down to a stream of events or a heap of different constituents, one's vision of the world is altered. The tables melt before our eyes into streams and complexes of events; trees go into a kind of haze of elements and processes; people, even such as Sophia Loren, lose their charm in their aggregation of bones and blood and pus and grey matter, dissolving thus from the glories of personal presence and sometimes fleshly attraction into a skin-bag of bits and pieces. The soul likewise is not to be found and any sense of immortality rots away under the eye of analytic introspection. The many categories and lists of Buddhism thus serve a very salutary purpose. All the old charm of the world goes once it is broken down and looked at with the eye of true insight. So the curved finger and thumb of the teaching Buddha's hand is a sign of the importance of knowledge. The aim of the Teacher is to bring about that knowledge in us. Consequently the ceremonies of Buddhism ultimately are just a dressing around the Dharma, which has to be heard, and being heard has its inner effect. So the Buddha's long commitment to wandering around discoursing, organizing the Order of monks and nuns and so ensuring the continuity of the message, is no surprise. His destiny was as the great teacher, and he is unlike those strangely inward-turned Pratyekabuddhas (Research Buddhas I call them) who have enlightenment but cannot pass it on, who cannot make what they have seen understood to others.

Emptiness and Substance

One could see all this as the recognition that the world ultimately has no power. And behind it there lies no power. The world is only dynamic in the sense that it is in ceaseless flux; otherwise it is hollow, a vast complex swarm of processes, each evanescent, and with nothing permanent in them, as they tirelessly fade and rise, only the patterns into which they form themselves remaining stable, giving off thus a spurious sense of permanence. But that picture is not what the Christian doctrine of creation paints. It is true that as the hymn writer has it 'Change and decay in all around I see'. But the world is shot through with the power of God. It is not a series of separate independent powers, but rather a great material expression of God's creative power, ordered – once Greek and more modern science had overlaid the picture – according to the rational principles issuing from God's mind. This cosmos, this divinely ordained thing, may have an origin in time and it may ultimately pass away or somehow be utterly transformed, but it is not just a hollow swarm of short-lived processes. Rather it is created beings in motion and interactions, created and sustained by the one Being, the one holy Power. Indeed it is by the transformation of the material world that salvation is to come, rather than by insight which 'sees through it'. Thus the Buddhist and the Christian see the world about them in quite different ways, or so at any rate it so far seems. For the one the trees melt, as we have observed, into a haze of elements and processes; for St Francis they are signs of God's goodness and glory. If things are a problem for the Christian it is because they are finite; the only true satisfaction and joy is to be found when they are seen not as finite things in themselves but rather expressions of infinite purpose, for it is with the infinite that ultimate joy comes. Or perhaps things are a problem in that the human being is fallen, and perhaps with him the whole created order. The good purposes of God have been perverted mysteriously. But such reflections are very different from those of the Theravadin. For they are reflections which see the non-eternal in the light of their created relationship to the one divine Being. But (will it not be said?) the Theravadin has also a concept of the Beyond. Does he not see the events of the world against the background of the transcendental, or Nirvana?

The Meaning of Buddhist Transcendence

There is indeed a transcendent in Buddhism. As a famous passage puts it:

> There is, Bhikkhus, a not-born, not-become, not-made, uncompounded, and were it not for this not-born, not-become, not-made, uncompounded, no release could be shown for that which is born, become, made, compounded.

The words just preceding this often quoted passage are more geared to experience:

> There is, Bhikkhus, that plane where there is neither extension nor movement; beyond the plane of infinite space and of that of neither perception nor non-perception; where there is neither this world nor

another; neither the moon nor the sun. Here there is no coming or going or staying or ceasing or originating, for this is itself without basis, without continuance, without mental bject: this is the end of suffering.

In other words, not only is there a transcendent state, but it is to be found in and through higher experience, lying beyond 'infinite space'. For in the Buddhist texts the planes of infinite space, neither-perception-nor-non-perception, etc., are stages of meditation – stages of the so-called *jhānas*. Nibbana from this point of view is the cessation of craving, the elimination of the 'influxes' of desire, wrong view and so forth which stain men and make them continue in the round of rebirth. From another point of view we can see it as a state of personality: the disposition of one who has achieved liberation, *vimutti*. But from another point of view it is the one unconditioned state, the one unborn something or nothing, which is not a set of processes, or an element in the ongoing turmoil of events. So beyond the cosmos, so to speak, there lies nibbana, the transcendental state: something which can be given in experience and yet is not an object of experience in the sense that the object can be distinguished from the subject. The two are if you like one, except that in the Buddhist analysis there is no ego, no subject.

Since this point is often misunderstood by Westerners and others who approach Buddhism from the assumptions of our usual ways of thinking, and who perhaps also seek in it more exact parallels with other mystical or contemplative religions than is in the end justified, let me spend a moment or two expanding what I have said. It is not uncommon for the mystic to say that in the higher reaches of interior contemplation the distinction between subject and object disappears. Mystics do not always say precisely this, and the theistic contemplative is often keen to retain at least a hairsbreadth's distance between the soul and God, for the blasphemous and destructive. But still, there is a strong drive towards ideas of unity, identification, the disappearance of subject and object. In the depths of the self the ordinary structure of experience is said to disappear. And why indeed not? The extraordinary discipline of the contemplative, the great struggles of the yogin to control his senses and his wandering thoughts, the amazing drive to blot out at will the deliverances of the seductive senses, the purification of consciousness through the most rigorous exercises – such heroisms of the inner life would presumably issue in something remarkable: so why not indeed the crumbling of that 'me-here-those-things-there' and the 'me-here-you-over-there' structure of perception and the dualities of thinking, remembering and the like? So then let us accept the disappearance, for the time being, of the distinction between subject and object. No wonder then that those who believe in eternal substances think of the attainment as the arrival at the very ground of the person, the Self; or the very ground of things, Being itself. The Brahman-Atman equation makes sense partly in this context of the postulation of a divine Being and the subject-objectless non-dual experience another thought. Let us see it in the context not of substance but of process.

For the essence of the Buddha's metaphysics lay in his perception that the world is a swarm of evanescent processes. The idea of impermanence belongs to his first sermon. It is true that there is much more to his teaching than just this idea for he also stressed in a most original way the interlocking nature of what we divide as mind and matter: the world is not as we perceive it because we think of it somehow as static and independent of ourselves. Yet every perception is also a contribution to the world: it shapes what it sees – so that not only does the tree dissolve into a haze of green and brown processes as we note its impermanence, but it gives also dissolves mysteriously further into states of mind together with what gives rise to states of mind. In other words, the greenness and the brownish aspects of the tree, its shape even, are projections, though projections stimulated by something which is out there. However, leaving aside the semi-idealism of the Buddha's teaching, the doctrine of impermanence implies that when we reach the non-dual experience of nirvana it is not the attainment to a permanent Self, to a Substance. To the permanent in a way yes; to a Being, no. Many commentators have wrongly made the step from seeing the contrast between the impermanent and the permanent as also a contrast between process and substance, between the impermanent and some Eternal entity. This is a mistake. For the doctrine of impermanence and egolessness is the teaching that nothing underlies the shifting changes of the world. If though there is an unconditioned, an unborn, then the perception of it is not dual, is not subject-object in character. A permanent State has come to be interpolated so to speak in the stream of conditioned events. A lot of conditioned non-substances are replaced by an unconditioned non-substance, not by an unconditioned Substance. So nibbana can only be understood in the context of non-dual contemplative experience multiplied by the whole teaching of impermanence and the Buddhist attack upon the philosophy of things. For this reason too the Tathagata, the Buddha, is unfathomable, trackless.

So though the Christian worldview and the Buddhist both have the sense of the Transcendent, the context and character of that Beyond diverge greatly, at least as we see the conception from the directions of Kandy and Constantinople. Nirvana, to put in a concrete fashion, is not Creator or supreme Object of Worship. It is not a personal Being. It cannot even in the Theravada, and only very doubtfully in the Greater Vehicle, be thought of as Ground of Being. It is the *summum bonum*. But it is not the origin of the world, the Logos. One cannot thus write 'in the beginning was Nirvana' or that 'Nirvana is God'. This though should not stop us from seeing that in some ways the impulses towards the Transcendent both in Buddhism and classical Christianity may have a convergence in the mystical life. The negative way of Pseudo-Dionysius is not untypically closer to the multiple negations of the Buddha. The Neoplatonic tradition in any case echoes with that of India, and there may indeed have been some real contact between the East and Alexandria, and who knows what traditions lay behind that mysterious teacher of Plotinus, Ammonius Saccas? It is nice to think, though it may alas be only wishful thinking, that there is a strand of holy thinking issuing from the Ganges into the very lifeblood of the Christian tradition, through Augustine and others.

Christ and the Buddha

The difference reflects itself naturally in the way in which the Buddha and Christ are seen. The Buddha is one who arrives at the end of the world, at the end of his world. He has a strange transcendental aspect, for he has interpolated nibbana into his stream of consciousness: he has seen the nature of things and seen them from that transcendental point of view. His faint smile is a smile from that Beyond, but a passing smile also. But the crucified Christ, even he for all his humility, humiliation, yet has traces of the great Power he has left behind. The halo of the Christian tradition is a light that shines from the world beyond the world, the gold to be seen in heaven. Thus forever in the Christian tradition is this old problem of how the two natures are combined – how the eternal substance is somehow combined with the human. Thus we find St Thomas Aquinas considering the problem of how it is that God who is changeless can become man (for does not this imply a change?):

1. It seems that the statement, 'God was made a man', is false. For since 'a man' signifies an independently existing subject, to be made a man implies an absolute beginning of existence. But it is false to attribute an absolute beginning to God. It is, then, false to say 'God was made a man'.

2. Moreover to be made a man is to undergo change. Yet God cannot be the subject of change, *I am the Lord and change not* (Matt 3:6). Consequently it appears that the statement *God was made a man* is false.

It is no surprise that Thomas resolves the problem by distinguishing between intrinsic and relational changes. A person can remain unchanged even if someone shifts from standing on his right to standing on his left. There has been a change of spatial relationship though not a change of the person 'in himself'. Of course, it is to be doubted whether Malachi in the Old Testament meant more than that the nature of God is unchanging (his character) and that he is everlasting, rather than any stricter sense in which he is changeless. But let us not worry on that score, for it is surely typical of the classical tradition of Christianity both East and West and partly because of the use of the categories of Greek and Roman culture to treat God as changeless. This is in line too with most of Indian tradition. The transcendental is the changeless. And of course the great intellectual problem of all such theologies is how there can be any living juncture between what changes not and what changes. The question for the Theravada is how it is that the Buddha so to speak makes his way to the Unconditioned. In Christianity the question is how Christ makes his way *from* the Unconditioned. But as we have noted the presupposition of the one concerns power and substance; the other diminishes powers into causalities and substances into processes. For this reason, the one faith takes sacramentalism seriously and the other does not, though admittedly each faith came from a quite different direction (the one had Jewish sacrifice as the form of sacramentalism which it was to transcend; the other had the religion of the Brahmins to reject, save in so far as the ideal Brahmin was still respected).

Priest and Monk

From the perspective of Sri Lanka the Catholic priest has a quite other function from the monk. No doubt merit accrues, as is thought in Ireland or Italy, when a son becomes a priest. It rebounds well to the credit and piety of the family. No doubt too it is a good and worthy thing to respect priests and to give money to keep them in sufficiency. No doubt too the priest is supposed to be a good example of holy living, but his prime duty is something intrinsic to sacramental religion. For it is primarily through him, in classical Christianity, that the power of the divine is channelled. Or at least he administers such channelling. That is the secret symbolic logic beneath his celibacy, for through that he is set apart from the ordinary householder. His clothes too have that special character to indicate divine office. Now it is true on the other hand that the glorious saffron of the bhikkhu's robe in Sri Lanka, deliciously orange against the backcloth of green plaintain trees and the fields of greening rice (orange and green, but not the violence of Ireland), signals that the monk is special. But in a different way. For the priest, sober by day and as he moves among his parishioners, is in the candle light of the mass in blazing gold and red, decked sometimes baroquely with lace. He dons these magnificences to show forth glory: the glory which should surround the sacrament which in turn reflects the light of redemption. The priest thus becomes part of a drama in which old events are re-enacted, for the resurrection of Christ is for ever renewed through the sacrament, as his death also is remembered. Thus the priest helps to present an action in which the power of the divine is operative, and the substance of God made available to the faithful. But this complex of ideas surrounding the Mass is something which is not natural to the Buddhist. For the Buddhist there is no holy Being to make manifest his power. Everything is impermanent, even the most numinous and useful of the gods inhabiting his beautiful island.

The sense of power in Christianity and in the classical Mass in the Catholic tradition is one that is in accord with the numinous character of God as experienced and worshipped; and it is indicated by the very architecture of great cathedrals, as well as by the arrangements of Orthodox churches. These reflect two ways of symbolizing the numinous, and there is nothing parallel to them in the Theravada. For the old Catholic arrangement suggested the long approach to the altar. From the altar the holy accoutrements of liturgy face downwards towards the congregation. The raised altar suggests spectacle as well as the symbolism of height. If soaring arches reach upwards to heaven, the raised hands of the priest with the wafer in them as he offers them in a high gesture to the Source which is somehow present in it are there for all to see. The faithful come to hear Mass, and to see the sacrament, as well as to participate in the rite. Indeed for long periods the Church's main piety was less one of eating the bread, sharing thus in Christ's body and blood, but more one of being present to the very power of the liturgical event. The congregation itself gained substance from the invisible throbbing power of Christ at the altar. Out of such a conception, of course, there arose a whole host of practices in which the power of God was fragmented, controlled, displayed, mediated – the reserved sacrament, the monstrance, even perversely the black Mass.

Though some of these practices and the ideology of the Church-mediated powerful liturgy came under much criticism at the Reformation, as though salvation could somehow be dispensed in doses and given out in response to determinate acts of piety, the general notion remains classical: that Christ is specially present in the sacrament. He is god and so numinous, broken and so bread to be eaten. But the arrangements of orthodoxy express the numinosity quite differently. For the golden action of the liturgy takes place substantially behind the screen of the ikonostasis, and only partially and in glimpses can the faithful see beyond into the holy sanctuary. The movement of the priests in procession outwards into the congregation signals the coming forth of God into the midst of his people, and the coming down of the divine from heaven to earth. Thus is symbolized by the screen and the partial sight of what lies beyond a whole diagram of the numinous. The holy Being is screened from us, and yet is revealed to us: he is invisible, but yet sometimes the veil concealing him is lifted. Thus too we may conceive of the whole cosmos as a kind of screen which (so we know, if we are among those who have faith) has the Godhead somehow behind it. In similar fashion the ikons themselves are meant to show what cannot be shown, to reveal something of heaven through earthly forms. Thus the arrangements of East and West differ in emphasis. The soaring Cathedral and the raised hands of the celebrating priest show the *tremendum* as being *fascinans*; the ikonostasis shows the sacrament as being a *mysterium*. The one elevates the divine, the other gives it half-hidden glory. But both arrangements conduce to the same end for in the language of action, architecture, painting, vestment and candle they seek to convey something of the power of God in Christ, and to express his presence to us here and now, as well as in the Beyond.

In a sacred rite, a sacrament or a sacrifice – some religious action in which the operation is conceived as more than mere symbolization of memory or whatever – in such a rite a change is held to occur. The bread and wine become

Christ's body and blood: they are communicated to the faithful. Something is given, something is received. Such a transaction is a conveying of substance or power. The faithful appropriates to himself something of the divine substance. This is why the term *bhakti* in the Indian tradition which of course means loving devotion has a root which has to do with participation, taking a portion of. The devotee in coming close to God receives something from God. In sophisticated terms (though one does not for that reason need to use technical jargon), such a portion of God is his grace which is bestowed on the believer. In order to understand the logic of the sacrament, then, it is necessary to see how the notion of substance works in religion and life. Here I use the term not in that more austere way in which it serves as a term of art in philosophy, and in such formulae as 'Three Persons in one Substance'. But I use it more freely, as noted above, to provide an expression which can be used both in the field of the history of religions for what is sometimes dubbed *mana* and in more secular contexts, as we shall see when we come to contemplate nationalism.

The Existential and the Holy

We may look upon the holy as a special case of the high concentration of existential power. I say 'existential' meaning that feelings are involved. That which is existentially significant is as it were laden with a certain power, and emanates therefore a kind of substance. It is liable so to say to leak forth from it of its own accord; but it can also more particularly be conveyed, canalized, controlled even by ritual gesture. Consider for instance an instinctive (but actually in part culturally conditioned) reaction when one encounters a strangely unkempt beggar in the street: it is to back away, to avoid. It might be rationalized by saying that he is unhygienic and maybe indeed he is, but even notions of hygiene have a symbolic loading, a less than scientific gestural and ritual component. Putting a little space between oneself and the beggar – walking pointedly on the other side of the street – is a gestural way of saying that one wants nothing or as little as possible of his substance. For it is negative. He is lack of success incarnate, and bad luck perhaps. He is one who rejects the rules of decent society, and so vaguely is a menace to good order. He is vagrant when he should be staid. No suburbanite carries this sort of threat to stability. (Note how vagrancy is a negative way of saying wanderer: the happy wanderer is a different case, rising perhaps above the rules, not sinking Calibanesquely below them, undermining them therefore: also consider the divine wanderer, the *sannyāsin*, the Buddha himself as holy peregrinator.) Many metaphors there are which are used to refer to the miasmic effect of the transfer of substance – as though invisibly we received good and bad invasions, balm, blessing, merit, grace; pollution, stain, curse and so forth. The holy, as an especially concentrated value, contains dangerous power; and the rituals with which people deal with it are intended to make sure that the good or positive value emanating from it is properly conveyed. Thus the person who approaches the holy Being circumspectly, confessing his sin and so averting hostility, that is the destructive interplay between the holy and what is alien to it, hopes to receive something good – the substance of the divine, or rather a portion of it.

This might sound mechanical. It can be, because it is possible to conceive of the Holy as simply a non-personal force and to use sacramental transactions as a way of manipulating the world. But we have to take into account that a power or substance has a certain character, and often is figured as personal Being. As such its behaviour is unpredictable and certainly not just at the disposal of the worshipper. Worship itself may be regarded as being the gestural or ritual acknowledgement of the superior power or value of the Focus of worship: and such an acknowledge-ment of superiority cannot be maintained if the worshipper also holds that he is capable of manipulating the substance of that Focus. Thus there are necessary reasons why it is that the Holy is outside human control.

Self-help and Other-dependence

Thus the idea of grace, so central to devotional religion, arises from the recognition that the superior personal Being of God (the immeasurably superior Being) is in no way beholden to the worshipper: the latter if he is wise recog-nizes God's utter power and beneficence and relies there-fore in hope upon the divine mercy: hope, rather than absolute certainty, because it depends only upon God, and cannot be fully measured by human calculations and predictions. Consequently the atmosphere of salvation or liberation must be quite different in such a religion of worship than in the more orderly (perhaps) and rational-seeming system of the Theravada. For the Theravadin the words of the Buddha are a prescription for self-liberation. The idea that there is any ritual relationship between the goal and *summum bonum* on the one hand and the adherent on the other does not make real sense. The individual has to do the best he can, within the structures permitted to him by his karmic situation. Self-discipline, moral training, yoga, keen attention to the Dhamma and to his psychological condition – such striving is the condition of making progress towards the transcendental goal. Religion – such as the feasts of temple and procession – is a colourful means to stimulate imagina-tion and effort and to give occasion for the gaining of merit. Thus the Theravada can be classified as a faith of self-help, rather than other-dependence.

Buddhism itself later was to make this distinction when in the high Mahayana it was theorized that in latter decadent days, so far away in time and spirit from the teachings of the Buddha himself, men would be unable to achieve their own salvation, but would need to look to the assistance of a celestial Buddha or Buddha-to-be, such as Amida or Kannon. It is true that even in the Theravada without the intervention of Gotama in human history there would have been no prescription, no Path, which men could follow. But given that Path they can tread it for themselves. It is like a do-it-yourself building kit for a radio: this implies that you can make the thing yourself, though of course there would have been no radios without a Marconi. But by contrast Christian faith is most markedly other-dependent. It is on the grace of God in Christ that the Christian must rely. It is through God's various interventions into history, through the Law and through the atonement wrought by Christ above all, that salvation is given to men, if they can only avail themselves of it. The alienation from God's good substance brought about by Adam's act requires a divine and not a human remedy. Here too we note another divergence in atmosphere.

The Buddhist explains our problematic condition through the chain of causation going back to ignorance, that is the failure to have insight into the true nature of the world and of ourselves. It is an analytic explanation. By contrast the Christian explanation of the problems of men is cast in the form of a myth, a story of primordial times. Christianity displays itself here as elsewhere dramatic rather than analytic in style. In brief then: it is not just that Christianity involves the idea that it is by God's act that his beneficent substance is conveyed sacramentally to mankind: it also implies that in receiving Christ the Christian acquires something of his character. The numinous nature of what is Beyond the world is what gives the basis of the belief in grace: but it is reinforced by the personal nature of God and his particular character as revealed in the drama of redemption.

The Shape of Sacramental Power

For a gesture or sacrament is not just the establishing of some general link or channel of communication. There is the particular form or character of what is conveyed. A kiss conveys love: folded hands reverence. So the bread and wine of the Christian communion is intended to convey an inward and spiritual grace no doubt, but grace of a special character, for it is Christ's body and blood that they are – the essence of Christ. In other words the Christian shares in the very drama of Christ's life, his character and his acts. The divine substance is communicated thus in a particular configuration. This is where the Eucharist is a performance very different from just the telling of a story. It is true that we sometimes look on a narrative as making the events it describes live again. They are present to our imagination and feelings, it is true. But the conveying is more solid in the case of a ritual re-enactment. The replay of the Last Supper makes Christ present, really, to the participant here and now. It involves a kind of time travel, the bridging, in the light of eternity, a gap of many centuries. So there is we say a double movement implied in the celebration of the Mass: the movement from the Beyond to this side of the veil, to the world of men; and there is the movement across time from those days to our days. No doubt it is easy to represent this as rather like magic and no doubt the Church has sometimes acted as if it had magical powers to conjure Christ from there to here and from then to now – but such 'magic' is of course not consistent with the idea of the divine power or initiative, which is the numinous premise from which theistic experience starts. If the Theravadin finds a parallel to such Christian notions in his ancient traditions it would be in the Brahmin sacrificial religion which the Buddha rejected: but the whole context there was so very different that only formal parallels remain – the notion of divine power or substance. But Buddhism demythologized all that, and rejected ideas of the mysterious efficacy of rite and language. They were assigned merely a psychological power. But for classical Christianity psychological power was not a sufficient account of the mysterious transactions whereby saving grace was channelled to the faithful.

Sacramental thinking makes a profound difference even when secularized, as we shall see in greater detail later. But let me here give a foretaste of that deduction. The sacramental is a species of the performative act, whereby with gestures and words something is done: where language is not just describing but in an intimate sense doing. When I say 'I promise' a promise is made and it is no use for the bridegroom, sceptical out of the vestry, trying to go back on his words and to claim that before the altar he was lying. 'I will' can be no lie. It is a part of a sacred contract. It is through such acts that things and persons can be said to have performative substances. The officer in the army has such authoritative substance partly in virtue of the commission handed to him by the State and partly in virtue of the 'recognition' of authority in such acts as saluting. It is true that sometimes authority may derive more 'naturally' so to spak from brute facts: the man who carries the gun has power over me in virtue of my fear of him and the threat he possesses. This shows how the web of performatives, in relating to acts and feelings, is continuous with what is existential. The existential power in things and people toarouse feelings and reactions in us is expressed linguistically in a range of performatives, such as exclamations of surprise, amusement, horror, delight and so forth. In the light of such brief reflections, it is not difficult to see that the very notion of the person – the supposedly sacred basis of modern individualism and personalism, the basic time in the pantheon of the humanist – is one with a performative cast. A person is someone towards whom one is expected to act in certain ways. Dehumanization occurs when, for instance, elementary decencies are not observed, when the performances of 'Good morning', of respectful attention, of the handshake, of the giving of privacy, of the use of the right name – such acts are no longer operative. Or it occurs when men are put simply into a machine environment, when they no longer have anything serious but mechanical transactions with their environment. Hence the pathos of *Modern Times*.

The sacred performative lies, then, at the heart of classical Christianity; and its offspring, the idea of substance to be conveyed, transformed, transferred also is vital. This helps to give the Christian life a special flavour, in regard to identity. For instance, the concept of original sin is that all men are in a state of solidarity or identity (of a sort) with Adam, the first man. This was once figured as the actual transfer of that sin through the act of generation (just as we think now that nationality, for instance, basically is so conveyed). Salvation involves the Christian in acquiring a new identity, with Christ the second Adam, through baptism and the other rites of the Church which, taken in the right spirit, bind people to Christ so that they are 'in Christ', and Christ is 'in them'. There is a slightly strange dialectic here – for the Christian is one with Christ in somehow sharing his substance, and yet different from him, in that Christ being divine must be Other than any creature. Similarly the Christian receives God's grace, which is the presence of the divine substance in him; though he does not thereby become God. And that grace both expresses the Christian's likeness to Christ but also enables the imitation of Christ to occur – the imitation which is the ethical translation of the idea of taking on the configuration of Christ's substance. To put it in another way, the Christian's life takes on the pattern of the divine drama.

Thus again we see a contrast with the Theravadin ideal. The stories of the Buddha's previous lives in various human, animal and other forms make for enlightening moral inspiration: they are the Aesop's fables of the East. And the story of Gotama's own life is also good to exhibit the finest qualities to folk. But that which in the last end the Theravadin imitates in the Buddha's is his knowledge, his gnosis, his insight, in the context of the stilling of the flames of passion, the going out of the fire of grasping. But it is not so much knowledge as action that the Christian is called on to imitate: not so much insight or wisdom as love and humility. It is not from this point of view so surprising then that the atmosphere of the one is analytic, the other dramatic. And yet it may be replied that after all the Theravada stresses *karuṇā*, compassion, and *mettā*, loving-kindness. There is surely not a great gulf between the Buddhist and the Christian ethic. Surely not. It is striking how much there is of solidarity between the two. Yet even so the context and the nuances differ. Christian *agapē* has the suggestion of reverence, while Buddhist compassion has the nuance of concern. The one sees in the human being the image of God; the other sees in the individual the sufferer. The two are not incompatible or in contradiction. It is just a divergence of emphasis.

The Self and the Non-self

This of course brings us to what for many commentators has been the strangest split between Buddhist East and Christian West: the doctrine of non-self, the denial of the immortality or eternity of the soul, the rejection of a changeless something within the person. Much has been written in recent times, sometimes with a view to trying to establish somehow that despite everything really the Buddha did not deny a higher Self, but rather only used rather strongly a *via negativa* in case anyone should mistake the higher with the lower self. There have indeed been cultural reasons why some have wanted to escape the relentlessness of the Buddhist denial of the self. From the perspective of Western attitudes and categories there has been something especially uncomfortable and difficult in the Buddha's analysis of the individual into the *skandhas*, or groups of factors. Perhaps too the thought of a religion without God has been hard to take: the idea of a religion which does not have a soul either is especially contrary to many Western preconceptions. At the same time it has been in the interest of those, like Radhakrishnan, who espouse and express the modern Hindu ideology of the higher unity of all religions, to try to show that after all there is not much difference, other than words, between the Buddha's negative way of putting things and the more positive teachings of the Upanishads and the Vedanta. Shankara too has helped to bridge the gap between Hindu being and Buddhist becoming. Yet on the other side we have the overwhelming testimony of so many Buddhists over so many centuries, the struggle which the personalist 'heresy' inspired – thought darkly to reintroduce the *ātman* into Buddhism – the inconsistency between belief in the Self and so many texts. Moreover, what good does it really do in the circumstances to interpret Buddhism in a way not accepted by the weight of Buddhist interpreters? It may of course be that there are theoretical reasons why such a majority should be mistaken; but that itself would be a hard thing to establish. I think it is better to accept a little more starkly that there is a great gap indeed between standard Buddhist analysis and classical Christian belief.

But the gap should not after all surprise us. The non-self idea in Buddhism is in its own way simple and perspicuous, once a certain premise has been accepted. After all it is a simple deduction from the more general thought that everything which we encounter in the world is impermanent, that is it consists in a complex flow of processes. Once we accept this, then clearly there is no point in making an exception for living beings. This must especially be so in that once we look into our own minds and feelings we do not find anything permanent, but rather a whole series of short-lived often very fragmented experiences, ideas and impressions flitting past, so to speak, the mind's eye (itself a wavering and intermittent set of processes). What good would the permanent soul do? It would be changeless and so incapable of doing anything for us or even of binding early stretches of life to later stretches since it would have no special connection of a real, effective kind with either. Consider: if I am thinking now of the blue sky and in a moment's time of the battle of Waterloo something must have brought about the change. But it is no explanation to say that my soul brought about the change unless it itself changed in some way. In that case it too can to all intents and purposes be broken down into a series of changing processes. If by contrast we think that it really is changeless then its existence or otherwise is irrelevant to the transition from the thought of the blue sky to the thought of the Battle of Waterloo. So the soul is empty, nugatory, a useless extra. Or it is just another name for an aspect of our changing life. It may be noted that the argument I have presented can also be considered to be an argument against an unchanging Soul of the universe and by implication an unchanging God. In some sense, as we have noted, God does have to change to be the Creator; and the chief point of believing in a single Being is that he or it somehow lies behind and is the ground of the universe which we see and inhabit. But if we abandon this sense of an ultimate Power and see only changing processes, then it is inevitable that the very notion of static Being and with it the idea of the soul or eternal self will vanish.

This is one side of the Buddhist analysis. Another side is to be found in the actual analysis of the living person into his constituent processes – those of physical form, of feelings, of perceptions, of dispositions, of states of consciousness. Buddhism's actual psychology is a detailed one, and so is its diagnosis of why it is that the living being and the human person in particular is bound to be the ceaselessly changing world of *saṁsāra*. Briefly: perception, presupposing consciousness, operates by contact. Such contact inevitably generates feelings, both pleasant and unpleasant (on the whole, by the way, in the human condition pleasantness predominates, despite all the talk about suffering *dukkha*), and these feelings generate differing forms of grasping. The cure of course is to gain insight into the human state through both increased existential awareness and rigorous analysis. In any event, the way the living person is presented is not vague and not just pictorial: it includes a fairly detailed psychology. For this reason we can see Buddhism from one point of view as a form of therapy, congenial to certain motifs in modern psychoanalysis. Classical Christianity also evolved a complex scheme, especially through the introduction of Aristotelian psychology into systematic theology. Nevertheless, in origin the Christian ideas are less analytic, and again more mythic. Thus the drama of salvation implied that somehow the human being may be restored to a state of beatitude in relationship with God. For varying reasons, such a relationship was figured both as resurrection of the body and as dwelling with God in heaven. Not unnaturally Greek notions of the soul which had a mystical context and importance were also woven into the fabric of thought about the afterlife and the final judgement and transformation of the human person.

The Drama and the Centre

The scheme of classical Christianity is more centralized, moreover, than that of Buddhism, and the central point is man. The great drama of creation is played out in relation to the world of men. It is true that Christianity conceives of angels and devils, of beautiful spirits freely and deliciously praising God in heaven and acting as his messengers between the other world and this: figures notably human in guise, so ikons and art would indicate and the imaginations of the pious, but mysteriously endowed with wings and a kind of luminescence – and figures too more grudgingly God's agents, the Devil and his hosts of assistants ranging earth and the underworld, torturing the damned, putting on strange forms to tempt the living, disguising themselves in sexual beauty and the pride of the flesh, lurking within the seats and corridors of power, ready to lead men into the deadly sins. Perhaps in our day this picture of the ghostly world of angels and devils has faded. We no longer save rather quaintly and spookily (for the benefit of the media) cast out demons; but rather, armed with Freud and electric shocks, bash and cajole the neuroses and psychoses which infest the spirit. Nor does the vision of the angel any longer command much loyalty save briefly at Christmas and for the benefit of children. And perhaps in a way such fading is not altogether untrue to the tradition, for though the angels and demons undoubtedly exist there, they are after all only personifications of divine powers, which centre their attention upon the human world. And why? Because it is in that world that God's creation has its highest expression, for are not human beings not only made in the image of God (whatever that mysterious notion means) but also given sovereignty over the living world? And was it not above all as a human being that God's son came to Earth? His human nature and destiny was there so to speak in the very beginning of time. The fall of Adam was a *felix culpa*, free and yet part of the plan: against God's will and yet part of his purpose: the occasion for the unfolding of the paradoxical power of the second Person of the Holy Three – come with glory, but yet in the shape of a servant. The everlasting Servant. That perhaps is what is a bit unnerving in these latter days with science fiction. Moon landings too have made us see ourselves in a truly existential way, almost a mythic manner, as dwelling on that luminous, blue but oh so fragile ball, swimming and turning so peripherally through space. So the centre seems to have somehow gone. But that was not of course the vision of the classical faith: the wondrous hierarchy of being, the threefold cosmos of heaven, earth and underworld, the great scenario of Dante's epic, uneasy melange of Greek and biblical cosmologies.

The drama for us is frighteningly brief. One life and then the Judgement. No wonder at times the Church could feel itself entitled to inflict pain and torment in order to fix up lives hereafter, if all was to be measured by our sojourn on this earth – like a long visit to Japan, by the time you have adjusted it is practically over. Immanuel Kant could introduce the notion of modifying the schedule, and adding gradualism after death; and the Western tradition could also hark back to the reincarnation of the Orphics and the speculations of Plato's immortal *Phaedo*. But rebirth never really has taken firm root in the Christian West; and purgatory remained as the chief concession to the gradual spirit. But of course early Buddhism is drenched in karma and the cycle of births. A concession to popular imaginings? It is hard to think so, so central is it to the understanding of the whole scheme of liberation in the Theravada. Moreover the Buddha has unmistakably some spiritual relatives in the ancient world out of which he spoke and thought: the Ājīvikas, the Jainas, the Sānkhya tradition perhaps in its pre-historical form. Among the holy recluses, the *śramanas*, sacred and speculative counterparts to the Brahmins, the doctrine of rebirth seems to have been common. Out of this milieu there came that strand in Indian thinking which was to invade the Brahmanic world of the Upanishads, to form the thinking of the *Gītā*, and to shape later Indian consciousness. It is hard to look on the Buddha's simply adopting the belief as a concession to weakness; although it is true there have been interpreters of the tradition who have greatly underplayed karma and rebirth, as devices, *upāya*. But it is not a doctrine which can be erased from the Pali Canon without great devastation, nor can it be erased from the minds of those Sri Lankans who are, for us, guides through the image-houses and around the dagobas, through the monasteries and along the paths which lead to hermitages and to Adam's Peak.

Rebirth and Karma

Indeed considering the trouble rebirth causes when it is combined with the theory of non-self it must have been deeply entrenched in the tradition to have survived at all. For consider: there is nothing permanent to carry from one life to another. There is a chain of rebirths but no individual running through the whole series. There is a path but no one walking along the path. The only link between lives is causation, is the way one set of processes gives rise to another set – the way my last acts of consciousness give rise to new acts of consciousness associated with another complex of groups or *skandhas*. Looking backwards memory can also serve as a link; my early years have set up a chain of processes leading to my present tendency to have certain memory images taken by me to be faithful representations of those events in my life. So just as I am linked to my past through a complicated and turbulent long swarm of processes, so I am connected to previous lives. Here is no idea of a permanent soul. The only thing which is permanent is liberation itself, the transcendental Non-Process set over against the processes of the world and interpolated sometimes into them through the mysterious destiny of Buddhas and of those who sucessfully follow Buddhas to the high mountain of nibbana. But of course rebirth does more than indefinitely extend individual careers; it partially dehumanizes them. I am not likely to be reborn as a human being for did the Buddha not think it was like the case of a blind turtle living at the bottom of the ocean, only rising to its surface once in a hundred years, and of a wooden yoke floating on the surface, namely that the chances of the turtle's coming up inside the yoke are about as great as yours or mine are of being born in the next life as a human being? (So make the most of this wonderful, almost unique opportunity to grasp for that higher insight which brings liberation.) Far from being born as a human next time, I am more likely to emerge as a fish or animal or ghost, though godlike existence or purgatorial suffering is a possibility too. The living world contains unseen reaches; and in any event this world-system is only one among an uncountable number, as we have seen. The pattern of rebirth is thus widely diffused throughout the whole vast cosmos. And though human beings may be important, for only humans can be Buddhas, and only those who know the nature of existence as discovered by Buddhas can gain liberation, yet the human condition is not so centralized as it is in the case of classical Christianity. Curiously, but this is a matter for later reflection, karma, which goes classically in India with a diffused cosmology, represents a problem for scientifically oriented modern Buddhists; while it is the teaching concerning the uniqueness of man, which makes for a tidy, small universe, which is the cause of Western uneasiness in the face of modern biology and astronomy.

The theory that living beings reap the fruits of their actions in former lives and in this life is most attractive as a way of dealing with the misfortunes and inequities of the world, as at least it first appears. It creates a very comprehensive framework for viewing virtue, vice, good and ill. It also makes possible a certain stratification of holiness: that ordinary folk may not have to strive so strenuously as the monk in the pursuits of self-control and liberation is a sign of their karmic unpreparedness for the higher life. It lends itself thus to a spiritual elitism. It also lends itself to a gradualist approach to the education of the masses and in general to missionary work. It may be that Buddhism's astounding past successes in spreading over so great a part of Southern and Eastern Asian culture is a tribute to this rather leisured method. The Christian picture of redemption has been more urgent, harsher in many ways, but replete with energy. Moreover it has much more than Buddhism expressed a community ideal in salvation – the communion of saints is a heavenly counterpart to the new Israel upon earth. Thus when the family groups and individuals come walking to the temple to pay their respects they are it is true consciously part of a social fabric: but the rite is more individualistic. The Christian style of worship is more resolutely congregational.

Yet there is a nice paradox about the mysticism both of East and West. The contemplative seems to be on a voyage from the alone to the Alone; or from the non-self to the Empty. Seated, for instance, on a level piece of ground beneath a spreading tree, the Buddhist yogi is looking inwards. He seems to be profoundly by himself. Similarly one might think of St Anthony and other heroes of Christian asceticism, who played a part in the rise of the Christian mystical tradition, as being loners. The paradox is that it is typical of the mystical traditions that the loners band together into groups: the Sangha, the monastery, the Sufi order. There are various factors at work: the mutual help, the need for spiritual advisers, the demands of discipline, the economic fruits of piety, the concentration of cults, etc.

We have in the course of this exploration seen a number of the primary ways in which the Theravada and classical Christianity diverge: in cosmology, in the valuation of history and the drama of redemption, in the attitude to the question of Creation and the existence of a numinous Being behind the world and working through it, in the sacramentalism of the one and the more analytical approach of the other, in the great difference in career and atmosphere between Jesus and the Buddha, in the analysis of the troubles of mankind, in the matter of belief in an afterlife, in the relationship of each to worship and the idea of God. For all the sympathy which can flow outwards from Christian love and Buddhist benevolence and compassion, the gulf between the two systems does indeed seem a large one. What are the bridges that can reach across the chasm? Can we explain why it is that great religions should start and develop in such divergent ways? Are there after all some common characteristics, or some fundamentally similar basis and means of reconciliation of the two worlds? In brief, how do we diagnose the difference between the faint smile of the Buddha and the dark power of the Pantokrator? The answers to such questions are part historical but part philosophical. So let us turn then to reflect about the two faiths, as we have glimpsed them so far.

4

Reflections on Buddhism and Christianity

Pattern and Accident in Religion

To try to bring understanding of how it is that the Theravada and Christianity differ so much and yet may belong in their own ways to a general history of religions is a great task. But it is one which can yield fruit. For nothing is more barren than accepting at the start that the divergences are mere accidents of history and culture. That there are accidents of history and culture who would deny? The shape of Indian religion is, for instance, partly determined by adventitious geography: the Himalaya range, for instance, has had a powerful effect on Indian symbolism. Given the great 'snow-store', the vast upthrusting mountains, the cascading streams tumbling down into the plains, the rarefied air and the arching effect of the peaks – it was no surprise that India should often think that the continents were clustered around a vast mountain, Mount Meru. Still the details of that magic mountain may give us some surprise. It is traditionally thought to have been 80,000 leagues high. Round it are great circular mountain ranges sticking out of the ocean, the seventh and outermost being a mere 1,250 yojanas high. Outside of it are the four continents, including the southern continent, the island of the rose apple tree, Jambudvipa, often identified with India, or else with the whole of the known world. Of course, once one begins to look at such mythic geography

one perceives that certain less accidental features have
entered into traditional Buddhist thinking. Mount Meru
itself represents the axis of the world, the great thrusting
central pole going up through the earth to the heavens: it is
the path up which the holy man may in his strange
experiences ascend. It is the symbolism of the centre and
the symbolism of height combined. And such spatial
symbolism is characteristic of human culture: archetypal
one might wish to say. So we will generally find that men's
systems of belief, their worldviews are like much else of
their cultural existence, a mingling of pattern and serendip-
ity, of theme and accident. It is characteristic of the human
being to try to make sense of the accidents, to weave
personal or collective existence into a kind of collage
(nothing changes so much as the past, we might say). So
though we must look to the genesis of Christianity and
Buddhism necessarily in certain configurations of particularity, there may nevertheless be some recurrence of theme
and contrast of pattern which may make sense of their
divergence.

We could of course look at things more concretely, and
less from the point of view of the history of religions, but
from the angle of commitment. What is the Christian, for
instance, to say about the Buddha's teaching and experience, given that in the Theravada at least it is hard to
discern anything approaching a personal theism? Putting it
crudely: Did the Buddha see God but not realize what he
was apprehending? Conversely, the Buddhist might ask
what is to be made of the whole history of Christian theism
given that it seems to rest (according at least to Buddhist
analysis) on a mistake? Can one deflate it by supposing that
it has a Freudian origin – that the Christian God is Dad
projected large, and has no external substance? Or is it
possible that some Christian contemplatives – men such as
whoever it was wrote the works ascribed to Dionysius the
Areopagite, and Eckhart and others who have emphasized

the unknowability of God, his ineffability – have in fact reached the higher stages of contemplation even if they have failed to draw the right conclusions from their experience?

Again, we might see the faiths from a Marxist or humanist angle, and consider them ultimately, for all their nobilities here and there, to be delusions. But even here there is the unnerving question as to how it is that alienation should take such differing forms. But these questions – of secular analyses of religion – I shall leave to the second part. For the time being, let us try to look at the two religions (or phases of religion) from the perspective that, given their differing accounts of the world and of the way to release and redemption, there may nevertheless compatibly be a manner of accounting for the differences that makes use of recurrent themes of religious experience and symbolism. And it seems that it is with the mystical that we find the best starting point.

The Purification of Consciousness

Mount Meru may remind us that the idea of an ascent up the *axis mundi* to the high heavens (as well as the idea of a trip to visit the land of the dead) is a theme of shamanism. It is, that is to say, a theme to be found among hunting cultures and projected symbolically into later civilizations. And we may think that there are relations between shamanism and the practice of yoga. There are also relationships to other styles of religious experience. Muhammad's night journey to Jerusalem is suggestive of shamanism, as also is Paul's account of how whether in the body or out of the body (God knows) he was taken up somehow into the higher heavenly world. It may be that we can see in shamanism a kind of prototype religious experience and symbolism which lies behind the varying patterns of religiosity later to appear in the historic era of men's life. So it may well be that Indian yoga was not without shamanistic antecedents. Even in the sophistications of Buddhism there are traces: the various levels of *jhāna* or meditation correspond to the various heavens as the adept moves to ever more refined planes of existence. Again, the heat generated by many a yogi of the Buddha's day and even of our own is reminiscent of the way in which fire is used in sweat lodges and the spiritual prototype of the sauna. Typically the Westerner sweating it out in the sauna is thinking of his waist line not of the higher purifications and ecstasies which heat can induce: transmute the spiritual into the physical – a typical ploy, perhaps a hangover of the sacramental attitude. Nevertheless, though the symbolic background of yoga is important, the way it developed in the Buddha's time was increasingly technical and analytical. It is as though the various factors and forces of the psyche had to be labelled and clearly distinguished as part of the whole project of mastering them and so gaining a state of pure and unruffled consciousness.

It is this purification of consciousness which in one way or another unites mystics or contemplatives from different traditions. True what is found in such a state is described rather differently: and it could be that purification is only so to speak a stage on the inner way. To questions of the relation between experience and its interpretation we must return a little later. But that the contemplative succeeds somehow in going beyond ordinary shifting thoughts and mental images, and cuts out in his interior life the external perceptions of ordinary life; that he or she finds himself experiencing something to which the usual distinction between subject and object is no longer quite apt; that in such a state time so to speak stands still, and a kind of experienced timelessness appears; – about such descriptions of the inner mystical life one can find very widespread agreement. But the yogi or mystic does not just of course live in this rarefied state: in his return from the mountain, so to speak, he confronts ordinary life, and therefore there must emerge the relationship between the higher state and everyday existence, between the imageless and the images, between the timeless and the temporal. The varied interpretations of his experience provide that bridge between the two realms, that way of relating. They also may have been part of the ways used to approach the higher state: the worldview of the contemplative already determines much about his quest, its shape and feeling. More than that: there may be a dynamic interaction between the purified state of consciousness and the concerns to understand and cope with the world with which the contemplative may already of course have been wrestling. And in the case of the Buddha one can say something like this: not only had the Buddha in his quest for spiritual depth practised various forms of yoga, powerful elements of which were to be incorporated into the Buddhist tradition; but also he had explored various speculative, spiritual and philosophical analyses of the way the world is. He was concerned not just to find peace (one aspect of the stilling of consciousness in its higher states), but also insight. And so the Dhamma which he taught was both contemplative and analytic: both a matter of experience and understanding. There has been a certain swinging as of a pendulum in later Buddhist history, now towards making it predominantly intellectual, now towards something of immediate experience. But the intention is between the two, a kind of fused balance between what can be found in higher consciousness and what can be discovered through reflection. Philosophy is liberating if properly conducted and consciousness if rightly directed is philosophically illuminating. So we have to ask, regarding Buddhism as it developed into the Theravada, what reasons seem to have been behind the relentless drive to dissolve things into impermanence, and with them the substantial soul or self?

The Context of the Buddha's Search

One needs to see the matter in context. At the time of the Buddha there were various schools, with the leader of some of which he is supposed to have studied. Basically, as we have noted, they belonged to those movements known as sramanic, after the term *śramana* or wandering holy man. These were teachers alternative to and often in conflict with the Brahmin class. The latter sometimes joined with *śramanas* and took on their way of life and ideas, but in doing so they excluded themselves from the pukka tradition to which they belonged. That tradition not only gave them a preeminent place in society, but also entitled them to administer the sacrificial rites which had played so large a part in later Vedic religion and whose inner meaning was to be discussed so profoundly and mysteriously in the Upanishads. Roughly speaking we can say that such belief in a supreme God as the Buddhist scriptures discuss was that held by some or most Brahmins, and which gave a special place not merely to the great gods of the Vedic hymns but very centrally to Brahmā. This personal being, personal variant so to say of that neuter power *Brahman* which pulsed through the sacrifice and was part of the very marrow and substance of the Brahmin himself, was conceived both as Creator and of course as having a special relationship to the Brahmin class. Though the Buddhist scriptures incorporate a critique of theism (as the belief that there is an eternal God and that everything else is non-eternal), the primary concern was with the kinds of doctrine which were current in the sramanic schools.

It is reasonable to say that the theism essentially rejected by early Buddhism was that associated with the Brahmin tradition, partly because it was part of the sacrificial and class system which came under the Buddha's criticism. In other words, when we ask the question, perhaps too concretely: 'Could it be that the Buddha had experience of

God but interpreted the Transcendent quite differently?,'
we should at least recall that any rejection of theism had
little to do with the dynamic personalism of Jewish monotheism or the classical conceptions of later Christianity. It is
easy for us to be anachronistic and neglectful of context.
The fact is that the Buddha might have come to say
something rather different had he been acquainted with
Plotinus or Paul. This does not mean that it is incorrect for
Buddhists now on the basis of the canonical tradition to
undertake a critique of Western theism. The best Theravadin minds of today have been pretty much convinced of the
incompatibility of Buddhism and theism as understood in
the West. But once we remember the variation of context,
once we remember that rejections are themselves functions
of the beliefs which are rejected, then it seems more
reasonable to distance ourselves more from the concrete
form of the question we have raised above, and say
something more like this: 'Does it seem at all reasonable and
in accord with the facts of religious history to suppose that
the same transcendent X would be experienced under
different forms and in such a way that both Isaiah and the
Buddha might in differing ways have been in touch with
the same Reality? And could it be that the belief systems
emerging separately in differing cultures represent differing grids of interpretation, but because they point beyond
themselves to something (or some things) discovered in
revelatory or enlightenment experience, there may be some
higher level of interpretation which would help us to
understand the experiential roots of the different systems?'
In other words, it may be that a theory of types of religious
experience will help to make sense of the variations in
spiritual position most starkly perhaps represented by
sacramental theism on the one hand versus analytical
mysticism on the other.

Types of Religious Experience

My theory, already outlined, on this score is as follows. The mystical experience, which perhaps could better be named differently, and by which I mean the purified consciousness in which the eternal somehow presents itself, very often as a result of or in the context of a strenuous path of self-discipline, both physical and psychological, can occur in differing cultures but does not *require* for its interpretation the postulation of a God. It may be seen in the context of God. It may itself be interpreted as a kind of union with God. It may or may not be the case that somehow theistic mysticism incorporates into the yogic experience something which goes beyond or is somehow superior to that kind of consciousness-purity which does not. It could of course be the other way round – but note how terms like 'higher' are value-laden: our immediate task here is not to say what is true or better but to consider possibilities of how things actually are and have been in the actual operations of religious experience. The main point is that there is a kind of transcendental consciousness-purity which enters as a dynamic element into various religious traditions. The importance of this thesis is partly to be found in what it denies. What it denies is that such inner consciousness-purity is at all the same thing as certain other important modes of religious experience. The person who somewhat like Wordsworth feels a kind of unity with all that is, who identifies in his inner feeling with the natural world around him – such a person has an experience which taken in conjunction with consciousness-purity is significant, and which is relevant to it. But it is not the same. It is described very differently.

If we sometimes think that it converges it is because as a matter of fact a certain sort of monism can be generated from different directions. It can be generated from the experience we have just referred to. But it can in differing guise be generated because consciousness-purity when interpreted as an experience of the holy Being underlying the world can lead to the idea that the true self found in consciousness-purity is identical with that Being, for the subject-object dichotomy has disappeared. In one case the person feels unity with nature directly in experience: in the other case the unity is felt in experience, but via some interpretative steps of identification. Again: it is not only that unity-with-nature experience differs from consciousness-purity. It differs markedly from that which classically has been described as the numinous experience. Here the individual is confronted by something awe-inspiring out there. Or if he hears something as it were tolling in his head it is perceived as coming from an Other. The dualism of subject and object – of subject and subject, we might say, for the numinous Other is typically perceived as a personal Being: in the case of Arjuna in the *Gîtā* as a personalized nuclear explosion, it seems like – this dualism is intrinsic, vital, striking. It is true that we also have to consider cases of possession where something funny indeed happens to the subject-object dichotomy, but let us leave these cases on one side for the time being. The notion of the Other is not an equal one, either: as the use of the capital 'O' rather feebly points out. The Other is overwhelming, fearful, crammed with value somehow, of great and powerful substance. No wonder the person confronting the Lord in such circumstances finds his hair standing on end, or thinks that he is a sinful creature, or feels it would be safer if somehow the Lord went away. So it is not just that there is a twoness as between the Other and the subject: there is a qualitative difference in which the superior power and value of the Other is displayed.

From this sense of Otherness, superiority, so much else in religion flows: the sense of dependence, for it is presumptuous for the subject to suppose that he can truly influence the Other; the idea of grace, for power flows down from the Other to the subject, and again reliance on works would itself be a way of staking out an inappropriate independence; the sense of the supreme Power of the other which may imply that all of the universe flows from him in some way; the sense of holiness and goodness, for the good things of life including ethical conduct and good emotions, must be related to the Other's supreme concentration of value. Sometimes it may look as if the religion of the numinous involves a simple appeal to power. And after all God did in effect use that 'argument' with Job, in the end. But that in itself helps to reinforce the sense of the uncontrollability of the divine. How often do we hear that it is not right to try to make God conform to norms invented by men, and so it is easy to be critical of an appeal to holy Power from a standpoint that may after all not be quite appropriate, within at any rate the boundaries of religious experience and sentiment. Above all, the experience of the Other generates worship. The reaction of the subject in acknowledging the Other's majesty is something which in ritual can be formalized as liturgical worship. In that the sense of the Other is both acknowledged and stimulated, both expressed and evoked.

In the Theravada the saint does not worship nibbana. He may commend it as the *summum bonum* but it is not in any ordinary sense a source of power, nor is it the Other, still less a personal Creator. If in any way the consciousness-purity and the numinous experiences point to the same Something or Someone, then it is only so, so far as we can see, in virtue of some theory which seeks to show a rather complex relationship between language and practice on the one hand and the postulated Ultimate on the other. To that we shall come. But it is facile and logically naive simply to say that God is transcendent, nirvana is transcendent – so God and nirvana are the same. Or that God is *summum bonum*, nirvana is so too – so the two are one. Or that there is a supreme sacredness about both so that they must

somehow be the same. Or even that the X is beyond
language, so surely in the ineffable sky beyond the clouds
of language somehow the various different shapes of religion can meet, shining, unseen. The facts or supposed facts
to which I have alluded in hinting at arguments which
apologists for the transcendental unity of religions use all
may show that ultimately the identity of what the Buddha
saw and what Jesus heard can be affirmed. Can be, not
must be. They provide possibilities, not entailments. As
arguments in any case they are fallacious as they stand. But
in simplifying perhaps I do misrepresent.

Briefly, then, I would argue that there are different
patterns of religious experience, and it is in part because of
this that the great religions differ. The fact that the Buddha
was bound up as many of his sramanic associates were with
the practice of a kind of yoga aimed at self-control and the
increasing purification of consciousness meant that he was
not inclined much to take seriously the numinous gods. It is
a view entrenched in Buddhism that the saint can see the
gods in a way which even the Brahmin cannot; but in
seeing the gods the saint sees through them. It is as though
the power emanating from gods and spirits and from the
evil Satanic Mara were seen as merely transitory. The
numinous, in brief, was seen as a subsidiary thing, and
paradoxically of little power when confronted by the
emptiness of the pure consciousness.

The Numinous in Buddhism

Now maybe it will be said that this diagnosis is scarcely
true of the great Vehicle and the Vajrayana. The fearful
aspect of Tibetan divinities, the power which emanates so
beautifully from Amitābha, the devotion inspired throughout the Mahayana by the great Bodhisattvas, the fearsome
aspect of Nichiren – these and other evidences will be
brought in to try and redress my balance. I am glad about

that: because I think that precisely they reflect the truth – that in the Great Vehicle and the Vajrayāna (and especially in the latter) the personal Other comes to play a much more colourful and central role. The Great Vehicle is a weaving together of differing strands of religion. But at the moment I am reflecting about the Theravada. But even so (it will be said) I have maybe underplayed the reverence emanating from the Buddha images, the sheer numinosity of the Perahera, the marvellous powers of relics and so on. Perhaps I have. But let me explain such power in a special way. I shall use a perspective which much later on in my argument as to the ultimate meaning of the divergences between the Theravada and Christianity will be important and I hope enlightening. For the moment let me just state this view of the matter with a certain dogmatism.

We notice with stained glass windows how dull they are from the outside and how wonderfully they glow from the inside. So it is with the gods and the powers of Buddhism. Viewed from those as it were inside this world – the world beyond in a sense seems wonderful: the Buddha so to speak glows with golden light when seen from the angle of the ordinary world. But once outside this world the glories are nothing. In the light and open air of the eternal the individual no longer needs the shelter or the props of the church. The saint sees nothing in the outer show: what for others are beauties are neither beautiful nor the opposite. As when we look at a stained glass window from the outside: it does not seem very meaningful judging it on its appearance from there.

It might be worth noticing that just as the Buddhist may be unimpressed by the gods and even the great god Brahmā, so he might not be much impressed either by the great god Yahweh or the great avatar Christ, you could find quite a number of Christians who would be rather unimpressed by the yoga, the *dhyānas*, the purification of consciousness. Such meditations and self-control are rather foreign to the spirit of the revivalist preacher. But as I have said earlier, such confrontations have a certain anachronism about them. But it is worth briefly speculating about the Buddha in the Western Isles of Scotland, or of Billy Sunday (or Graham) in the rock temples of Dambulla, Sri Lanka, to realize from what different experiential premisses the two religions come (or at least the two sub-religions come). For it leads us to reflect about the ultimate meaning of these styles of experience in today's world. At any rate, the first part of any overall theory of religion will concern patterns of religious experience: and I have referred so far to three – the mystical or consciousness-purity type (which may itself of course have a number of forms), the numinous Other type (which again may have more or less personal forms) and the panenhenic type (to use the expression Zaehner used). I have also made some reference to shamanism, which may have within it elements that later were to be found distinctly in prophetism and in yoga. Because it involves ecstasy and possession by spirits, it exists as it were in a form which can move in either direction – inwards towards pure feeling, or outwards to what comes from outside in order to possess one. Possession, one may note, is a natural outflow of the numinous, in the sense that the Other breaks into a person's consciousness and this breakthrough opens up a channel so to speak through which there comes the substance of the divine. That substance may take on the particular configuration of the truth, as held within the Other in some way, and that truth, conveyed into the prophet or oracle, thus makes the person share a portion of the divine. So that when uttering that truth he speaks on behalf of God: 'Thus saith the Lord'. The spirit works within him, and so in a partial way he is possessed.

Substance and Sacrament in the Indian Tradition

Now we have also considered another polarity evident in the contrast between the Theravada and classical Christianity: the relationship to notions of substance and sacramental power. This is also, by and large, a contrast between Buddhism and the Hindu tradition. For Hinduism has much to do with the mediation of holy power, Brahman or more personally the Gods. The famed convergence between Buddhism and the Hindu tradition which made the former increasingly irrelevant because no longer a striking alternative had much to do with the Tantric emphasis, which reintroduced the *mantra* into Buddhism, the sacred formula, through which sacramental action is brought about. But perhaps we need to see the Buddhist tradition first of all merely as mystical, as tending to the purification of consciousness. Now other schools went in that direction too. And they evolved rather different worldviews, incorporating the idea of eternal souls or life-monads. We need to see the Buddha's originality against the light of his critique of the notion of substance and the reasons behind it. For it is highly relevant to the way in which we may evaluate the spiritual and intellectual aspects of a religion in interplay. It helps to illuminate why and to what degree a religion needs to be philosophical. So why was it, then, that the Buddha did not take what after all might seem to be quite a natural path, namely that if you can attain to purity of consciousness you come to the timeless essence of the human being, and this is a soul?

The Logic of Non-self

It solved, I think, a number of different problems. First of all it brought the doctrine of liberation closer to experience. If the whole point of the teaching was to lead people to the Unborn, then let it alone stand as the ultimate 'reality'.

What is experienced there has no structure, for consciousness has been purified in the most extraordinary way. Why not let liberation, so to speak, explain liberation, without bringing in a timeless self, which, after all, turns out to be superfluous once we look at the world in terms of combinations of conditions and combinations of processes. Second, in dissolving substances the doctrine also dissolved *Brahman* as a Being, and so dissolved the divine Reality of the Brahmins. Thus it is common in the Buddhist scriptures for the expression *brahmabhūto* to occur and other combinations where the holy-power word is used, but it is used in quite a dissolved manner – the saint is someone who is brahma-ised, attains the brahma-states, and so on. The emphasis is upon movements, attainments, processes, dispositions; not upon a static Something underlying the whole of reality. Third, it seems reasonable to suppose that you can work the contrast between the mutable and the eternal in a number of ways. For instance, you can have one eternal Substance which lies behind or gives rise to a host of mutable substances. Or you can have an eternal Substance which lies behind simply a lot of processes. If you do this you tend to treat the processes as modifications of the Substance, like waves on the ocean or bodily changes of a person: thus, more or less, Rāmānuja in the Hindu tradition. But why not have an eternal non-Substance in contrast with a whole lot of processes? Why not treat the Unborn not as a kind of superthing, but as a timeless state? This seems to be an aspect of the Buddha's originality, that he could see the possibility of a way of looking at the eternal in a manner which none of his contemporaries did.

Another thing which the total doctrine of impermanence achieved was a realization of the often misleading character of language. It is a matter of convention, not of intrinsic meaning, that words mean what they do, and this being so it is no surprise to discover that the conventions of worldly men have produced concepts which are all right for manipulating the world and for understanding it at a surface level but are misleading when it comes to the depth of things. Thus labels such as 'I' suggest that there are substances somehow beyond appearances, and selves and things permanently holding the world together in little packets, but this is largely an impression growing out of our perceptual and other apparatus. So the Buddha set his feet along that middle path between realism and idealism, which stressed how much what we think of as the world is the projection of our own psyches and our own structures of language. This momentous distinction between conventional language and a higher or deeper level of truth was developed in the Great Vehicle in a dramatic way, to which we shall later come.

The doctrine of impermanence by placing the emphasis upon change also of necessity raised the question of what causes change: it was the Buddha's perception that only a change can explain a change which gave his outlook such philosophical power. It also led the Buddhist into thinking about what the particular laws of change are. In particular, there was the role assigned to karma in the developing tradition. If there are no things which hold packets of events together it must be regularities or patterns which constantly reappear in the way the flux works its way onward – and that complex pattern known as karma was a way of explaining how individuals persist both within one life and from life to life. Thus a pattern of causes was the substitute for a soul, together with the promise of liberation. For all the eternal soul could really do was (spuriously) to offer continuity through a succession of lived experiences and to promise the possibility of its isolation from worldly experiences, namely liberation. Combine karma and nirvana and you have a quite sufficient account of reality, so far as the progress of the individual goes.

By breaking up substances also the doctrine of impermanence helped to dissolve conventional attitudes and to induce a new moral vision. A new vision – because all concern for a permanent and precious self had to disappear once one realizes one is but a conventionally named swarm of differing patterns of events, held together in unity by the warp placed upon them by the law of karma. And a break from the conventional view of the world since nothing now seems really as it appears to be. We swim as it were in a mist of short-lived processes, to which we contribute colour, feel and emotion as they interact with that swarm which constitutes ourselves. The tiny atomic processes in my eye spin outwards to meet the processes flying away from the so-called solid objects around me. And if the only ultimate satisfaction is a permanent one then there is nowhere amid these swarms of events that we shall find it. Nor is there an I on which to rely. In brief, the doctrine of impermanence has a certain speculative, analytic validity; but its attraction from the practical angle lies in the fact that it substitutes a new vision of reality which tends away from selfishness and towards a kind of higher neutrality of feeling. The criticism of common sense is an instrument in the leading of a life conducive in the end to the non-dual perception of that eternal state which is nirvana.

Buddhism as Pure Mysticism

The radical attack on ideas of substance and sacramental power means that Buddhism, so far at any rate as we have here encountered it, is a kind of pure mysticism: mysticism in the sense that it is contemplative in character and tends to the purification of consciousness and the perception of the Transcendent – and 'pure', if that be the right word, in the sense that it does not blend pure-consciousness with ideas of God or divine Substance. It does not interpret the highest stages of meditation with any foretaste of the beatific vision of God such as the blessed enjoy in heaven;

nor does it see in pure consciousness the Ground of Being or the sacred Brahman-Atman. Incidentally, it is this 'purity' of Buddhist mysticism which has for many Westerners a great attraction, in so far as they may have become disillusioned with the God of the preachers – a God sometimes perceived as abrasively human, patriotic, respectable, without psychological insight, in conflict with science. The inward thrust of Buddhism moreover chimes in with the introspection so likely to result from the atomization of society and its shifting reliance on good feeling as its cement.

Does this judgement about Buddhism, as pure mysticism, mean that the mystic does not see God? Or let me turn the question around and look at Buddhism from the angle of the theist. What, then, is to be said about the Buddha? Does he see God but not recognize him? Posing the question thus is maybe making things a bit too concrete. Still, it is a possibility, in the framework of my theory of types of religious experience, that the Transcendent can be perceived under different aspects. After all, it is frequent in the mystical traditions to speak of the ineffable, the cloud unknowing, the Abyss, the One and so forth: such terms are mysterious perhaps but they suggest a kind of experience which is beyond images, beyond relationship, beyond time. Even within the bosom of very personally oriented Christian mysticism such motifs recur. Why should it not be said that there is an aspect of the divine Substance which is not personal (is if you like transpersonal), which is timeless, inscrutable, dazzling? Why then not say that consciousness-purity is an avenue for the vision of God, even if this interpretation is not placed upon it by the Buddhist and some other non-theistic mystics? So my theory of types of religious experience is quite compatible with the claims of a theist, and for that matter the claims of a Buddhist. For the former, the mystical is one access to the divine; for the latter, there is no high evaluation of those factors in experience which may lead to and express belief in God – but rather mysticism is seen as sufficient in itself, if properly viewed through the lens of the Buddha's analytic teaching, to serve as the liberating experience of the Transcendent.

Though religious experience may be a dynamic aspect of the way religions develop, it is wrong to suppose that we can see them out of context. They have to occur within a framework of interpretation. Thus ultimately the question of whether an experience is 'valid' or not is a question to be addressed in a wider milieu. Moreover it is clear that interpretation so to say colours experience. The Buddhist practising the stages of meditation understands what he is doing against a whole frame of teachings and traditions; similarly the numinous irruptions into prophetic experience themselves are perceived against a pre-existing background, though they may give rise to revolutionary new accounts of reality. This context-relatedness of experience means not only that the comparative task is a delicate one, but also that we cannot simply treat autobiographical and other accounts of mystical or numinous experience as simple descriptions. Of course there is also a general question of validity which as philosophical folk, reflecting, we need to consider.

The Validity and Invalidity of Religious Experience

For it may well be felt by many people that this concern with transcendental experiences is after all a little precious and misdirected. What can one find in the depths of meditation but the bright reflections of a sense-starved brain? What is there is pure consciousness but an uninteresting blank? In an age of science in any case perhaps we shall be able to go beyond the dream of the Sixties – the dream that by LSD or other substances the gates of heaven might be swung open: perhaps by fiddling with the cortex through electrical currents and the like it might be possible to short-circuit human experience and climb by technology to the highest stages of Buddhist *dhyāna*. Or again, it may be thought that the numinous theophanies to which the prophets testify are only peculiar projections out of human wishes and fears. In brief, it may be easy to think that religious experience as such has no validity. We are, so to speak, captured for ever within the colourful prison of the empirical world, and can never break out of it whether by plunging inwards or by waiting for voices from afar. If it is knowledge we want, then this is yielded by the procedures of science, by criticism, experimentation, empirical enquiry: not by some crazed gnosis or grace whose provenance must lie in an earlier, prescientific world. Maybe.

But this life needs to be an examined life, open to the critique which comes from Beyond. We need a critical voice from the Beyond. The prophet and the mystic have only in past times provided this because they genuinely felt that they had perceived the Unborn or the Ancient of Days. But for the moment I do not wish to enter into the general question; but rather to look upon the dynamics of religion as they relate to different types of experience. So far then, I have characterized Theravada Buddhism as a pure mysticism controlled by a psychologically-oriented analysis of reality which helps both in understanding and in the path of self-training (that is, the philosophy is in an important sense pragmatic).

Prophetic Religion and Christ in History

The numinous experience of the Jewish tradition found its most obvious expression in the lives of the Prophets. Can one also speak of something sacramental in the tradition? The clear candidate is the Law: which was an objectified something through which God's mind was mediated to the Jewish people and which by its system of injunctions could produce behaviour that was holy, keeping the people of God apart from others and thus in a special relationship to his Power. Naturally, those who look upon the Torah as simply a set of regulations fail to perceive its sacred significance and the fact that it has a transcendental exist- ence beyond the words over which the learned can pore and contend. It is an unusual sacrament perhaps; but it does provide an outer vehicle whose inward meaning is a communication from God to his people. Of course, the Torah is a complex object: partly written, but also enacted and observed – in the sacrifices in the Temple, in the old days, for example. But side by side with the sacramental- ism of the Law was the critical voice of prophecy, stirred by numinous awe, and speaking, by a kind of possession, in the name of a God who continued to note the failings and follies of those with whom he had so generously entered into Covenant. Again, looking to theisms: the sacramental aspect of Islam can be seen as the Koran, the concretization of the Prophet's messages, but more than a book, for it is laid up in heaven, everlastingly as a kind of offshoot of the divine mind. Let the Koran suffuse your life, with its inspiration and its law, and through that will flow the merciful blessings of Allah, so overwhelming in his awe- some majesty. But in Christianity the sacramental motif took a very different direction: for in a sense Christ is the first sacrament, in that his earthly mind and body and career mediated a pattern of divine atonement to mankind. Secondarily, the power of Christ is mediated through the liturgy, preaching, etc.

There is hardly a question in classical Christianity of language's being misleading. It might be inadequate for speaking or thinking of God; but the world conceived was a real one, in which substances and powers have their varied effects on each other and on men and in general reflect the Creator's will, screwed up perhaps by the Devil. Apart from the fact that *Genesis* implied it, the reality of the cosmos was a reflection of the numinous polarity. If God and worshipper are two, then the worshipper is not nothing. Similarly in a very different context that great Indian proponent of the religion of devotion (*bhakti*), Rāmānuja, argued most vigorously for the reality of things, against the (for him) lethal illusionism of Śankara – lethal because robbing devotion of its ultimate meaning. Likewise Madhva in the Dvaita tradition, and the Śaiva Siddhānta, and the Lingāyats, and the Sikhs, and Caitanya. Wherever you get theism you get the reality of the created cosmos. It stems from the logic of the experience of the Other. All this was of course reinforced for Christianity by the Incarnation. It was not effective, so to speak, if Jesus was a mere phantasm. Norman Mailer once wrote of Nixon that he walked and moved as though his limbs were controlled by a hand inside his head wielding strings. How much more ridiculous would be the thought of Jesus the puppet, son of Mannikin, going through earthly motions for the sake of winning the faithful. No real suffering on the Cross: 'My God, my God, why have you forsaken me' a bit of a fraud. Worst of all: if he does not share human nature, fleshly, wartful, joyous and painful, then how can he expiate for human kind, and how can men genuinely be in solidarity with him in the sacrament and in the drama of salvation? It was this above all of course that moved the Fathers of the Church to resist the heresy of docetism, despite the painful cost of eel-wriggling and formulae required to utter the paradox 'Fully God and fully man'. A phantasm would have made the old monotheism easier. So, then, the Buddhist scepticism of language was not characteristic of the Church; and language too was conceived as part of the fabric of powers and substances impinging on us. It was a linguistic image which dominated so much thinking about Christ indeed: the Logos. And the performatives were conceived in seriousness in the Liturgy, and not just as instruments for inducing certain states of mind. Further a certain realism pervaded the whole mythic aspect of the faith – a factor with incalculable later effects on human history.

It is commonly said that Christianity and for that matter Judaism are historical faiths. This is both true and in two respects misleading. It is true in that the divine drama is played very much in the light of the ongoing swirl of human affairs, history concretely considered. It may be that modern criticism may induce worries as to whether this or that in the Gospels and so forth is true – was the trial of Jesus really like that? Such questions persist. But the fact that we may be in doubt about this or that does not detract from two things: first those who listened to the Gospels through the classical Christian centuries took them to be among other things records of actual historical happenings. And second, Jesus actually lived and in a certain environment. Some sort of history was going on through and around him. But the 'historicity' of Christianity can be exaggerated if it suggests that there is no or little historicity elsewhere in the religions. Moreover it may lead us to forget that it is not just history with a transcendental outreach. Without the conceptions brought to bear, of a transcendent God, of heavenly judgement, of God's dealings with Israel and so forth, the history would just be seen as human history. But for Christianity it is human history against a transcendental backdrop. Moreover, the realism on occasion wears thin and we do not know what to make of certain ideas and stories woven into the tapestry of biblical history. There is old Adam and the speaking snake and Eve's strange birth. There are the bloodcurdling shattering ideas of the last things and the Second Coming. Is this an event in history or out of it? Obviously most Christians in the early Church took it in a realistic not an allegorical sense.

The effects of historical realism in Christianity were to be profound. Augustine's great theory of history long dominated the Western imagination, and provided a charter for the medieval synthesis between Church and State. Various offshoots of theory spurred differing parts of the Church – for instance the idea of Moscow as the third Rome, destined to be the heir of the decadent and protesting West; and the sense of the struggle between Christ and anti-Christ in the historical events subsequent to the Reformation. But there seems to come a time in human affairs when the move is made from the personal beings of myth to strange, at best partly personal, forces and abstraction. Consider the Gnostic hierarchies, the ballet of the Sefiroth in the Kabbalah, the emanations from the One in Neoplatonism. In modern times there is the signal example of Hegel's tremendous dialectic, replacing the older more 'mythic' way of viewing the history of the world; and then of course the tremendous inversions of Marx, providing a secular account of the meaningful rhythms of history which has proved up to a point heuristically fecund and undoubtedly a wonderful (for many) way of dealing with their own problems of collective identity. Thus the Maoist version made a rude and rough sense of modern Chinese history, better sense perhaps than any alternative available; and with it thus was created a tool for action and a scheme through which the reconstruction of China could be perceived and made real.

Identity, Myth and Personalism

Collective identity? I mentioned this because a major function of a myth may be to create identity. Indeed a group needs to have a past, a lineage (or at least a serious, persisting group). So the history in which Christ is involved is not just a set of interesting events but provides the fount and origin of a new Israel, a new community, a new 'we' in which men and women are solid with Christ through the Church and the sacraments and thus as it were

become citizens of a new world. The old myth tied things
and people together very well, for a person had identity
first as member of the human race and thus somehow
participated in Adam's fall; second, the Christian participated in the new Israel, for which the old Israel provided
the background. But in modern times the first part of the
story has been shattered, with the coming of Evolutionary
Theory. It does not matter much whether Darwinianism or
Neo-Darwinianism is correct in the postulated mechanisms
of evolution; what is most important, mythically, is that the
picture of men emerging from a simian background and,
beyond that, various extravagant species way back to some
kind of primeval soup, has taken a pervasive grip upon most
educated people's minds. We need as it were a new theory
of affiliation, so that we may know who 'we' are. Another
feature important both as a deduction from prophetic
experience and from the belief in Incarnation is a kind of
personalism. Men are made it is said in the image of God,
and part of the reason for this is that men are capable of
communicating with God and, most vitally, of receiving
the influx of experience and teaching in which God reveals
himself. The incarnation implies even more intimately that
men are made in the image of God. Not only is God
human, but this was something ordained so to speak from
the beginning, at least as a possibility. So humanity is taken
up somehow into the Godhead. Because of this, and the
realism associated with the Jewish-Christian myth of history, there is for Christianity no question of the ultimate
perishing of the saved (or, more grimly it came to be
thought of the damned). Thus though Christianity has by
no means always been in the grip of the notion of an
immortal soul it has yet been in the grip of the idea of some
kind of God-derived immortality. In the course of the
evolution of European culture, then, certain values stem-
ming from the numinous and sacramental aspects of Christianity have acquired a life of their own: the idea of Nature

as something not only distinct from God but actually emptied of all the other gods; the idea of realistic history as the scenario of salvation and the guarantee of identity; and a strong personalism.

The Mystical in Christianity

And what of mysticism? Was Christ perchance a mystic? We know nothing really of his inner life. But he called God 'Dad', and the main trend of his activities once he 'went public' was not towards contemplation. The fact that there are identity statements in the scriptures ('I and the Father are one') in no way entails anything mystical, for there are many varieties of identity statements in religion and else-where – e.g. 'This is my body and blood'; 'A cucumber is an ox'; etc. Moreover some forms of mysticism, notably the Theravada, do not go in for mystical, that is consciousness-purity, identity statements. Moreover in Jesus' immediate Jewish environment it is doubtful whether we can speak of mysticism proper – thus attempts to trace Jewish mysticism back to Rabbi Akiba seem to me to founder on the problem of definition. Perhaps he would more accurately be likened to a shaman in certain respects. It seems, then, that consciousness-purity as an aim, even without the context of a search within for the great Spirit ruling the world and vivifying the hearts of men, is not a serious motif of early Christianity. This is not to say of course that Jesus and others may not have been visionaries: perhaps indeed though we do now know it Jesus had some kind of encounter with Satan in the desert and some encounter with his heavenly Father that spurred his mission. Consider Paul. Consider for that matter the ambience of Easter and Pentecost. But of the yogic type of quest we do not find serious traces. Yet is was not so very long in the evolution of the Church before gnosis beckoned, and the Desert, and asceticism leading to inward control. And out of such movements

there distantly came the great glories of both Orthodox and
Catholic mysticism: Hesychasm, St Gregory Palamas, the
Jesus Prayer, Dionysius the Areopagite, Erigena, Eckhart,
Suso, Teresa and so on. It should not surprise us. Monasticism, a great womb of interior religion, provided an ideal
of purity once the Church had permeated the secular world
– here was a new 'kingdom not of this world'.

Moreover, the life of prayer itself can take differing
directions, for the self-naughting implicit in adoration can
also develop into techniques of self-purification leading
ultimately to a kind of consciousness-purity. One should
also remember that the great synthesis which Christianity
achieved in its imperial days – the binding together of
Graeco-Roman culture and the prophetic and sacramental
traditions of the old and new Israels – involved taking up
the Neoplatonic tradition, which itself was a noble working
out of Platonism in the deep ambience of the mystical. So
various impulses came together in the formation of Christian mysticism – the new quest for apartness, asceticism, the
intensification of prayer, the other self-naughting side of
adoration, the heritage of Plotinus, the rhythms of monasticism. It is perhaps not surprising that the Reformation
was not so favourable to the inner quest of this kind: was it
biblical? (it could be asked) and did it not depend too
closely on (non-biblical) monasticism? But of course here
certain criteria of judgement were being used. It seems to
me quite valid to say that the evolution of mysticism is itself
in some degree revelatory; and it certainly has (as Merton
and others have shown) been a bridge to Asia. But of course
even here the bright obscurities of the Western mystics
involve a differing ontology from that which we have been
looking at in the Theravada.

Instead of nirvana, a Godhead beyond God; or a super-
essential nature not to be got at by affirmations but rather by
negations, and yet somehow existing or if you like super-
existing beyond the personal nature of the Highest. It is a

bright dark substance which the Christian finds, exuding a kind of love in the melting union, touching inward the very apex or depth of the soul of a person, providing a foretaste of the beatific vision and yet somehow constituting no vision but rather a kind of uniting, a merging, a birth of Christ in the soul. But still different as the framework may be there is a hint of complementarity. The bent perhaps of evangelical Christianity, harking back to prophecies and rather literal tales of scripture, is anthropomorphism. True, the ikons and the plaster saints are banished in the Baptist chapel, just as Cromwell looked sternly on the aids to Catholic piety. True, it is firmly held that God is a Spirit and must be worshipped in spirit. But yet such faith often expresses itself with astonishing anthropomorphism. God speaks, guides, is a Father, punishes the wicked, fights for us, gives us commandments and so forth. Can it be denied that all this is scriptural? It seems so, and yet it is not checked by those elements which exist elsewhere – the traditions of scholastic theology or allegorical interpretation, the work of Rabbis and so on. For much of evangelical Christianity such intermediaries are irrelevant, and an obstacle. But the danger is that God becomes too vividly an old man, too vividly that Father figure which we also experience in childhood, and too easily an unseen spokesman for current human values. Divine anthropomorphism is itself under suspicion because of the changes in modern visions of the cosmos under the staggering impact of science and history. What for many Christians is a kind of comfort, an accessible God to talk to, is for many others an intellectual obstacle. But be all these things as they may, the Buddhist drive in the opposite direction, towards non-personification of the ultimate (and indeed of ourselves), represents a counterbalancing motif. Not surprisingly the Neoplatonist 'higher agnosticism' has been in the Christian tradition a main force in counterbalancing the figure of God as a human person painted large, infinite.

Emptying in Christianity

The self-naughting of the mystical path is of course part of the imitation of Christ. For Christianity contains within itself a strange dialectic. For on the one hand the Christian in being in sacramental communion with Christ not only overcomes that alienation from God which is the source and expression of sin and so of death; but also on the other hand he is a participant in the deathless, partaking that is to say of the divine substance and so gaining an ineffable security. He gains more than the whole world, the pearl of great price. So the Christian has, through the sacraments, the highest possible access to divine power and substance. What more in the whole wide world should he want or need? He is like a god. Christ became man that men should become gods. But though he gains this marvellous power, the form of that power is the opposite of what might be imagined. The power comes bearing a certain configuration and it is by conformity to that shape or pattern of the divine substance that the Christian expresses his oneness with Christ. That configuration is the story of Christ, and that includes at its central point the Crucifixion, the dark culmination of that whole process of self-emptying through which God became man and shed his glories and overriding powers. Dying on the Cross God in Christ felt himself forsaken, since this was true death and true humiliation, not just the playing out of an earthly charade. So too the Christian though he may be destined to rise again yet is destined to follow the Master through Gethsemane and Calvary.

In brief, the power of the divine substance is great, but its form is self-naughting. The Christian gains the highest possible security for his ego, because of God's promises of salvation, and yet at the heart of that security lies the call to shed the securities of the world and of the 'successful' ego. Christianity is markedly at its mythic base not a religion of success. And so though Christians may begin from a different picture of the basis of the world, from a different ontology in other words, the effect of their conquest of power is the losing of the self. By contrast the Buddhist more directly attacks the ego by sweeping away the whole basis of substance and so the acceptance of a substantial self. Instead the world is so to speak neutralized, analysed away so that it no longer has its usual stirring impact upon us. This is self-naughting by analysis and the cultivation of neutral feelings; the Christian case is a kind of self-naughting in which the glories of immortal substance are found to be self-emptying. In both faiths there is a kind of emptiness then, but the styles of emptiness emerge from differing backgrounds and conceptions. But this is one of the ways in which there is a certain complementary between the religion of the Buddha and the religion concerning Christ. The one transcends the search for individual security and seeks to banish it by dissolving all identities. The other accepts the search for security and the need for meaningful identity, but binds the believer, in identity, to one for whom one should lose one's soul in order to save it.

A Final Note on Christian Mysticism

We raised the question of mysticism within the Christian tradition. It has a natural place there, for reasons to which I have alluded; but yet there is a question mark about it because for some Christians it is not easily found in the Bible and it is mostly associated with classical Christianities which were under fire from reformers. If there is a question about the place of the inner quest in Christianity, is there not a converse question about the devotional worship which came to emerge in the Greater Vehicle tradition? Again it may be in some sense a natural and a valid development, and yet it is strikingly at variance with the Theravadin thinking about Buddhahood. This is not to say that the Theravada necessarily represents 'primitive' Buddhism and that Mahayana represents a growth upon that. For much of the Theravada is later development, and the one time fashionable picture of the Theravada as 'primitive' is not accurate. Rather, there was some early Buddhism which in its old form is lost to us, save in so far as we can look at it through the lenses of the various schools. Still, there is a certain puzzlement, even given all this, about the growth of the Mahayana, and in particular the ideals of the celestial Bodhisatva and of the semi-creative Buddhas ruling over paradises and the like. Why *bhakti*, then, in Buddhism? It is at this point suitable for us to move further in the comparisons of Buddhism and Christianity and to observe some of the characteristics of the Mahayana. I shall relate the *bhakti* element to the main impulses of modern Protestantism. For though *bhakti* is and was vital in Classical Christianity, it was a main force in the newer forms of Christian piety. To that we now turn.

5

The Great Vehicle
and the Protestant Spirit

The Logic of Devotion

The Mahayana has been of course a vast and rich phenomenon, a soul for the diversities of Asia. If one were to choose
from it the main motifs they would, I think, be as follows.
These are, incidentally, motifs which can in a simpler or
more rudimentary form be found in the tapestry of the
Theravada, but often without much prominence. One
thing that immediately stands out is that which we have
already seen – the great development of loving adoration,
bhakti. But *bhakti*, often so reminiscent of the warm piety of
Christianity, especially in some of its Protestant revivals,
needs an object, a focus. One cannot adore oneself. One
adores someone Other. That someone took many forms of
course in the Great Vehicle, celestial Buddhas, divine
Bodhisattvas, in Tibet Taras, those luminous goddesses;
and so on. But above all there is the adoration directed
towards the great Amitabha, Buddha of Celestial Light,
Amida to the Japanese, creator of his celestial paradise the
Pure Land which is light years to the West of us, but is the
haven where the faithful may go. And there is too the great
Buddha-to-be Avalokiteśvara, the Lord who looks down
upon the world in compassion for the struggling and
suffering living beings caught in the web of samsara. All
this embellished by statues, from Gandhara, in Mathura,
later in Loyang and in much of China, and the great figures

to be found at Kyoto and elsewhere in Japan. So one begins of course in certain ways to feel affinities between such worship and adoration and Christian piety. Is not Buddhism in all this verging towards theism? So much so, it seems, that for such Japanese saints as Shinran and Honen faith becomes everything, grace infusing the adorers, everything thus dependent on the Other for salvation, not at all upon one's own efforts. The ambience and atmosphere may be very far removed from Wittenberg and Oxford, but the sensations seem sometimes those of Luther and Wesley. First, then the Great Vehicle bred *bhakti*.

Novelty in the Great Vehicle

But some would see that as very secondary, just a sign of the adaptation or skill in means which the Buddha himself displayed in his teaching and which is carried on in the tradition. For ordinary people the religion of adoration is a suitable way of bringing them on to higher things. Or else in a degenerate age, for according to Buddhism, as we have seen, things are running down hill, this form of faith may be the best. But it must be viewed (it is sometimes said) in the context of skill in means, *upāya*. This doctrine gave Buddhism great flexibility and it is an idea which may well be most important for the Christian tradition. At any rate it has meant that apparently new scriptures and teachings in the Great Vehicle, often very greatly resisted by the more conservative, have been justified by an appeal to what the Buddha essentially taught. It is as though tradition and origin get mixed up together, since what now emerges with seeming novelty in the tradition really goes back to the Buddha's own teaching. The situation is rather different from that which occurred in the revolutionary age of the Reformation and beyond. The Reformers and more generally the Protestants appealed to scriptures and to origins in order to 'go back', to go to the core of the original message as exhibited in those very scriptures. The first and second centuries were brought in to redress the balance of the sixteenth. But the Reformers, though prolific in commentaries and Institutes, did not present hitherto unknown writings, but the Mahayana did. They only harked back in order to hark forward. Be that as it may, the second main feature of the Great Vehicle to which we can point is the idea of *upāya*, spiritual adaptation to the conditions of the hearer. So it was that Buddhism was able so amazingly to adapt itself to Chinese, Japanese and other cultures, very different from those of its native India. And so it was that Buddhism was able to ride and influence the tides of devotionalism to which the *Bhagavad-gītā* bears most eloquent witness.

Two Levels of Truth

But such adaptability came to be much bound up with an idea which was of profound religious and philosophical vitality, namely the conception of two levels of truth. There was the level of conventional language, useful for ordinary intercourse and for expounding the outer shell, so to speak, of the faith. And there was the higher truth, to which words might point as a finger might point at the moon – a higher truth to be hinted at in philosophy and to be experienced directly in the highest stage of meditation. In relation to this higher truth, conventional truth was really a means, really a way of expressing attitudes which might draw a person up higher in the spiritual quest. This two-decker idea of truth means that a distinction can be made between differing forms of religion or spirituality. So the ordinary person worships Buddhas and Bodhisattvas, and all the great rich vast mythic dimension of Buddhism, the galaxies of Buddhas, the wondrous figures on high, the suffering Buddha-to-be, the amazing paradises, the purgatories, the whole realm of merit and rebirth – all these in the last resort turn out to be representations at the lower level. The man of true insight (*prajñā*) sees beyond these images and wonders to something more still, more profound, more empty, more transcendental: in a word he looks to the Void, the Empty, Suchness, *Tathatā*, the blank and luminous essence of all Buddhahood, the heart of the message, the culmination of insight, the true nirvana.

Developments in Great Vehicle Philosophy

The notion of the two levels itself connects up with the extraordinary developments of Mahayana philosophy. Above all it connects up with that school known as the Middle One, the Madhyamika, doughtily articulated by the acute Nagarjuna, highly original, surprising, paradoxical. Sometimes too it is known as the Emptiness School or Void School (the *Śūnyavāda*), since it used the sword of philosophy to destroy all substances, all performances, all views, all anchorages of the mind, leaving the essence of the world empty. Empty it was of course so that the higher level of experience could be manifest, for philosophy and meditation marched here, as they always classically should in Buddhism, hand in hand. There were other schools of course, and we shall look too at the *Vijñānavāda*, the Consciousness School, and that fabulous Chinese synthesis the Huayen (and in Japanese Kegon). It would be wrong to ignore the diverse riches of the Great Vehicle philosophizing. But if anything is central to the Vehicle it is the literature known as the Perfection of Wisdom and the philosophy known as the Madhyamika. And these pointed unmistakably in the direction of emptiness, Suchness: the direction of the critique of all worldly and conventionalist theories. So it is reasonable to look upon the classical Middle, Void doctrine as at the heart of the Great Vehicle philosophy. So far then we see four motifs, interconnected: *bhakti* or adoration, devotion; the system of skill in means, *upāya*; the notion of the two levels of truth; and the 'doctrine' (for can it really be a doctrine?) of Emptiness, *śūnyavāda*.

Nirvana is Saṁsara

Another characteristic Mahayana idea is that strange paradox, the identification of nirvana and *saṁsāra*, of ultimate liberation and the world of ordinary, revolving, flowing, suffering existence. How can this be? Are we if we only knew it free, even within the apparent limitations of the flow of life? Precisely. If we only knew it. The accent here again is on insight, on knowledge that goes beyond theoretical knowledge, to the experience of it, just as I cannot know what love or a headache is like without having undergone it. Still, why should nirvana and samsara be one? It seems to shred the very distinction upon which the whole pattern of Buddhist aspiration is modelled. It abolishes the distance between the struggle and the goal. The answer, very roughly, is like this: that nirvana after all can be nothing different from the transcendental state which the person of insight experiences. But that transcendental experience is of the Empty. It is a non-dual encounter with Emptiness. So nirvana is after all the Empty. It cannot be seen as different from it, because of the non-duality and yet the very stuff and marrow of the world is Emptiness. 'Stuff and marrow' I say for the sake of the lower level of truth, for in higher truth nothing does have stuffing, nothing has marrow. Things are but empty turbulences on the surface of the world as it is brightened and confused by conscious perception. So the inner X of everything is the Empty too. So if nirvana is truly the Empty, and if the true nature of the things of samsara is the Empty, it is logical to see nirvana and samsara as identical. And it is more than logical: it has a practical meaning, which was to find high development in medieval Japan and in Zen. For the world of the laity was as pregnant with the higher life as the life of the monk. It was possible because of this doctrine, and for other reasons, to practice a life of meditation within the midst of things, to gain insight by archery, wisdom by swordplay, vision by tea-ceremony.

The Bodhisattva

Another and much remarked feature of the Great Vehicle in its rich proliferation of mythic themes was the ideal of the Buddha-to-be, the Bodhisattva. Not just the earthly Buddha before his attainment of his Enlightenment; but now more vividly the conception of one who puts off his liberation for life after life in order to sacrifice himself on behalf of living beings, drawing them upwards out of the suffering of the world to higher joy and insight. We have something of course of this spirit in the *Jātakas*, those compassionate Aesopian stories of the prior lives of the Buddha. But in the Mahayana the whole apparatus of the Bodhisattva's compassion, the various complex states of his path, the conception of the thought of Enlightenment and the Great Vow which set him upon his path – all these ideas became very central to piety and the religious imagination. They incorporate even the idea of the transfer of merit – that the Bodhisattva through his immense services on behalf of living beings, services which *ex hypothesi* (for he is putting off the liberation to which his merit so to speak entitles him) earn a vast pile of merit which is from his point of view superfluous, and which he can give away to those who need it. So we have here an analogy to the idea of grace: the freely given merit of the compassionate Bodhisattva. Thus, as one text has it:

. . . It is surely better that I alone should suffer than that all these beings should fall into misery. There I must give myself away as a substitute through which the whole universe is redeemed from the terrors of the purgatories, of birth in animal form, of the world of Yama and death, and with this my own body I must feel, and in this I speak with truth, the whole mass of all painful experiences . . .

Many have noted a congruence of a sort between this compassionate and self-sacrificing ideal and the classical Christian idea of the way Jesus suffered on behalf of all men in his own flesh. But there are obviously some differences. For one thing, who is the Bodhisattva? Who was or is Avalokiteśvara and the others? Even regarding the historical Buddha the accounts of his previous lives cannot be checked: they seem like fancies and wise tales. But they are not embedded in real events. Maybe it is only a Western prejudice to opt for the real, the historical; rather than for the imaginative, symbolic. But the contrast is there. And yet from another point of view the Bodhisattva is real enough, for the path of the Bodhisattva is not just the career of some legendary being – it is a pattern of living for the here and now, for those who set themselves in compassion and strenuous activity in the line of conduct expected of the Buddha-to-be. So at one level the Bodhisattvas are mythic beings, recipients of worship, dispensers of grace and merit; but at another level they are the best of us, here and now in the world of struggle and sorrow. This is partly how it came to be that the Bodhisattva ideal dealt with the problem of higher selfishness which the *arhant* or Lesser Vehicle saint might be subject to. For if a person rigorously pursues the path leading to his own nirvana, conceived as liberation from the round of earthly *samsāra*, then is he not to act with high prudence? But is not high prudence in the long run selfish? The saint seems to be looking after Number One. One is reminded of that gentle passage in the *Questions of Milinda* where the Greek king, mindful of all the

talk about the impermanence and unhelpfulness of the
body, suggests that the Buddhist monks look after theirs
pretty well. But, points out Nagasena, when one has a
wound one dresses it tenderly, takes trouble with it and so
forth: likewise with the body. But the suspicion remains
even so of a kind of selfishness. But the Bodhisattva ideal
transcends such ego-orientation, since one steps along that
path in principle puts off, gives up, his own liberation.
How can he be happy when others suffer? Selfish pursuit
of liberation is itself not consistent with the demands of
compassion. And the Bodhisattva is compassion incarnated, *karuṇā* in the flesh. In brief, then, the Mahayana
incorporates the motifs of *bhakti*, skill in means, double
truth, emptiness, and the ideal of compassionate Buddhas
and Bodhisattvas. There are other motifs to come to, but
these are the most important; and they are perhaps well
synthesized together in that middle Mahayana teaching
known as the Three-Body Doctrine, with its ambient
values and philosophical ideas.

The Three Bodies of the Buddha

The three bodies or aspects of the Buddha provide us with
a hierarchy in the splendidly imaginative cosmos of the
Great Vehicle. It is not to be thought that when we speak
here of the Buddha we mean just one being (though
admittedly all Buddhas are identical in the *Dharmakāya* or
the Truth aspect of Buddhahood). One must imagine many
many Buddhas. This is not only because there were
Buddhas on earth preceding the last one Gautama, together
with the future Maitreya; it is also because each world
system has such Buddhas. But more: at the level of the
heavenly life – beyond the immediate veil of the impermanent world in its deeper but still impermanent reaches –
there are innumerable Buddhas. They form a rich pantheon, scattered in the various corners of existence, brilliantly

reposeful in meditation, astonishingly creative in paradise-making, given to luminous interventions towards creatures below, and indistinguishable from their bright confreres the great Bodhisattvas. The role call even of the principal Buddhas is impressive: Vajrasattva, Aksobhya, Vairocana, Ratnasambhava, Amoghasiddhi (great Dhyani Buddhas these, powerful in meditation), Amitabha (or Amitayus), destined to have a brilliant and profound career in China and Japan. There are the Bodhisattvas to consider – Samantabhadra, Akṣayamati, Kṣitigarbha, Akāśagarbha, Ratnapāni, Sagaramati, Vajragarbha, Avalokiteśvara, Manjuśrī and many others. But in principle the Buddhas and Bodhisattvas are as numerous as the grains of sand along the great River Ganges. A whole cloud, a host of divinities rises like a million exhalations of spirit across the wide cosmos: and the eye of the Buddha can see the vast numbers of Buddhas and gods and beings throughout the infinitude of galaxies, while the ray of light emanating from his forehead lights up, to the eye of the faithful, all these systems and marvels. And consider too the earthly Buddha, Gautama, Kasyapa, Kanakamuni, Krakucchanda and the rest, stretching back into the ever more heroic and splendid past. This is not to take account of the Brahmas, the Maras, the yaksas and devas, the various realms of spirits and living beings. It is altogether a vivid and astonishing cosmos to which the hierarchy of the three Bodies holds a central place.

Transformation Body of the Buddha

To begin below: the Transformation Body or *nirmāṇakāya* is that mode of manifestation through which the Buddha appears on earth: and so it is that the essential spirit of Enlightenment, the supreme Suchness, as it were reveals itself in a form adaptable to the human state – a form which not only enables the Tathagata to teach but also gives encouragement to human kind in that he the supreme Teacher is himself human. Those who follow him can attain to the highest wisdom. In fact if they only knew it each one is a Buddha in principle and can tread that path which will bring him to supreme insight. There is in much of Mahayana thinking about the Transformation Body a suggestion of its unreality, as though the Buddha on earth were a kind of fantasm, a condensation of apparent flesh. This is partly because in any case the two levels of truth (as we shall see) when brought to bear on the Three-Body Doctrine assigns the Buddhas of this world, whether on earth or in heaven, to the lower realm of conventional (and misleading) truth – truth which dissolves into the fictive untruth when it is transcended through insight into what lies higher. There is always too the problem of the juncture between the transcendent and this world. They join in the figure of the Buddha, but does this not make him a kind of amphibian, a being of (so to speak) two worlds? It means that he defies human categories, for though he is human he has a transcendental dimension. He thus has a magical quality to him, hinted at by the mysterious marks which he bears upon his immaculate golden body and at the strange events surrounding his birth. At any rate, there is an air of magic pervading the *nirmāṇakāya*. The accent, though, of such magic is that it is in the service of transmitting the Dharma so that living beings might be refreshed, transformed, and in the end liberated.

Buddhas as Celestial

Upwards in the heavens we perceive the more numinous and glorious beings which exist through their subtle and brilliant bodies. This is the level of the Body of Bliss, the Enjoyment Body, the *Sambhogakāya*. Such Buddhas and Bodhisattvas as possessed such glorious identities were capable of great creative activity, even if none were creator

of the whole shoot. Waveringly, the Great Vehicle was
faithful to the old insight that nothing permanent could be
a cause of change... and yet, of course, there was always that
nagging question about the juncture between the transcendental realm and this world, for did not that in some way
imply a kind of creative irruption by the transcendental
into this world? Most luminous, the Buddha of infinite
light and age, Amitābha or Amitāyus, was the author of
that wondrous paradise: free from purgatories or painful
births or animals or ghosts, full of gods and jewels, emitting
many fragrant scents, rich in a great diversity of flowers
and fruits, adorned with trees made of jewels, thick with
birds which have sweet voices, resplendent in many colours, surrounded on all sides by great golden nets into
which are woven huge and delicious lotus flowers, each
emitting marvellous rays along which travel clouds of
billions of golden Buddhas speeding to all the world-
systems of the great universe, and watered by magical
rivers which are calm and lucid and whose waters are cool
for those who wish them cool and warm for those who wish
them warm. Truly a miraculous and joyous world, fit for
the faithful who call upon the Lord Amitābha for rescue. In
that world of true delight all beings have their minds fixed
upon liberation to which they will in the end win through.
And in all directions there are world-systems with Buddhas
and Lords as numerous as the sands of the river Ganges
who praise the name of Amitābha: powerful name indeed,
for through it those who hear it will turn away from lower
things and through rebirth in his paradise gain happiness
and final bliss. So around the Bliss Aspect of Buddhahood
one discerns many delights and many radiant beings. The
way it is described in the scriptures gives one a feeling for
the inexhaustible glories of the heavenly world as it is
conceived in the Great Vehicle. It all reminds one, though
the imagery is so different, of the bright glories of heaven as
depicted by St John in *Revelation*. Yet everything is on a

vaster, more extravagant scale. In brief, the Bliss Body of
the Buddha represents the numinous brightness and powerful compassion of the Buddha as a kind of divinity.

Buddhas: Gods and not Gods

The Buddhas have wonderfully multiplied. If it is polytheism it is one of an extraordinary and extravagant kind. But
oddly one does not think of such Buddhism much in such
terms. For the gods like Indra and Brahmā, Vishnu and
Skanda – these primeval personal forces ruling battle,
wind, cosmos, order, war and so forth are incorporated into
the Buddhist fabric but at a lower level from the Buddhas.
The latter scarcely ride the wind or stir the sea or thunder
off mountain peaks and fructify the bosom of the earth; nor
do they haunt the vine or stir the orgy, or sound the pipes
and rise in mystery caves. Or at least not yet. By the time
Buddhist Tantra has run its course, the Buddhas become
more like the old gods. But in the high classical Mahayana,
the Buddhas are not the many gods of the Indo-Aryan
tradition, nor are they part expressions of great natural
forces and other angst-laden powers loose in the world.
Besides, if the truth be told all the Buddhas are really one,
in essence. This is where we reach the apex of the threefold hierarchy. It is where we reach the Truth-Body, the
dharmakāya. But before we turn to that let us just reflect a
little further about the celestial Buddhas. I have said what
they are not. They are not the gods of old, rulers of a
tripartite universe. But what are they? They are in one
sense a creation of the Buddhist imagination, and yet they
stand for something real in experience.

The intensity which Pure Land Buddhism was to attain,
for example, is not just the spinning out of an easy theory
on how to shorten the long path of karma and so hope for a
cosy, quick attainment of salvation. It is not a philosophical
construct. Of these there are of course plenty in the Great

Vehicle. It is also a product of a real kind of encounter: the encounter with a personal focus of faith, to whom the faithful indeed can pray and enter into a spiritual kind of dialogue: for from the power of Amitabha there emanates something like grace, vivifying the individual and assuring him of rebirth in Paradise. In short, the Buddhas are foci of *bhakti* religion, and this has its own kind of experience and dynamic. It is the kindly face of the numinous in action, such as we discover in so much of later Indian devotional religion. In brief, the Mahayana through the figures of the celestial Buddhas and Bodhisattvas gives expression, among other things, to the devotional strand of numinous religion, in which the worshipper is in warm encounter with a great Being who will help in his striving for redemption, or the kind of holiness which belongs to the Focus. But it should be noted that the relationship is so far – that is before the emergence of the Vajrayana or the Diamond Vehicle, whose main modern incarnation is in Tibetan religion – not a sacramental one.

The Unity of Buddhas and the Non-dual Experience

But as I have said, really all the Buddhas are one. Why is this so? Is it simply men's relentless quest to try to simplify things? There is a beauty about beginning with One. You can have multiplication later. Well, this may have been a motive in the evolution of the *dharmakāya*. But more important were the logic of experience and the philosophical thought of the Great Vehicle. The logic of experience? The point is that as we have already seen the highest mystical experience the apex of the meditational quest, is one which is often interpreted as if it eliminates the distinction between subject and object. The Void is so to speak neither here nor there (neither here with me nor over there in some 'objective' manifestation). The difference between the Buddha and the ordinary person is that the

Buddha has attained the highest insight.

Let us simplify what this latter insight is and reduce it to the experience (though of course it includes the context, a certain illuminated framework of ideas). So then for the moment we can consider the transcendental nature of the Buddha: what sets him apart from mere humans is the experience and what is manifested in experience. But this is not something other than the Buddha, for it is non-dual. Moreover what it is in the case of one Buddha cannot be distinguished from what it is in the case of another Buddha. If it could be there would be a sort of duality in it. So at least looking at the matter negatively there is no difference in the Empty essence of the numerous diverse Buddhas. They all (putting it positively) have the same nature. That nature is pointed to by the Truth, the Dharma. So it is the Truth-Body of the Buddha. Thus all Buddhas are in a sense united in their Dharmakāya. That, first, is the argument from non-dual experience. We can note that as the Dharmakāya is highest in the hierarchy it bridges the distance between conventional truth and religion on the one hand and the higher transcendental truth on the other. In other words the non-dual experience of Emptiness is given the high honours, while *bhakti* and the spirit of the numinous – the religion and faith of duality – retains lower status only, conventional, provisional. The commanding heights of the spiritual economy of Buddhism are still held by the contemplative life and experience.

The Philosophical Argument for Unity

In addition there is philosophical argument. For the dialectic of the Madhyamika and the whole thrust of that literature known as the Perfection of Wisdom (that is to say Perfection of *prajñā*, wisdom or, perhaps better, insight) is destructive of substance and indeed of all theories concerning the world. The patterns of existence may be explained in terms of cause and effect, but even these come under the ban of philosophical acuity on the ground that they contain within their very inner marrow contradictions. So even karma falls; and (worse still it might seem) the Law of Dependent Origination taught by the Buddha himself. Yes, even the Buddha's teachings leading men on to liberation are in the last resort found to be self-contradictory. What then can the Buddha do or mean? He can *point*, to the higher truth. It is not for us now to question whether the whole Madhyamika position is coherent, for it might well be thought that such a relentless negative way ought to collapse into nihilism and not into a new interpretation of the Buddha's teaching. But at any rate it leaves the nature of ultimate reality (well, can we call it reality?) mysterious. But the Great Vehicle exponents were widely though not universally agreed that it is best to refer to the ultimate *Tathatā* or Suchness, or as the Empty or Void, *Śūnya*. The transcendental is not to be described discursively, though it can be reached in thought through the process of philosophical thinking of the negative kind described and it can be found in experience in the ultimate apprehension of the non-dual. It follows from all this that Suchness is not a sort of thing. And it certainly cannot be many things. Again, looked at negatively, you cannot speak or think of a plurality of such blank ultimates, and so if one speaks conventionally it is best to say that there is one. Thus all the Buddhas are united in the *dharmakāya*. In this way the Three-Body doctrine managed to synthesize differing strands of Buddhist piety and practice. In brief: *prajñā*, meditation, adoration, compassion and analysis are brought together in one coherent collage.

The Devotional Turn

Emphasizing the devotional aspect – this brought the piety of the Pure Land schools, in which Buddhism begins to take on a very tender face of theism. Emphasizing the meditation and the idea of levels of truth – this leads on to Ch'an and Zen, respectively infused also with the spirit of the Tao and of Japanese values. Though Zen may be very different in various ways from the Theravada it does, though, retain strong affinities, for its concentration is upon meditation. But the Pure Land sometimes makes one feel: Are we here beyond the limits of Buddhism? How can what has so centrally been a non-theistic religion take on so many of the attributes of the sweeter kinds of Christianity? How can it be that self-help is replaced by devotionalism and the idea of grace, help from the Other?

Belief and the Buddhas

It is useful now for a moment to stand back. The modern person may well ask himself how the classical Mahayana is relevant to contemporary life. One can understand that for other ages it was a wonderful way of bringing together philosophy and popular religion, and of giving a new dimension to the Buddhist ethic of compassion. And yet can we really any more believe in those myriad Buddhas? We may believe in a sense in the world-systems, for is the cosmos not a vast swarm of galaxies? But we can hardly suppose that in one of those galaxies there exists a Pure Land full of trees made of and bearing jewels and of miraculous rivers adapting themselves to the every wish of the fortunate faithful. Can we not look upon it all as we might look upon Dante's great work – a wonderful and imaginative figure of many things, but only, after all, a set of pictures neither fact nor fiction, but a gallery of images, from which we can receive impact and instruction, but yet which correspond to nothing which is truly out there in or beyond the cosmos? So too the wondrous picture of swarms and clouds of Buddhas and Bodhisattvas is nothing other than a waking dream. A projection, perhaps: and maybe it is the genius of Buddhism that it provides suitable objects of devotion.

Buddhism and the Business of Rent-a-God

There is a serious thought here. Perhaps Buddhism is the best in the business of Rent-a-God. After all, there are many devotions and passions and urges for meaningful service floating around. They are indigenous to the land of the human spirit. They are especially evident now, in the multiplying of cults and movements. The warm ecstasy of dancing before Krishna, the zealous millennarianism of the Unification Church, the deep, deep longing for security among the Jesus people, the semi-deification of Che Guevara, the flight to gurus, the desire for a God to lay one's troubles and energies before – such phenomena live around us, across the wide world, and even within the more forbidding zones of Marxist influence. But it is not always clear that the gods which the floating devotion latches on to are good gods. Jones took devotees to vulgar unnecessary death in Guyana, and one can name other leaders who do not seem worthy of the devotion of their followers. It is, of course, hard to apply criteria, for men differ in their estimates of the fruits by which they should be known. But even so: the gods of the contemporary West are not always good gods. At least the Buddhas and Bodhisattvas of the Great Vehicle shine wth compassion, a great degree of powered gentleness and an ultimate concern for peaceful insight. They are not bad gods. They may not exist, but their influence seems to be benign.

Pure Land and Martin Luther

But as I have said: the Buddhas are not just projections, or if they are such they are also importantly objects of experience. What the mechanism is of supposed projection in the case where there are visions, encounters and the like needs separate treatment. Especially where Buddhism takes the Amida turn, the turn towards the specially fervent faith in faith itself and in the Buddha Amida who is its source and focus, one is inevitably reminded of the pietism which flowed forth from the Reformation, partly in its Radical form and partly in the development of inward-nesses which hoped to vivify the structures of the magisterial Churches. Consider the following passage:

> . . . he who relying on his own power undertakes to perform meritorious deeds has no intention of relying on the Power of Another, and is not the object of the Original Vow of Amida. Should he, however, abandon his reliance on his own power and put his trust in the Power of Another, he can be reborn in the True Land of Recompense. We who are caught in the net of our own passions cannot free ourselves from bondage to birth and death, no matter what kind of austerities and good deeds we try to perform. Seeing this and pitying our condition, Amida made his Vow with the intention of bringing wicked men to Buddhahood. Therefore the wicked man who depends on the Power of Another is the prime object of salvation. This is the reason why Shinran said 'If even a good man can be reborn in the Pure Land, how much more so a wicked man . . .'

One is reminded, is one not, of the whole debate about grace and works in Christendom, and the fervent reliance of the evangelical Christian on the Power of Another. Similarly Shinran got married, and his followers, on the ground that celibacy is self-reliant or, as we might say in the West, a matter of works: and it is not by works that the person is saved but solely by repeating the Nembutsu sincerely, that is to say Nama Amida Butsu or in other words 'Homage to Amida Buddha'. Or as might be said in the West, it is *sola fide*, by faith (in Christ) alone that one is saved. One is reminded of that famous passage in Luther where he expounds his liberation from the sense of sin and hopeless struggle in the times when he was as other monks relying on himself to strive for perfection through the imitation of Christ:

> At last by the mercy of God meditating day and night, I gave heed to the context of the words, namely 'In it the righteousness of God is revealed, as it is written "He who through faith is righteous shall live" ' (Rom 1:17). There I began to undersand that the righteousness of God is that by which the righteous gives by a gift of God, namely by faith. And this is the meaning: the righteousness of God is revealed by the gospel, namely the passive righteousness with which a merciful God justifies us by faith, as it is written 'He who through faith is righteous shall live'. Here I felt that I was altogether born again and had entered paradise itself through open gates . . .

Naturally, the whole cultural and religious context is very different, but the elementary notions and feelings correspond: the sense of dependence upon the Other, the sense that works are not enough. The logic of it all is that only from the holy Power itself, himself, can the individual's holiness derive. The individual is too immersed in sin and passion to be able to get out of the stream himself: only through a helping hand can he be freed. There is another congruence which is important.

The Dramatization of Experience and Grace

Part of the revolution which Luther brought about was that he released new forces of religious experience; and thus set in motion changes which gradually, and sometimes dramatically, eroded and weakened the older sacramental system.

The Church's administration of that system was under fire because it suggested that by doing certain things the faithful could be assured of salvation or at least some remission of their purgation in the next world. The keys to purgatory were useful ones for a priestly class. But Protestantism came increasingly to substitute for the formal sacraments inner dramatizations of experience which were effective signs of grace. Thus the very stress on adult baptism which was so vital in the evolution of the Radical Reformation was much more than so to speak the displacement in time of a sacrament: it was predicated on the argument that the individual must be self-conscious enough to be able to make a choice. He must be old enough to experience Christ. This was beyond the capacity of an infant; and by consequence infant baptism took on (according to its critics) a magical air: the transformation of the status of the baby without reference to its feelings, belief, commitement, experience. Thus it is no surprise to discover that the ideal of the Christian 'born again' in experience, the sense of conversion, the conscious acceptance of faith, the realization in the heart of healing grace, the sensation of being transformed into a 'new person', came to figure as vital in modern evangelical Protestantism. Nor is it surprising that for many Protestants the true meaning of the Lord's Supper is that it is a memorial of Christ's last days and promises. It is not a special canalization of Christ's presence: a communication of substance and power. Rather it is a means collectively of affirming something and of mobilizing people's feelings. To put it all somewhat crudely: the direction of Protestant piety was towards the dramatization of Christ in individual experience and away from external and ritual transmission of divine grace. It is true that this tendency was modified by the principle of *sola scriptura*, for the appeal to the Bible also of necessity raised questions about the nature of baptism and other sacraments. Also the Bible itself came to be a kind of sacrament

– the Word concretized into the words of the printed book. It thus itself became a matrix of experience, giving shape to men's interpretations of their own lives and experiences, and so providing the pattern of life which could be relived. Naturally the Bible as matrix is very different in character from (say) the *Lotus Sutra* or the *Sukhāvatī-Vyūha*. Thus the piety modelled upon it has a very different content and flavour from that modelled on the Buddhist texts. Yet still there is a correspondence of the inner logic of experience.

The Vitality of Numinous Dependence and the Question of Validity

But again, some may feel, in this modern world how seriously are we to take the sensations of dependence on the Other and the feeling of being 'born again'? All that can be said at this stage is that the feeling of the personal Other is a very widespread one, for it is this that animates the enthusiastic and gripping faith of Islam; it is central to both Christian and Jewish piety, though in differing forms; it is probably the most vital force in modern Hinduism and shines forth in the cults of Vishnu and Śiva, and in the faith of Ramakrishna and other modern saints; it is of the essence of Sikhism; it is as we have seen at the heart of the Pure Land; it can be found in many smaller 'Third World' religions; it is often the dynamo of new religious movements both North and South. It is not reasonable to take traditional religion seriously and not to take such *bhakti* seriously. This indeed is a main criticism of rationalist forms of religion, boiling it down to theoretical theism plus ethics, somewhat in the manner of Kant. The sage of Koenigsburg did not take seriously those aspects of religion, the deeply experiential, which were to be explored by Schleiermacher speaking to those cultured despisers of religion who were cultured despisers of the numinous and personal *bhakti*. Such experience is one kind of pointer to the Transcendent. It is of course another matter whether we are to take the latter seriously. I reserve that question to a later part, for it is my contention that the Beyond is an important direction, without which a certain shallowness and cruelty may pervade the material world of rational enthusiasts. At any rate we may provisionally claim that the realm of *bhakti* is one which is vital in the mosaic of religions. Where it pushes forward to become the dominant force in a religious tradition it may well be rather free of sacramental context and finds its force in those experiences of loving dependence which release men from a sense of the oppression of evil, the entanglements of the world, and which create so to speak a certain drama within the soul. The myth lives thus not so much in ritual as in living experience.

The fact that we can move from the self-dependence of the Theravada to the Other-dependence of Shinran is surprising, as though Buddhism has a certain formlessness. But the move is covered by a theory of history: the degeneration of the Buddha's teaching in the lives of men eventually means that because of our immersion in passion and ignorance there is no way in which we can jack ourselves up out of this slough. But it is also covered too by the idea of skill in means. Now though the Christian faith has no such explicit teaching, it may have come, above all in these latter days and by a very different route, to a similar conception; or at least to a predicament where it has taken advantage of a quest for adaptation which may have a like effect. (It is true too that some may feel that a certain formlessness has crept over the Christian faith.) Let me attempt to retrace this history, for it too is something which owes itself to the Reformation among other things, and is where paradoxically also there is a certain congruence between Protestant faith and aspects of the Great Vehicle.

Self-criticism and the 19th Century

One of the main achievements of the German universities in the 19th century and of the Protestant faculties of theology in particular, was the use of the new methods and theories of historical and philological enquiry upon the very scriptures of the Christian tradition. for some it seemed and still seems like blasphemy. Were not the books of the Bible a sort of written sacrament, choc-a-bloc with living power and hedged round by the promises and authority of God? It seemed grubby, disrespectful, sacrilegious, atheistic to poke around in the words of holy writ as though it was merely a human document. All the old security goes once one begins to ask ordinary questions about it. It is like cross-questioning an Emperor about his sex life or his bank accounts. The Bible which has had a certain ritual and performative use and which lives in the hand and the mouth of the preacher now became a set of documents to be probed like any other collection of ancient writings. It was a tremendous, but unnerving achievement, the embarking upon the critical path of enquiries into the Bible. What did it reveal? Many things as we know and yet also an increased uncertainty. The man Jesus seemed to take differing forms, and *The Quest of the Historical Jesus*, to use the title of Schweitzer's epoch-making book, has in fact revealed much more than Schweitzer imagined. We now know more about Jesus' Jewishness, his Aramaic, his eschatological thinking the milieu of the early Church, the trajectories by which certain motifs moved from his time into the context of the Hellenistic world. But the net result is something of a mystery, and rightly and naturally so. For it is evident that Jesus himself used various categories of his time and yet in a new way: he himself partially fell outside the conceptual apparatus both of the Jewish movements of his time and of his hearers. It is this mysterious transcendence of categories in the figure of Jesus which helps to account for the varying directions which Christianity has taken.

A Comparison of Jesus and Muhammad

We can see this very clearly if we contrast the case of Jesus with that of Muhammad. Now of course Muhammad did not claim in any way to be a Son of God (perhaps Jesus did not quite claim this either, though also . . .). He was a Prophet of God. Moreover what corresponds to the incarnation in the Christian tradition is not really Muhammad: it is the Koran. It is the Koran which is the Word which was in the beginning with God. It is the Koran which became the concrete earthly manifestation of the will of Allah. It is itself not God but it is everlasting: it is as it were a concretization of part of the divine mind, adapted for conveying the truth to men. Thus Islam from the earliest days has a very detailed self-revelation of the divine will. It was moreover 'composed' in a very short time. There are relatively few mysteries or worries about the validity of the text. It is quite credibly the *ipsissima verba* of the Prophet or rather of Allah speaking through his messenger. Everything thus has a high degree of articulation and clarity, especially as many of the features of a legal system are laid out in it. The clarity of course also has around it a halo of the numinous and of the mercy and power of its Author. But still, Islam has much less of obscurity and potential for argument about its founding document. This is a great strength, though it is a weakness too. (In my opinion, for reasons which I shall later come to, the tragedy of Islam is its very clarity, but of that more in the sequel.) But especially since the rise of modern critical enquiry into the New Testament so much of it is laid open to question and obscurity. There is the tension between Jesus and Paul, between Hebrew style and Greek thought, between the differing models of Christ, between modern notions of what is historical and the old genres of religious writing, between the older mythic structure and modern cosmology. The New Testament in its modern milieu presents the faith with a vital and hard question: the question of how it is possible to have a critical theory of tradition (this is part of a more general problem, of course, for all human communities have mythic pasts which they need to retain for the sake of identity and which they need to transcend for the sake of the hardly avoidable changes which a critical outlook implies). The critical mind of the 19th century, carried forward into the 20th, has naturally provoked reaction: there is the conservative, or fundamentalist, stance of those who see themselves robbed by criticism of the power and certainties of the Word of God which they prize so much in the insecure vagaries of a stormily changing world. Sometimes such conservatism itself leads to a form of criticism in reverse: for the critical mind often contains its own sometimes too cosy presuppositions. But conservatism also leads to the denial, sometimes, of what is manifest: thus often the deliverances of science are rebuffed in a manner which can only serve to isolate the faithful from the intellectual main-stream. But their reactions perhaps only serve to make more vivid the problem: How can Christian origins retain their inspiration and living force while at the same time subject to the scrutiny of the critical mind? How can tradition and new thinking blend?

Fruits of the Critical Mind

It needs to be repeated that no religion other than Christianity, and mostly Protestant Christianity in particular, has ever turned such strong and unrelenting critical light upon its origins. It is a remarkable fact, and something which may owe itself to the essentially critical and even iconoclastic aspect of the Protestant mind. (Protestantism is not all critical, as we have seen: but it has a radical wing at any given time which is dissatisfied with authority.) An effect of this is that modern Christianity has found itself in a strongly experimental mood. By a very different route it has come to a Western version of *upāya*. This can partly be explained by a theory of analogy: If that is what the faith meant in the milieu of the first and second centuries, then what should it mean in the milieu of the 20th century? Thus Bultmann's famous, though confused, project of demythologization involved the following thought: that which the myths then expressed to the hearer of the Gospel can now be expressed through a version of personalist Existentialism. Naturally such analogical reasoning often produces great strains. For often the faith has been projected into later centuries retaining the forms of an older time, and so later generations no longer see the good news as new, but rather as good traditions; and they no longer perceive Christ through the eyes of their own age but mediated through the customs of older times. There is nothing too disastrous in all this (if one were to make a judgement about it), because conservatism is a method of trade across the centuries: it uses the ship of tradition to ship what is first century into our own times. Without such shipping we would not have the goods available. But still having found the goods the new Christianity of the post-critical period is almost bound to try to adapt them to the new feelings and the new minds.

There is another fruit of the critical mind. It is that a certain sense of the mystery of Christ is restored. By probing the words of the Bible the critics give new life uncertain though, to the various categories and images surrounding the figure of Christ. It can well be argued (and I shall do so later) that the very mysteriousness of Christ in the New Testament and more broadly Christian origins, the manner in which he breaks through existing categories both in the way he was perceived and acted as a human being and in the way he was later perceived in the resurrection experiences and in the early liturgy – this strangeness was powerful: it was dynamic obscurity, which has given the Christian tradition considerable richness.

For after all, though the critical mind has accelerated the process of seeing the multifaceted and peculiar nature of the New Testament, one could also point to the tradition itself as eliciting the various figures of Christ – as ruler, judge, victim, priest, ethical teacher, miracle-worker, bringer of the kingdom, Good News in person and so forth. The images of Jesus have shone through the various liturgies and art forms, through lives and hymns, through the varied preachings and codes of the tradition – a tradition ranging from Coptic Ethiopia to Swedish Lutheranism, from Orthodox Moscow to Catholic Ireland, from the Quakers to the Latter-Day Saints, and so on. Mystery means flexibility, pluralism, richness (but it can also mean softness, corruption, domination by the powers of this world). So in Christianity we have a marked contrast to the certainties and clarities of Islam. These are two paths for universal theism of the Western kind. Both have produced great civilizations. It is, as I say, arguable that the more chaotic, mysterious path is more adventurous and liberating than the other. But such a value judgement is one which goes beyond the descriptions and the analysis, and carries us into the later reflection upon the philosophical and spiritual evaluation of the contrasted faiths which we have been looking at.

So far I have detected a kind of *bhakti* in Christianity, especially in its non-sacramental form, and in the Great Vehicle; and I have seen the evolution of a kind of Christian *upāya* which may have been unconsciously played out in previous traditions but which rises to the surface of consciousness through the impact of the critical mind in the 19th century. But it can be said that after all the Pure Land, and especially in its most radical Japanese forms, is not central to the classical Mahayana. For in the classical Great Vehicle as we have seen the commanding heights are still commanded by the yoga of consciousness-purity. Moreover the picture of the world presented by the dominant philosophies differs greatly from that which we associate with the Protestant tradition. Yet here too there is a possible convergence which I can hint at, and discuss a bit more fully later on. But let me just sketch two alternatives to the radical Madhyamika, which are important for a delineation of the Mahayna mind.

Buddhist so-called Idealism and the Problem of Representation

One vital philosophy was the *Vijñānavāda*, 'Representation-only', often interpreted as a form of idealism. Another which I shall sketch is the Chinese Hua-yen. For it is unwise to see the Great Vehicle always through South Asian eyes, since so much of its flowering was destined to be in the angular strange mountains and great plains of China and in the sea-washed islands of Japan. Buddhism flowered far beyond the rose apple trees of Jambudvipa, amid the almonds of the Empire and the cherries of the Shogun. By looking at these two philosophies perhaps one may bring balance into the picture of Buddhist philosophy, especially as we can see them with the Theravada too in the back of our minds. As we shall observe, the divergence between these pictures of the cosmos is not as great as is often imagined. For Buddhism swings uneasily like a pendulum across the midpoint of its path – sometimes swinging over towards the ideal, sometimes to the real, sometimes to subjectivity, sometimes to objectivity. Between the reality and the feeling there falls the conception and it is here that the midpoint in a way is found.

The correct interpretation of the *Vijñānavāda*, often translated 'Consciousness-only' is subject to some dispute, as are some of the historical questions about one of its prime exponents, Vasubandhu. It is typically thought of by Western commentators as idealistic, and Edward Conze refers to it as similar to Berkeley's philosophy. But perhaps such ways of looking at it are misleading. One reason why it may be called 'Consciousness-only' is that it identified reality, Suchness, with pure consciousness. This has some-times made it fleetingly seem like Hindu non-dualism, as though *vijñāna*, consciousness, is a kind of super-soul. Not so. There is no call to look on the consciousness as eternal. Rather it is the luminous state of the yogin who achieves the highest insight. It is not for nothing that the school saw itself as Yogācāra – the Practice of Yoga. But it is assumed that this luminous pure consciousness enables the illumi-nated one to see the true nature of the world. And this is where the philosophical arguments about reality meet up with the saint's vision, as they should always do in the Buddhist context. The reason why the doctrine has been seen as idealistic is this – that Vasubandhu and others continuously and importantly stress that objects in the world once they are grasped by us through our minds become in a sense illusory: they are not really 'in them-selves' as we grasp them. As it were we impose our minds upon them. And except in the state of pure luminous consciousness there is always the subject-object dualism of the grasped and the grasper, of the representer and what is represented.

One way of seeing where the illusion comes from is set forth most clearly perhaps by Dignāga, the later logician and theorist of knowledge. He denies vigorously that there are real universals. That is he denies that there are real universal qualities like blue and roundness which we can detect in the world. Once we admit such universals we are stuck with problems: for one thing it really, despite what some earlier schools thought, ran contrary to the whole Buddhist tradition of the criticism of language: for if there is something universally blue out there in the world it is this to which 'blue' refers and there is nothing misleading about ordinary language. Dignaga does not consider that the way we classify things is based directly on perception, but rather is the result of a kind of inference. It is the result of systematic sorting by us of the given patterns of the world. Thus to put it briefly: All the general things which we say about the world, and all the general concepts which we bring to bear upon what is given in perception, are products of the mind, imposed by ourselves upon the world about us. They do not properly describe the way things are. All that we are given in perception is a swarm of particular things, or rather events, about which in truth nothing general can be said. Thus the world presents itself to us as a swarm of particulars, upon which we project our conceptions and classifications. Every act of consciousness other than consciousness-purity is an interplay between the graspable and the grasper (between object and subject) and so involves a kind of distortion.

Buddhism between Idealism and Realism

But what of karma and the whole process of rebirth? This is accounted for in the system by reference to the so-called Store-Consciousness or *ālaya-vijñāna* which contains within it the seeds of the future. The evolution of beings out of this so to speak primeval consciousness containing within it the germs of that graspable-grasper split, which is the way ordinary experience presents itself to us, is one main factor in making commentators look upon the Consciousness-only school as subjective and idealist, for it seems to imply that the essential stuff of the universe is mental. At any rate it illustrates a difficulty with the Buddhist tradition. It seems that it was part of the Buddha's original teachings that the world as it appears to us is not the world as it really is. The cosmos is as it were a result of an interaction between events out there and events in here – namely in the psychic apparatus of the person who perceives it. Thus there has to be a balance kept between simply saying that the events out there do not exist and saying that (as they are presented to us and as we grasp them) they do exist. If the Theravada and even more the Realistic school, the Sarvastivadins, tended to lean in one direction, we see the Consciousness-only school leaning in the other. Moreover it was clearly part of the Buddha's message that liberation is possible and this meant or involved some kind of purification of consciousness. Because of this it is easy to think that in one sense there is an end of the cosmos, namely through liberation, when the false constructs which we project on to the world disappear and when moreover karma has exhausted itself. The constructed cosmos has an end, by liberation (though of course part of the construct is that there are other beings still awaiting that final freedom). Anyway, it appears that Consciousness-only, while being compatible with a kind of pluralistic realism in which the events of the world swarm and impinge on us, but in an indescribable way, also in its doctrine of karma gives a higher place to mental interactions than to physical ones and so in this sense tilts towards the idealist position.

The Hua-yen Variant

The further extension of some of these ideas, but within the ambience of the Chinese tradition, is interestingly undertaken in the Hua-yen school and above all in the thought of Fa-tsang. The interest here lies partly in the fact that Fa-tsang exhibits a Chinese tendency, towards a totalistic or organic view of the universe. Thus every event is in the nature of a cause, and directly or indirectly is in interaction with all other events. Thus the universe is a total interacting organism, or to use a metaphor which was used, it is like the marvellous jewel net of Indra in which each jewel reflects all the others. This vision of an orderly, causally interconnected universe in part has Chinese roots, going back to Taoism and to Chuang-tzu. But it also reflects an aspect of the Buddha's own experience as it is described in the scriptual tradition. The Buddha, as we have noted, did not just have a brilliant experience of consciousness-purity; but he also perceived in the light of that and of his strenuous analytic reflections that the whole world was ordered according to causal laws (to which, together with karma, he gave a highly original interpretation). It is also (apart from the Buddha's analytic interest and concern for the 'scientific' diagnosis of men's ills) a kind of religious experience to see everything somehow in a state of sublime interconnection. In the West this is for cultural reasons often figured as the pervasion of the world by one Spirit. As Wordsworth has it ('On the Power of Sound'):

> By one pervading spirit
> Of tones and numbers all things are controlled,
> As sages taught, where faith was found to merit
> Initiation in that mystery old.

The sense of unity in diversity, of the harmony of the cosmos, of the interconnection of things under a law, is something which often affects people with a powerful existential force: such holism is no doubt related to the panenhenic experience. Sometimes such holism is thought of as a kind of pantheism; but that is misleading in that it can be stated without reference to a Spirit. Thus in the Hua-yen it is *Tathatā* or Suchness which is so to speak the inner essence of whole. It is true that also the higher Buddha-nature, identified with Suchness, also manifests itself as Vairocana as a kind of universal Buddha. So Hua-yen is Janus-faced in that the cosmos from one angle is characterized as Suchness and Consciousness-only; and from another point of view is seen as condensed into the symbol of Vairocana. One is reminded of Spinoza's *Deus sive Natura*. We should say: *Buddha sive Natura*.

The Modernity of Buddhism

One of the main attractions of Buddhism is the modernity of its ideas about events and causality: for in reducing the visible world to a vast interconnected swarm of events it echoes the findings of modern science. An event is where a certain characteristic manifests itself at a particular point in space and time. Its coming into being is due to a set of conditions, themselves similar events. In Hua-yen's extension of this picture each event is a result of the total conditions of the universe and likewise is itself part of the conditions which brought about the state of the total universe. Because each event is empty of 'own essence' in the sense that its nature arises from the conditions which bring it into being, every event is, considered in itself, empty. Moreover the Mahayana metaphysics echoes the kind of view of reality which we find in science in that we transcend, in the latter, common sense and common perception. The theoretical constructs of science are very far removed from what we perceive with our sensory apparatus. The latter simplifies the world, and presents it to consciousness in a way which suggests substantiality, relative permanence, large-scale qualities such as broad patches of colour and so on. But actually behind the ways in which the mind sifts and translates the messages coming into the conscious organism are a vast swarm of small-scale events and processes. Buddhists atomism is more advanced, from a modern point of view, than Hindu atomism, where atoms are everlasting, tiny building blocks of the universe. There is no need for the hypothesis of lasting atoms: better to see the world as a vast set of short processes, the one giving rise to the next according to a complex pattern. Perhaps too we may say that modern science has acquired a sense of philosophical idealism, in that discovery is the result of an interplay between the scientist and the natural world in which constructs, theories, revolutionary new conceptualizations play a vital part. It is folly to think of theories simply standing in one-one relationship to a reality out there. The correspondence theory of truth, which implies this kind of mirroring by language of what it is it describes, is naive. So it is not possible really to say how things and events are in themselves. Rather it is possible to say that certain theories in a general way give a kind of purchase both in understanding and in practical manipulation on the facets of the world which they are 'about'. There is a beginning and a schematic account of this relationship between things in themselves and our thought in Kant: though it would be much better to think of 'processes in themselves'. Given this modification there is a strong affinity between Kant and the Buddhist semi-idealist metaphysics of the Great Vehicle. In brief, there is a congruence between this metaphysics and the situation in which modern knowledge about the world finds itself. This undoubtedly is one of the latter-day attractions of Buddhism. It seems not to have those clashes between the spiritual and the scientific which have seemed to plague Western faith.

To some degree this impression is delusive. If we took what the Buddhist scriptures say seriously and in a literal manner there would be lots of difficulties for the modern person. In the *Sutta of the Great Decease*, for instance, which tells the story of the last days of the great Teacher there is an account of the various causes of earthquakes, which would scarcely be taken with anything but levity by a geologist worried about the San Andreas fault. Again, though Buddhism postulates many world systems they are roughly speaking cylindrical in shape, ranging from subtle heavens down to grim purgatories. This of course is a mythic picture no longer seriously viable. One can of course make the heavens and purgatories into states of mind and there is some justification for this, but Mount Meru and the continents and the floating lands would have to go in the process of Buddhist demythologization. Again, in early days men were of great height and the world was rich and plentiful, but it has gradually degenerated until present times. This myth of history has no basis, for the directions ran otherwise, and out of evolution. Early men were no golden giants; and if their lives were not nasty, brutish and short, they were doubtless hazardous, restricted and uncomfortable. Further, there is a serious problem about karma itself, which in the age of modern genetics and other conceptions concerning the formation of character and so forth runs into trouble. That trouble may be avoided by various ruses, as we shall see, briefly. But it still looks to be a difficulty for modern scientifically trained Buddhists. Now it may be answered to all this that part of Buddhism's skill in means is that it already builds into its teachings a method of demythologizing.

Buddhism and Myth

The modern Buddhist does not need to be encumbered by the charming wiles of tree spirits, or the hauntings of ghosts, or the thought of a personal Devil pacing the world in anger and scheming, or the geography of Jambudvipa and the crazy dimensions of Mount Meru, or the miraculous achievements of Buddhist saints, or real belief in poor old Brahmā. The modern Buddhist can reduce these things to the austerer categories of the Abhidharma, the analysis of teachings which on the whole dispense with the thought forms of Asian agricultural society. Given such a way of thwarting the mythic, a modern Buddhist can certainly construct a very scientific framework of belief: using the ideas of the flashing jewel net of Indra, the interpenetration of processes in the organic universe, the difference between processes in themselves and the constructs which we impose upon the world, the extravagant dimensions of the cosmos as perceived, though mythically, from earliest

times in Buddhism; and all this does not include the whole
and subtle apparatus of Buddhist psychology, which gives a
new and special perspective on the inner workings of human
kind (new, that is, from a Western point of view): a view
which may perchance be able to marry itself to Freudian
psychoanalysis, but which at least provides a map for those
healing voyages which the practitioner of Buddhism may
make among the turbulent processes of his non-soul.

Still, Buddhism does not find itself standing still in the
face of modern knowledge. It too has to make adaptations,
though the direction of these changes is as it happens rather
different from those which have characterized modern
Protestant Christianity especially in the 19th and 20th
centuries. To a great extent, the problem for Christianity
has been the doctrine of man. It is true that once
Archbishop Ussher had calculated that the creation of the
world took place in 4004 BC, there was bound to be a
question about that too. But it is readily seen that it does
not matter to a great God whether he made things with a
big bang billions of years ago or whether, more cosily, he
fashioned things out of nothing just a few millennia back.
But the publication of the theory of evolution (and it does
not much matter whether the mechanisms whereby new
species have come into existence are as Darwin or Neo-
Darwinians say or have some other shape: what is important is the general principle of the gradual emergence of
living forms through to man in a related manner) – the
publication of that theory made the whole mythic story of
men's origins as described in Holy Writ virtually unten-
able. You could hide Adam in the interstices of our
ignorance of prehistory. You could think that God infused
a soul into an animal body, so that we owe the hair on our
chin to ancient evolutionary genes but our capability of
salvation to a more direct act of God. But these are stop-
gaps. You could transfer the Fall to a trans-historical plain:
a war in heaven before the creation of the world. But the

old anthropology necessarily crumbled. Now the story is for the most part treated by Christians as a symbolic way of expressing the human predicament, our alienation. Moreover, not only was it difficult to have that smooth transition from Adam through to the history of Israel: it was also to be increasingly hard to make older distinctions between body and soul, so interwoven are they in the nets of our physiology.

Religion, Science and Symbolic Values

At base, it was the question of man which had been the trouble over Galileo and the pre-Copernican cosmology. Of course Aquinas' marvellous synthesis between faith and Aristotle has been of great power and symmetry, with the imperious charm of the eagle: and it was an eagle in the service of the great demanding Church, sensitive as to its authority. But why did the system compel the marrow of men's feelings? Why did it have such an inner rightness about it? Because the drama of redemption was central to the whole creation, to the whole rationale of the coming to be of this world; and because Christ's taking on of human flesh most appropriately – that is to say symbolically – should take place at the centre of creation. Anyway, the notion of men's home as being at the centre is natural to the symbolism of space to which we are all deeply heir. Such symbolism was dislocated; as indeed was the pattern of myth by Copernicus. It could of course be said: But after all, the old cosmology is only a picture a way of guiding our practice and experience, and can we not continue with the old mythic structure even if our science has changed? If one were to follow certain thoughts in modern philosophy of religion it might be possible. But the difficulty is that science itself has symbolic value. Or to put it another way: The cosmos itself functions symbolically, and inspires certain kinds of feelings; but the symbolism and the feelings

themselves are in part a function of the way things actually
are. Consider, for instance, that beautiful picture of the earth
which was swum so decisively into modern consciousness
because of the moon trips: that picture of spaceship earth
already gives us a new vision, a new symbol, a new way of
feeling about our fragile, beautiful home.

I have said that science itself has symbolic value. It gives
insight; it produces power; it promises effective knowledge
related to those things in life and death which produce
angst – it can help crops, childbirth, contraception, health.
It has some of the old properties of magic, not so much
because it is magic, for its rationales are different, but
because it enters decisively into confrontation with many of
the magical aspects of traditional religion. It also, up to a
degree, represents a different establishment, a counterpoise
both to Church and State: a new intellectual and economic
force injected into the ongoing structures of society. Thus
it is not surprising that modern Christianity, and especially
that critical form of it which grew up within the matrix of
19th century Protestantism, has tried to reshape the intellectual content of faith in order better to conform to the
shifting and growing insights of science. This we find in so-
called liberal Protestantism a forward-looking attempt at
synthesis. But as we shall see more than the content of
belief and symbolism is open to change: because of the
methods and inner structure of science, old ideas of authority are under fire. This shows in another context the
importance of a critical theory of religious tradition. How
can Christianity simultaneously preserve its past liturgical,
spiritual and biblical riches and at the same time adopt a
critical attitude towards its own ideas?

Convergence of the Great Vehicle and Protestantism

Thus we find both in regard to the Great Vehicle and to
modern Christianity a convergence on the question of the

scientific character of religious belief. Of course a spiritual outlook is not itself a kind of science. The reason for living among the glittering interfaces of the jewel net of Indra are primarily to do with vision, vision which indeed may trace itself back to the Enlightenment of Gautama the Buddha himself. And the doctrine of the creation of the world by God can no longer be regarded as a scientific hypothesis; but is something based at least in part on the experience of dependence, and on the practice of the presence of God in and through the glories of his creation. But yet, though the root of these visions and doctrines is not itself scientific, it needs somehow to take account of our new knowledge of the world – precisely because the latter gives a special configuration to the cosmos which God creates (or the cosmos which is the great jewel net of Indra). In the next chapter the time will have come to give a final estimate of the relationship between the two systems of Buddhism and Christianity. But let us note here that we have seen that for the most part the Great Vehicle maintains the ultimate supremacy of consciousness-purity, interpreted as lying well beyond the categories of personal encounter. On the other hand the Great Vehicle is most hospitable to the sentiments of *bhakti*, that loving encounter with the personal Other which also in a differing form animates so much of Christianity and which lives in a relatively unsacramental form in Protestantism. Hence the convergence of Luther and Shinran, of Spener and Honen. That hospitability to the experience of *bhakti* may not be surprising. What great religion ultimately excludes it? (What major religion conversely in the last resort excluded the quest of consciousness-purity?) So we might wish to pose the question of the final relationship between the Christian and the Buddhist ways as having to do with the relative vitality and importance of these two main motifs of existential religion. But as we have noted, there are other contrasts at stake. For one thing classical Christianity has a strong

sacramental heart. This is something which came to be in
Buddhism only with the emergence of the Mantrayana –
the 'Sacramental Utterance Vehicle', better known in the
form of the Vajrayana or Diamond Vehicle. For various
reasons I do not here wish to open up this branch of
Buddhism; partly it is that in a way the convergence with
sacramental theism is too great. The Void becomes positive: diamond hard, a kind of primeval substance, per-
sonified through the Adibuddha or Original Buddha, a sort
of positive primordial creative divinity. Of course the
whole mythic content of Himalayan Buddhism is very
different from that of Christianity, but the logic of its forms
is close. But the challenge to Christianity in regard to most
of Asia comes from the limpidities of the Theravada and
the Great Vehicle – ultimately (it would seem) non-theistic,
not devoted to substance and sacraments, wielding power
through non-power, saving souls through the denial of souls,
tending to the bright darkness, the foll void, of the blaze of
non-dual consciousness, transcending personal relationships, ahistorical, riding loose to the mythic, concerned
more with ignorance than with sin, with patterns rather
than persons, giving a special vision of this world, but
eschewing the feeling of dependence, cultivating *bhakti* and
yet going beyond it. It is foreign it seems to the Liturgy, to
the Fall, to the idea of salvation by substitution. It looks on
Christianity from afar, perhaps seeing Jesus as a kind of
Bodhisattva; but unhappy that the matrix of the faith
should be Jewish rather than Indian history; skilled in
dialectic, timeless, rich, extravagant in symbolism. What
can it make of the dark ikons of the Pantocrator? Yet we
cannot feel anything but uneasiness at the fact of two such
noble, but differing, traditions. In the sequel I shall reflect
philosophically upon them, and establish a certain sense to
the idea of complementarity.

6

The Buddhist Meaning
of Christianity:
The Christian Meaning of Buddhism

The Relationship between Buddhism and Christianity

For those who take the existence of the great religions
seriously, the relation between Christianity and Buddhism
perhaps lies at the heart of the problem of diversity. But
our task of elucidating the modern meaning of these faiths
is of course complicated in the fact that these religious
traditions are faced not only by other religious alternatives,
such as Islam, but by the secular ideologies. What use to us
now is the quest for the Beyond, the Transcendent? This is
part of the problem of religion in the modern world – the
assumption that there is no Beyond, that weal and woe are
just to be influenced by events here on earth. Ruling out the
Transcendent, the rationalist rules out the particular forms
of religion. And he no longer takes seriously religious
experience or religious practice. But in one way both the
theist tradition of the West, emerging out of ancient
Judaism, and Buddhism favour secularism: not in the sense
of diminishing the importance of religious experience and
practice, but in the virtual elimination of the gods associated with particular cosmic powers. The jealousy of
Yahweh issued in the driving of the gods out of the
universe, no longer to stir ocean or thunder, or fructify

177

crop or herd. All devolved upon the one Creator. Hecatombs roasted for the pacification of Poseidon became an irrelevance in the world of monotheism. Yet despite this so-to-say 'secular' dimension of theism, there remained some claims which were ineluctable: one was the notion that theism concerned a living God, that is to say a God who lives in the experience of human beings; and another that he is beyond the cosmos, which is his creation. Conversely Buddhism sees a differently described Beyond, the non-dual void, nirvana: but again it is 'living' for it is something which ultimately has to be experienced in the lives of human beings. In brief: what the great religions claim, against radically secular ideologies, is that there is a Beyond or an Unborn; and this is somehow accessible to the religious experience of the human race, and is not just a philosophical speculation or a theory about the world.

Experience and the Transcendent

So in a way our question is: Why should we accept the validity and importance of religious experience? In modern times we have seen the great success of a certain kind of empiricism: of the appeal to what can be found out by using our senses, amplified by the various probes, from the telescope to the electron microscope, which technology has devised in the service of increasing our powers of scanning the world. There seems by contrast something primitive even about the wild ecstasies of the shaman, the visionary ecstasy of the prophet, the introverted silence of the contemplative. Is this the way to find things out about the world? About the world, or about what? Though there is no reason in principle why meditation should not enhance memory or be coupled with telepathic powers; nor is there any reason why prophecy should not also be associated with an acuter perception of political and moral realities –

the main thrust of such experiences is not their powerful side-effects, if there indeed are any. The main thrust is that they give knowledge somehow of the Transcendental. In a sense it is not knowledge 'of this world'. In a moment we need to consider how we divide worlds. What is here and what is beyond; what is in this world and what is Transcendent? But let us assume some line. Thus (it may be argued) the deliverances of the main religious experiences in the great traditions may refer to things in this world, but essentially they have to do with what is not in this world. This is where of course there may be a query from the other flank. If from the Beyond, if from another world, how can such experiences help us here, for it is in this world that we live? Or is it? Naturally, the question of whether religious experience gives us a kind of access to the Beyond is also the question of whether we do in fact live solely in this world or whether indeed we are after all amphibians, swimming in the flux down here yet capable of standing on the rock which lies on the farther side of the stream. So religious experience raises the question of what vision of the total universe we have: what vision of the whole of reality. Does it include only this cosmos; or do we see this cosmos in the light of what lies beyond it?

Clarifying the Concept of Transcendence

It is maybe not clear what Transcendence amounts to: what it means to speak of that which lies beyond the cosmos. I have hitherto been using this idea uncritically. It is now time to try to make it clearer. First, if we look to the notion of what is transcendent from the point of view of classical theism, it first of all amounts to this – that God exists or somehow is (for we might want to reserve the notion of existence to what lies within the webs of space and time, within the cosmos) apart from the world. That is, even if the world did not exist God would exist. (From the point of view of classical theism one could conceive that God might exist even though the world does not; but it would not be in some other sense possible for the world to exist without God, for God is its presupposition and creator.) So God and the cosmos are distinct. Thus God's existence is not a case of his existing in space. For this reason when we say that God transcends the cosmos, and use the notion of trans-, that is to say of his being 'beyond', we use this last word not in a literal manner: for in its literal sense beyond implies that if A is beyond B then A is in a different location from B: roughly it means that a line drawn from where I am or we are through B would if extended pass through the place where A is. But of course if God is beyond space then he is not beyond in this sense. It is a metaphor or analogy. It is maybe like the idea that my feelings lie (from your point of view) beyond my eyes: as though they are inside me in a special place; but thoughts and feelings cannot in the strict sense be located (leaving aside bodily feelings, like pain). The metaphor perhaps too implies that the world is so to say a veil: it is a kind of screen which keeps the invisible from our gaze. Thus we often think of revelatory events as ones in which in some way we penetrate the veil, for we are given a hint at least of what lies beyond. This metaphor of course fits in with the notion of holiness: the holy is often figured as hidden, and on occasion literally is hidden, behind doors and curtains, in the inner recesses of the sacred shrine, in the 'holy of holies'. In brief, we picture beyondness as implying that the cosmos conceals the divine, is dependent on it, and is distinct from it.

The Transcendent and Empirical Access

But such Transcendence is not accessible to empirical investigation, or at least not as we usually understand that. Not by seeing, or peering or observing, or hearing, or feeling, or by using telescopes or microscopes can we hope to penetrate the veil of material existence and discover what lies behind it. Even when we think of God as working within all things (and immanence is but the reverse side of transcendence's coin, for 'within' is as much a metaphor or analogy as is 'beyond'), we do not suppose that by sifting the atoms we shall find God. Even 'within' he is beyond. So the Transcendent is not something which we can establish by some kind of scientific procedure. Maybe we could make its postulation more plausible by inference, as scholasticism and the Nyaya tradition of India supposed. It might not be surprising if we were to begin to think of the Divine as being somehow a regulative idea, rather than something which from within the context of human knowledge can be affirmed to exist. But this is precisely where the problem of religious experience comes in. For though we may not pierce the veil by means of scans or probes or observations, it has generally been thought in the spiritual traditions of both East and West (and North and South) that there are bright clues to what lies beyond the veil, and these clues are found in religious experience, and the numinous encounters between what is Beyond, and us. In other words: it is not that God is the object of scientific enquiry; and it is not as though religion is simply a matter of ethical values (and God some kind of presupposition of objective morality). There is a third way. That third way is to be found in the (from a religious point of view) realistic notion that it is in certain profound and dramatic experiences that the veil is most luminously lifted – though one should also not neglect the daily and less startling sensations of those ordinary transactions with the Other discoverable in the life of prayer. So then there is a special gnosis, a special kind of encounter, a special avenue of knowledge which falls outside the other categories of human enquiry, and this is the avenue of religious experience.

The Paradox of Religious Experience

This must be seen however in context. Clearly, as we have been at pains to point out hitherto, an experience occurs within a certain living context. Maybe sometimes the impact of the experience leads to a change of worldview, as in the case of a conversion; or when a prophet sees things new in the light of the revelatory vision he has had; or when the mystic finds a new map of the world by consequence of his deep insight. But still we cannot treat religious experiences as 'pure', detached from context. The context enters into the fabric of the visions themselves. So the question of how far some experience can establish the truth of a system of belief and values is a hard one. But within such a context, a religious experience is gripping, often overwhelming, stamped it seems with truth and power. But because in the modern world especially the worldviews differ so greatly, and because for a wide swathe of human beings there is no question of their being a Beyond, we find a curious situation: for many people the appeal to their own or others' religious experience seems convincing, in order, natural; while for others such experiences seem to be bizarre, without importance, projections, delusions. Thus Christians listen with reverence to the account of Paul's conversion, or react with piety to testimonies of conversion; while Buddhists naturally look back to the Enlightenment of the Buddha, and are ready to accept that Buddhist masters know in experience the nature of suchness. But for others, psychoanalytic explanations come to mind in thinking about Paul; or thoughts or projection account for the way in which the pious seem to hear God 'out there'. They would regard the Buddha's enlightenment as being now of antiquarian value. There is no Unborn, Unconditioned, Transcendent. There is nothing beyond the material world as we ordinarily understand it and which we can best probe by the methods of science. So then: there is a notorious split, a gulf between those who entertain the living possibility of the Beyond, and those who consider that they have left behind any religious vision of the cosmos. For the first, religious experience has impact, truth-potential; for the second group, it has no impact, no truth-potential. This is a curious split, as I have said, and its strangeness can be brought out in the following way.

As we have seen religious experience is a major expression of the impact of the Transcendent. The Beyond finds a major mode of self-revelation, we might say, through the forms of religious experience. And it might well be thought that you could scarcely wish to find any better evidence of the Transcendent than the experience of it. What could be better than direct encounter? Yet if we look at that encounter from the standpoint of those whose worldview is secular and who rule out the Beyond from their scheme of things, the knowledge-value of the experiences is trivial. They cannot reveal the Beyond for there is no Beyond to reveal. So the best possible evidence seems within one general context extraordinarily powerful and fruitful in a living way; but in another general context seems altogether to droop, to be quite enfeebled as to its power and fruits. Yet here a qualification needs to be made and I shall come to it in a moment. Let us just dwell a little further, though, on the paradoxicality of the situation: For those who believe in the living possibility of the Beyond the spiritual encounter with it in experience is the best possible proof of the reality of the Beyond; and yet this proof value depends itself on the prior acceptance of the real possibility of the conclusion. Believe in the Beyond and you will have proof of it. Disbelieve and nothing can serve as proof. But now to the qualification, concerning the fruits and powers.

The Power of Experience

The secularist would be of course quite wrong if he thought

that because religious experience is (for him) based on a delusion that it can have no real power to move men. The question of the justifiability of a belief or the truth-value of an experience must be kept quite separate from the question of what kind of impact the experience may make in a living context. It is part of the task of the phenomenologist of religion to try to delineate the ways in which the experiences of the Transcendent which are reported in the history of religions actually change the ways in which people behave. Very often our prejudices about truth get in the way of this empathetic and delicate task. But for purposes of history and of the analysis of religion the truth-claims have to be suspended in our own minds. It is not for us to impose our own worldview on the material which we are contemplating. Thus we have to get at the human facts. We do so in a mood of epoche or the suspension of our own beliefs and presuppositions. We do not need to say that there is here or there an encounter with the Beyond, but only that there is believed to be: that the experience, real enough in itself, is taken to be an encounter with the Beyond. It is in this sense that Kristensen was correct to say that the believer is always right. Now from this standpoint of course the actual effects, the actual power in life, of the Transcendent (of what is taken to be Transcendent) need to be described. The historian of religion tries to bring out the thunderous impact of Muhammad's prophetic visions, the way they entered into his thinking and feeling, ultimately dynamized him and deeply impressed (after a struggle) many round him: how they came to have living power through the Koran. In all this those visions of his turn out to be an explosive factor in history. To put it too simply: the turbulences in the consciousness of Muhammad, like the tolling of a bell within his skull, those superficially tiny events were in a short time to lead to the formation of a whole new empire and with it a whole new civilization. So too the strange experiences which some of

the followers of Jesus had after his death led to transformations of behaviour and the creation of a vigorous new faith
which, too, though more slowly, was to change a world and
to bring into being a new civilization. So it is that we can
sometimes speak of the great power of religious experience
(but it can also prove feeble, overridden despite fancy
preachings and stupendous claims, by other forces such as
greed or patriotism). It is then the task of the historian of
religion, among other things, to try to delineate the living
impact of the experiences of those who have faith and of
seminal figures in the evolution of religious processes. In
brief: the Transcendent may be bracketed, but its manifest
powers are not bracketed: they are seen as fully as possible,
and shown in interaction with other forces in the human
psyche and in human society. But this procedure also leads
to a strange thought, one which is in parellel with the other
paradox which we have been describing.

The Existence or Non-existence of God: Does it Matter?

The paradox can be put most sharply by saying that after
all it does not matter whether God does or does not exist:
his powers would still be just as great (or just as small). For
if the Beyond is mediated for us in experience, and if such
experience and its dynamic can be described, then the
power of God in human life is after all something empirical;
and so it does not really matter if God exists or does not. If
he is real in life, such reality is enough. What does the
transcendental reference add to God's power? It seems
nothing. Well, it might be replied that God, if he is the
God of classical theism, does more than stir up human
beings. Admittedly this aspect of his activity could be
adequately described in a manner which exhibits the
impact and powers which he putatively has upon his
followers. But this does not deal with the way in which
God is the Creator and Sustainer of this whole cosmos: in

every leaf that pushes forth there is the inward power of God; in the sun, moon and galaxies; in all the vast incredible processes of the universe, there is God at work. But again we are led to ask: What kind of knowledge is this supposed to be, the knowledge or at least faith that God is Creator and Sustainer of the world? It is not a scientific hypothesis, is it? Perhaps in the days of scholasticism there was some difficulty in drawing the line between science and non-science; and God does after all have a sort of scientific role to play in the Aristotelian picture of the cosmos. But we seem to be beyond this. If God transcends the cosmos in the manner we have described then it is impossible to see how God himself can enter directly into the fabric of scientific explanations, which are, after all, ways of organizing and linking phenomena within the jewel net of Indra: within this cosmos. So what is it to see the cosmos as the creation of God? It is a kind of regulative vision: vision, because it is a way of seeing things (a case of seeing as); and regulative, because it directs our attitudes in certain ways – towards wonder, acceptance of suffering, co-energy in the work of creation, and so on. It does, then, make a difference as to whether God is taken to be Creator, but it is not a difference that has to be settled by relation to the facts which we can observe, probe and so forth. Of course, the idea that God is Creator is a wider idea than that he transcends the cosmos. But the fact that God is held to be transcendent does show that the notion of creation is not an empirical one. But in both cases – the transcendent as a presupposition of religious experience as classically inter- preted, and the transcendent as an element in a transempir- ical way of looking at the cosmos – the idea of the Beyond points to something which is inaccessible in itself, beyond the experience of the faithful. One might schematize the situation as follows: that the Transcendent has a subject and a predicate: the subject is in itself inaccessible, and the predicate is that configuration which is ascribed to it on the basis of experience and the context of experience. That configuration enters into human life because of human encounters with the Transcendent and because of the kind of vision of the world and of our life which the configuration creates. The subject is the ultimate Focus of belief or aspiration; and the Transcendent in its fullness, that is as both subject and predicate, can be considered as the real focus of faith, which is both a dynamic phenomenon in the lives of people and a kind of illuminative idea for the guidance of their feelings and their conduct. If we do not postulate the ultimate Focus, the subject, the inaccessible X lying beyond the contents of belief and experience, we might consider the real Focus as it enters into lives itself to be a projection. It is not my intention to rule this out as a possibility, for after all it is a necessary part of the apparatus of rationalism or secularism. The rationalist might in the end be right, in his battle with theism, and with all forms of belief in the Beyond. And religions have to be judged by their real Focus, that is by the particular configurations which they present and the particular dynamisms which they generate. There can be no blank cheque for transcendental religion.

The Need for the Focus

The upshot of these reflections is that the concept of the Beyond is a necessary ultimate Focus from the standpoint of the believer. The afirmation of this Focus confers 'objectivity' upon the real Focus which is how a religion's central value enters into the lives of human beings. That real Focus is what the historian or phenomenologist of religion is concerned about, and it is that which he wishes to delineate. From the point of view of the history of religions it is neither the case that the ultimate Focus exists nor that it does not. There is suspension of belief. Likewise, the real Focus as it enters into men's lives is not judged as good or bad, for the aim is to present it rather than to estimate it. From the point of view of philosophical reflection on religion, on the other hand, the question of the ultimate remains of course important: but I have tried to indicate that looking through the lens of human experience the existence of the ultimate is presupposed if experience is to be evidence for it; while if we preclude the ultimate, no evidence from experience can be enough. The way the issues are settled, if indeed they are settled, is a more subtle interplay of factors. How plausible, how persuasive, how important are the claims of one way of looking at the world over against another? The question of the existence of the ultimate is something which has to be settled at the lower level of the real focus and in terms of our total knowledge and estimate of the world in which we live. The tests are softer, stranger, than any proofs or verifications, less decisive than falsifyings and disproofs. If religion dies it dies the death not of a thousand qualifications so much as the death of a thousand awkwardnesses and a thousand flickerings out of dynamic power.

But Affirmation does not add Power

But the affirmation of the inaccessible Beyond does not add somehow to God's substance. It may express faith, but it does not strengthen the divine. It does not even strengthen God conceptually, as a kind of thought experiment. The ultimate who exists, because anchored in the Beyond and operative in human experience and in vision, does not have some extra power which the real Focus of religion fails to have, as we chart that in the history and the scientific study of religion. There we are methodologically agnostic: but if perchance we were to affirm theism, though it is inappropriate within the temple of the religious sciences, this would not be to add an extra factor, an extra grain or mass of energy to the encounters which men already report as experienced by them. The inaccessible subject, that trans-cendental X, that dark to us background upon which we may perceive the play of light, does not throb with its own extra configurations of power. It is true that the faithful person may think of God as having infinite power, that is power beyond any that he has so far manifested or might have manifested: always something in reserve as we might say. But this idea of the power of God is something which already is built into the Focus as he conceives and as he encounters it. The function of the ultimate X is to serve as the subject of such predication, to be the core as it were behind all the manifestations and configurations. So then the affirmation of the ultimate does not add to power: it does not indeed add anything beyond the condition of being, upon the divine. The core of the divine power is itself, so far as power goes, neither here nor there: it is a kind of suchness, a sort of emptiness. Nevertheless, that ultimate does, despite its inner powerlessness, have a marked impact upon human life, in so far as it is part of an affirmation among men.

For the question with which we began remains an important one, especially in the contemporary world. The affirmation of a Beyond is itself a condition of speaking from religious tradition and experience; and this may itself be an important ingredient, as we shall see, of the criticism of contemporary thought and values: a criticism which has its roots in heaven, calling into question the values of those who treat one another as merely earthly beings, denizens of one reality and not amphibians in a wider total system which goes beyond the cosmos as we know it. To that confrontation between secular ideologies and the systems of the Beyond I shall come more directly in due course. It needs to be borne in mind that we should not be concerned to defend religion so much as to defend humanity with whatever seems right in insight and attitude. Religion is not just a theory or a speculation: it may be for us a living anchor in the storms which the grandiose secular ideologies have stirred in the waves of a suffering race. But of that more anon. Meanwhile, though, we can return to the question of the relation between the Buddhist and the Christian worldviews.

The Beyond in the Buddhist Context

Hitherto in discussing the Beyond, I have been using the theistic context. It is important to connect up this discussion with the somewhat different flavour of the Beyond in the Buddhist context. There the Beyond is the unconditioned: it is something discoverable in non-dual consciousness, beyond perception and non-perception, in the most luminous refinements of the contemplative process. It is also the Empty, lying at a higher level of truth than the discursive knowledge of this world. It is how things truly are if we were to see into their ultimate essence. I think it is useful here to separate out two sides of this transcendent coin. One side is the Unconditioned which can be encountered in non-dual consciousness (how awkward and stumbling must language be here, for how can we speak of encounter, experience and so forth when there is no other to encounter, no datum out there to be perceived, but only a kind of . . . well, as I say words are awkward, and partly, largely fail). The other side is the theory of two levels of truth, the conventional and the higher: the one which accepts the superficialities of the world but is useful in manipulating it, the other which points with smile, finger, empty expressions (like Emptiness) to what is in a sense beyond: at least, beyond the conventional. As to the first side, because the ultimate as experienced is non-dual, it does not have particularity and does not enter into the flux of causes and effects. It is timeless (the immortal place as it is sometimes called).

So if we define the cosmos itself as a web of causal

relationships in space and time, then the ultimate in Buddhism is 'beyond' the cosmos. But there is of course no idea of its somehow standing itself in a creative relationship to the rest. It is not the source, still less the living source, of the cosmos. This of course represents a genuine conflict between Christianity and Buddhism. But it does not follow that there cannot so to speak be a 'side' or 'aspect' of the divine which the experience of the Buddhist saint illumines and encounters (again to use this unfortunate language). In any event the notion of an unconditioned timeless X is a conception of the ultimate which is itself compatible with the conception of the Beyond as we have delineated it in the case of theism. So there may be a hidden complementarity between the Buddhist and the Christian positions, and between the forms of life which they generate. As for the two-level side of the transcendental coin, there is a way in which this is in my opinion a highly salutary doctrine, for it represents immediately a criticism of our ordinary language, and a criticism of our usual ways of thinking. It also in religion represents a critique of our worship, our practices, our ordinary perspective on the divine. For after all, the Buddhas and Bodhisattvas are in their own gentle way divine beings, in effect, and yet in the last resort they may as it were disappear within the Truth-Body, or vanish in the blinding light of the ultimate experience of Emptiness. But the two-level theory is also involved in a kind of value judgement. There is something delusory about the world in which we find ourselves, for even if we were to replace our present ordinary language with something better, as say the Buddha tried in his teaching about the *skandhas* and the evanescent configurations of the human personality – even this improved language or better understanding of the plural world is itself defective. Well, in one way that might be right: we could perhaps go farther in our criticism and find the language behind the language behind the language. But nothing would satisfy the relentless criticism of the

Madhyamikas and other Buddhist dialecticians. The world as such as a plural set of fluxing events and processes is in the last resort at the lower level of experience. It is a kind of mirage in the light of the ultimate Suchness. Not all Buddhists of course in the Great Vehicle need take this 'idealist' turn; but it is worth considering as one version at any rate of what the teaching about two levels means in regard to attitudes. Now in this more extreme form it is in my view open to criticism. It is not necessary, nor in a way is it desirable, to think of the ordinary experienced world as being unreal. But the two level theory has great merit if it is used as a methodological tool in the critique of religion and life. Before I come to that, let me just comment on the inner meaning, spiritually, of the theory in so far as it relates to religious experience.

A Question of Priorities: Dhyāna and Bhakti

We have seen that for classical Mahayana the practice of contemplation and the yoga of consciousness-purity retains control of the commanding heights of the Great Vehicle economy. It cannot be said that the analogue in the Christian tradition, the contemplative life, has the same centrality. Moreover there would be many Christians who would wish to resist the notion that the 'personal' aspect of the ultimate is secondary, or even delusory. And there would to be many Christians who would resist the blankness (so to speak) of the ultimate in the *Śūnyavāda:* Christian mysticism has a more personal context. But even if the contemplative life is not so central in the Christian tradition it does have a noble place in it. Since the contemplative life is often itself an antidote to brash activism, and on the whole tends to peace and gentleness rather than militancy and hard lines of doctrine and authority, there is an important place for it in the total economy of Christianity, which has the diseases of its virtues, and among those diseases a sad temptation to violence and coercion. Thus we might look on Christianity and the Mahayana as mirror images: for the one the mystical life is secondary, and the faith of personal encounter is primary; for the Great Vehicle the mystical life is primary, and the religion of *bhakti* comes second. One cannot regard this diversity of balance, of priorities, as a sharp incompatibility, though it does represent a tension. And yet that tension may turn out to be a fruitful one, especially if we see the two-level theory not so much as containing levels as aspects: like a Two-Body view of truth, to go with the Three-Body view of Buddhahood.

The Two Aspects of the World

Let us look at it in a double way, first from the point of view of earth, and then in relation to heaven. At the earthly level the Buddhist critique of language is important (as is made clear by the way in which it anticipates certain central notions in contemporary philosophy) because it helps to deanthropomorphize the world. The world as we perceive it and classify it is presented to us in swathes of colour, in blocks of substance, in manifestations of power, in stillness and in motion. But behind these presentations lie processes which are beyond immediate perception, and both from the angle of science and in consideration of the way the world around us and within us 'really is'. Nevertheless, though such a critique of common sense is entirely justified, the critique itself must take a special view of the personal dimension of existence. Thus existentially the world of the swathes of colour, the blocks of substance and so forth, remains real for the person in the way he feels about things and reacts to them. More importantly there is the special world of interpersonal communication, where we do not only look upon the other as a great swarm of minute processes, but interact with macroscopic feelings.

The way of Buddhism is to transform feelings by inducing a special kind of deflation of the world and a special analysis of the personal, resulting in a new form of detachment and (be it said) compassion. The substances of the world and of other persons are empties. This is one path.

The path of Christianity is rather opposite. For the world is transformed not by a kind of subtraction but by a kind of enhancement, since it becomes symbolic of God's will, and shot through with the glories of the creative process; while other people are not just persons, but persons with the unseen halo of Christ, and stamped with the image of the divine. The reason for the difference in path are, as we have seen before, various. But the Christian emphasis on transformation, a kind of transfiguration of the world, even of its suffering, when seen by the light of the Beyond, connects with the sacramental heart of classical Christianity. For the language of substance, the transfer of power from one to another – much sacramental language fits with the personal and group senses of identity and participation which occur at the level of personal interactions. The bifurcation of the paths suggests a variant on Existentialism: that the world of the conscious individual is other from the world of things (which disintegrate into processes); and the conscious individual is in himself empty, save that he defines himself through his performative, symbolic relations to his neighbours and to his world. The language of substance is the language of perception and feeling, and the language of the symbolic transaction. The question remains as to the ultimate significance of the mere performative. This is where in due course we shall see that the sacramental conceptions of Christianity lend a transcendental character to the individual, and he escapes thus the fragility of human decisions about his worth. But to this variant on Existentialism we shall later return, in our discussion of the secular ideologies.

Neoplatonism and Buddhism

At the heavenly level the two-aspect of truth is especially important from the standpoint of theism. It was indeed a signal contribution of the mystical tradition of Pseudo-Dionysius and of the Neoplatonists that for experiential reasons it sought to vivify a negative way to counterpose to the grand and sometimes brash affirmations about the Divine. Thus we have such fine and strange passages as this:

> The scriptures themselves teach us that no being is able to grasp the meaning of this Super-Essence that transcends all essences, this good defying the description of all words, this mind which escapes every mind, this word beyond experience, insight, name and category, this cause of all being that does not itself exist, this Super-essence that is beyond all being and revelation save its own self-manifestation.

For, to put matters in the terms I have used, if the Transcendent Focus of faith has as its core or subject something which is blank, which is ultimately inaccessible, then this already suggests that a critique of anthropomorphism is always in order, to preserve the Beyondness of the divine. It can be seen that provided we do not make a hierarchy out of the dialectic which Pseudo-Dionysius expresses, that is to say provided we do not say that somehow the Super-Essence is real but its self-manifestation is unreal (which was indeed never the intention of most Christian mystics who followed in this tradition of the negative way), then there is a remarkable congruence between his teachings and those of the Great Vehicle. But to repeat: this is provided that the personal aspects of Buddhahood themselves are not just treated as mere lower truth and delusory. Of course we may say even in the case of Christianity that we do indeed suffer from a kind of illusion if we think of the personal qualities of God in a literal way. The anthropomorphic illusion is pretty common in a certain kind of brash evangelical Christianity (not all evangelical Christianity is brash, needless to say). It is as if God were at the end of a short telephone line, like Nixon talking to Armstrong on the moon. So the two-aspect theory of truth is a useful methodological principle for the critical evaluation of our religious language. It can be used as part of the approach to a critical theory of spiritual traditions which needs to be incorporated into our thinking, for reasons which will emerge more clearly later on.

The Relation of Criticism to the Spiritual

But perhaps many people might worry at this accent on criticism all the time. Is this not a weakness of religion today, that it nurtures too many critics from within itself, who undermine the more confident fabrics of faith, who cast doubt upon verities, who cause rocks to crumble? Many, surely, need assurance and hope, and do not need all the time to have their faith picked at? Such indeed is a natural reaction. Perhaps demythologization, shocking the bourgeois with new theories about Jesus, new airy tele-visual discussions of the difficulties of belief – such an atmosphere of criticism is rather destructive. Yet if such is the atmosphere of criticism of much British discussion of religion, consider how frequently there is the opposite extreme in America: the shouting of certainties from evangelists clad in double-knit suits (knit again Christians) flourishing Bibles with fabulous confidence, frenetic in their assurances that Jesus loves us and all is well with the world. Both syndromes are open to criticism. But, and this is where the two-level theory may also be salutary, the whole point about doctrines is to do with their spiritual referent. Religious externals, whether in words or acts, are fingers pointing at the moon. The two-level theory draws us to consider that criticism has to do with spiritual meaning: it is its whole point. Religion is not a game or a piece of science or just philosophy. Its meaning lies in its ultimately spiritual goals. So when we are valuing criticism it must be from a spiritual angle. The fact that a Christian apologist may use a bad argument, or that the surface meaning of the Bible is in some particular unacceptable, or that earlier Christian presuppositions have to be replaced: such thoughts are important from a spiritual point of view because truth itself is part of the fabric of genuine religion, and because older myth may obscure rather than enhance insight. On the other side, the criticism of criticism itself as being destructive of certainties is itself open to criticism. For why is it that there is a yearning for such clear-cut faith? Why is it that faith has to be so rock-like? The problem arises from insecurity. The sense of diminished identity, the desire for an infusion of substance to make up for the isolations and fragilities of the ego, implies a need for sureness. For uncertainty itself reduces the strength of substance. Thus a bird in the hand is worth two in the bush: an uncertain chance of glory tomorrow gives me less than glory today. But though the sight of such a thirst for substance may fill us with compassion there is a real critique to be made of it: for it has not yet come to terms with the suffering of this world, or of the veiled and mysterious character of true redemption. At any rate, the two-level theory, incorporating a kind of negative way, is a useful and vital methodological guide in the criticism of the concepts of religions, provided it directs itself along the path of that finger which points to the shining silver moon: the ultimate as perceived in a spiritual way. Of course, it should be added this process of criticism is a continuous one, and means self-criticism. For any critique which we may make itself may be infected by the ignorance and lack of insight which is so often the human lot.

Complementarity between Theism and the Great Vehicle

So far, then, we may observe a certain complementarity between theism and the Great Vehicle. The convergence is made more manifest in the modern world, as Christian theism progressively rids itself of the remnants of old polytheisms: where, that is to say, the postulate of the Beyond is disentangled from suggestions that God appears in particular natural forces and phenomena – where indeed he suffers in comparison with the old gods. No longer Poseidon, he is driven from the sea; and yet lives on here and there in little miracles or unexplained areas of knowledge, the so-called God of the gaps. Rather Christianity progressively has, I think, come most clearly to perceive that the Creator is continuously active everywhere in the natural order, in the great swirl of processes which makes up the jewel net of Indra. This has always been implicit in classical Christianity: did not Augustine say that preservation is continuous creation? But Aristotelianism perhaps muddied this clarity of perception. Because the Creator is immanent in all processes, he is in fact revealed by science but is not himself a scientific postulate. The world shows us the mind of God (and strange indeed it turns out to be); but we do not need the conception of the mind of God as the constituent of any scientific theory. It may be true of course, as some have argued, that this notion of the rationality of God as evident in his creation was a powerful impulse in the generation of the modern scientific outlook. But though it might be important as a regulative idea, it plays no part in the constitutive theories of science. So in modern times most luminously perhaps it is possible to perceive the holiness of God as having its twin roots in the Beyond and in the existential experience of those whom God encounters. In other words, it has its twin roots in the Transcendent and in the fabric of human reactions. From this twin standpoint, a vision of the world is generated which sees in the universe the signs of God's painful glory and power. But this 'gnosis', this knowledge of reality, is feeling-knowledge, onlook-knowledge, faith-vision. It is not cool appraisal, or neutral theory. It is beyond science, even when science in changing the configurations of our known world alters our feelings about that world. And because God is not a scientific hypothesis, then the status of the theistic vision of the universe is analogous to the type of vision of the world generated by Hua-yen and other ways of analysing reality under the searching light of inner illumination.

The Problem of Karma

So far we have noted a congruence between the structures of the Beyond as depicted in Christianity and Buddhism. Yet we have also noted a contrast between the substance-oriented sacramentalism of classical Christianity and the non-substantial, emptying modes of Buddhist analysis. Beyond this, there are of course great contrasts in the content of the two sets of mythic belief: and the Buddhist teaching about karma gives it a very different flavour, at least in its traditional presentation, from the aweful brevity and finality of this life on earth. As we have noted, too, there is a general problem with karma from the standpoint of modern scientific knowledge. It would perhaps be unwise to be dogmatic here. There are curious evidences sometimes brought to bear to confirm the theory; though they ought of course to await the verdict of science, inasmuch as, traditionally conceived, the doctrine is an empirical one and so should be available to empirical testing. Of course, one can look on karma in another manner. The momentary flux of the person, on the Buddhist analysis, means that any concern which I may have for my future states, whether in this life or in the next, is a concern for states which really strictly are not mine. They are just consequences, or at least part consequences, of my past and present acts. To be concerned about my own future is no different from being concerned about another's – that is, if I see things truly as they are. Prudence about my future states becomes a kind of altruism. I exist briefly amid a sea of short lived sentient states, my own (as we conventionally say) and others'. Goodness is so acting that there is less suffering and pain around, more joy. Indifference to self and compassion thus go hand in hand. The idea of the self has disintegrated and with it karma itself merely draws attention to the way we live in our own jewel net of Indra: one act affecting other feelings and acts, in this ocean of living feelings and consciousness. From this point of view Buddhism demands an absolute self-naughting, and when this happens the doctrine of karma vanishes – merely a concession, a skilful means, a manner of leading people towards merit and beyond it, to the higher reaches of self-emptiness.

There is in this notion nothing unscientific: it is an alternative vision of the way we are and of the way compassion ought to be directed. But though this is in its own way congruent with the sort of self-naughting that the Christian should undertake: that radical humility through which a person may save his soul by losing it, the main problem with the Buddhist 'disintegration of the self' is that it only gives provisional status to the sanctity of the person. It is true that Buddhist compassion and benevolence have been so powerful that maybe this lack of a theoretical basis for the sacredness of the individual may not much have been needed. But in the modern age it is needed, a point we shall explore in the context of the secular ideologies. So I am inclined to the following complementarity: when I look to myself I should follow the non-self doctrine and the splintering of the ego into a myriad shining droplets of sensation; but in looking to others I affirm the sacredness of the soul. Can such a complementarity be consistent? We shall see.

Incompatibilities between Buddhism and Christianity: History

But nothing much can help towards making the Christian and Buddhist mythic structures compatible. The Christian view of history and incarnation is much at variance with Buddhist ideas. But both will have to undergo some radical restructuring in the modern world. The fact is that men's consciousness has for various reasons been transformed in the last century or more, and nowhere more clearly than in their view of history. In some measure the modern view of history is itself a distant product of the Christian myth of history. It has been natural for the West to see the processes of liberation or redemption in historical terms, even if in modern times the transition is made from transcendentally oriented myth, to a kind of post-mythic dialectical ballet of historical forces. A potent source, as we shall see in more detail later, of the new concern with history has been nationalism, for it has provided men with a new milieu of identity and that identity has necesarily had to present itself in historical terms. The 19th century was the great period for the supply of ancestors, for the tracing of histories, for finding roots. But it was not enough to have the old legends such as might have satisfied our forefathers, St Patrick casting out snakes, Queen Libushe, Romulus and Remus. The 19th century was one where the actual became the real: the actual, as found in historical enquiry or in scientific probing, was hard, genuine, tangible, full of value. Only the actual, or what was taken for it, could glow pregnantly with meaning. Mere legends were but icing on the cake, a fanciful decoration – perhaps suitable for fashioning into national opera; but insufficient in a hard-headed world to function with full symbolic impact. So history managed an amazing conjuring trick. On the one hand it was proud of its scientific canons: archives scrutinized, documents analyzed, archaeology marshalled, oral traditions dissected. On the other hand it told the story of nations, of identities, of ancestries. It was charged with existential power; but it disguised itself, not without reason or justification in a way, as being scientific. And if meaning further was to be found in history, why it was through dialectical and other hidden forces arising from the logic of men's economic and institutional structures. So old myth was replaced to great degree by histories and theories of history.

The Myth of History

This transition to a secretly soft hard-headedness has left its indelible stamp on nearly the whole of mankind. Peoples now look not to myths of origin, but rather to histories; not to transcendental soteriologies, but to dialectical patterns of human change and historical development. It is not a change that Christianity or traditional Buddhism can ignore. The old legendary accounts of the ages of men in Buddhism have to be abandoned, as we have already noted. But perhaps that is not too worrying for Buddhism. After all the core of the message emanates from the Buddha, and though historical enquiry may find that the quest of the historical Buddha is harder even than the quest of the historical Jesus, yet scholars are rarely if ever now going to deny that there was an historical personage who set the wheel of the Dharma rolling, and that presumably he was a person of considerable genius and illumination. And historical questions in general do not much affect the content of that message: it holds good in itself, and neither is Amitabha or the Pure Land seriously threatened by the new historicism. Still, though all this is true, it is important for the Buddhist to see the role of Buddhism in planetary history, to estimate its place in the heritage of particular

countries, to look to ways in which it may develop in the
future. In other words, Buddhism needs to be 'placed' in
world history. In regard to Christianity, though, the
situation is much more acute. For it is not just a question of
estimating the place of the faith in the history of the planet;
it is also a question here of seeing redemptive processes at
work in the course of human history. It was not surprising
that the liberal Protestants of the vintage before World War
I saw redemption in evolutionary and progressive perspective – the optimism of the late 19th century and the sense of
rhythm which both Hegel and Darwin imparted to the
processes of natural and cultural development quite easily
could lead to a new post-mythic (yet secretly mythic)
account of salvation. Much of that was stopped abruptly by
the sledgehammer blow of Barth and by the evil chatter of
machine guns along the appalling trenches of the Western
front. But still Christianity does not make much sense for a
modern man if it says nothing about the rhythms of
planetary history. It can neither affirm the old myth of
history in its classical form, nor can it take flight from the
historical in the privatization of belief, as a form of
ahistorical existential encounter between people and the
Beyond. So it is necessary for Christianity to come to grips
with human history in a way which Buddhism does not;
though all faiths need to see themselves in the perspective
of an emerging planetary culture. It is precisely because
preeminently in West and East Christianity and Buddhism
have the greatest planetary outreach that we have here been
considering their relationships as of special significance for
contemporary history and values.

Buddhism and Christianity as Mutual Critics

Because the history of the planet seen from the Christian
perspective has a central point, which is found in the life
and the beyond of Jesus, the faith has also a curious

relationship to the historical. For while Jesus lived at a particular time and in a particular culture, and thus attracts that 'scandal of particularity' which is worrisome for some people; yet that time and place is in a way universally available. It is through, above all, the sacraments, and especially the Eucharist, that the presence of Christ can as it were be found simultaneously in that ancient upper room and in the modern community of faithful Christians. It is as we have seen a kind of time travel: a channelling of old power into modern times, a making real of the historical configuration of faith's Focus to contemporary experience. It is thus particular history made (in principle) universal. If those historical happenings, including the resurrection, caused in effect a sea change in men's relationship to God: if through them there occurred a renewed deep communication between God and men; it follows that through those events as communicated to us in word and sacrament there is an access of divine power to us – a new availability of grace, a new fullness of the spirit. The story is strange, mysterious; but if it be true, then the Christian has all the infinite substance and power of God to sustain him. With such substance pouring into him, how can he feel any insecurity? If he has God's blessing, how can he fear anything in this hard and suffering world? The power of God is ultimate security, and in its operation as mediated through sacraments the Christian is assigned a kind of fearlessness, a transcendental destiny, a new glory, a transfiguration of his life. Perhaps he catches only a glimpse, for we see as in a glass obscurely. But that in principle is the deathlessness which redemption promises, to those who participate in Christ, the victor. This is the power of the Divine, as it enters into human beings. Yet what a victory! For as we have seen, though Christianity promises ultimate security, the love of God, the configuration of the divine substance is patterned through the life and death of Christ. At his death he was or felt forsaken.

For God's path is that of the sufferer, of the self-emptier. So there is at the heart of Christianity the paradox that God is self-emptying, so that the Christian receives in the same breath of the spirit the promise of the highest, transcendental power and glory and the imprint of human emptiness, losing one's life, maybe with a sense of tragic despair. The fullness of the Christian life has at its heart its own form of emptiness. So again there is a certain congruence between Christian and Buddhist ideals. Yet by what very different paths do Emptiness and kenosis meet! The one path is by meditation, self-analysis, the ideal of the Bodhisattva; the other path is defined by historical events, is sacramental, and moves from the experience of the numinous and the logic of the sacred performative. The one may detonate the ego from within: the other gives identity and security to the ego from without and then detonates the very power which gave balm. Because of this congruence it may seem ludicrous for Christians to try to convert good Buddhists; but the two faiths may serve, as we shall see, as mutual critics and give one another new resources of insight and symbol.

Religions and the Secular Ideologies

As I said, a transformation of human consciousness has occurred in modern times, with the rise of a new consciousness of history, and the growth of secular ideologies– nationalism, Marxism, Nazism, social democracy, Maoism. Perhaps in these latter days of the 20th century we are waiting for Godot (or Buddhot), in that to a great degree the ideologies are a spent force: humanism insipid, Marxism cruelly strait, nationalism largely fulfilled, fascism discredited, social democracy smug, and the world half starved, half consumerized, and stepping to the edges of nuclear warfare; bright dreams dimmed somewhat, even though many marvels have been performed especially in the capitalist countries of the white West. But torture frequent; racism abounding; cruelties many; bitternesses widespread; plenty of the old clumsy pain-dealing Adam. The claims of religion, the affirmation of a Beyond, the experience of divine power and ultimate emptiness, the heroic practice of inwardness, the configurations of self-sacrifice in Bodhisattva and Suffering Servant – these expressions of religion, East and West, are not just private things, though they have relevance to individuals. If they are to speak to the world they have to speak to the world of modern scientific knowledge and to the world, above all, of the modern ideologies. What has the Christian's access of paradoxical power to do with the swirling and striking forces of nationalism and secular belief? What has the shaved monk's great voyage inwards to do with the tremendous social changes which are transforming our planetary world? This is where we move into the second part of our inquiry, into the nature of the worldviews which have dominated so much of our contemporary world. But perhaps it is useful to give a hint of the relevance of the religions of the Beyond to the secular problems of our day.

Although Buddhism and Christianity have to undergo great changes as they swim onwards to the 21st century, part of the secret of their relevance lies in the way they integrate the past to the problems of today. For one thing, the Marxist perspective, as it is often interpreted in practice, fails to show forth the meaning of personal suffering, inevitable even in socialist paradises. Moreover, Marxist collectivism abstracts from persons and in doing so fundamentally conflicts with the principle of the sacredness of human life. That sacredness is from one point of view a reflection of the attitude of love and compassion; but from another point of view it is itself a performative concept. And, as I shall argue, it is seen best in the light of the Beyond, in which the performative life of the sacrament channels (so to speak) that deathless sacrality to the individual. Indeed the transcendental aspect of humanity is the

true guarantee of those rights which are so often crushed
today. The shaved monk too is a symbol of how men can
swim not only in this world but in a transcendent reality
too; and also Buddhism shines out as an ideal of that
ultimate peacebleness and insight which the world badly
needs. But all this needs to be seen in the realities of the
ideological drives of this modern world. To that I now
turn; but not before an expression of the synthesis.

Fearful tender one your transcendental gaze
Stirs the dancing atoms of my mind:
You who look down, stirring imitation,
Lord of Infinite light, ancient of days,
What lies behind your eyes? Nothing we can find,
Suchness and superessence, beyond explanation,
The highest immortal place. But holy power
Flows from your smile, conqueror, slave.
When you sprinkle rain the stars shower
And the moon finds a new halo in your light.
You make me command the whole world, brave;
Yet at your heart there lies the dark night.
   Holy too is the shaved monk who paces
   The warm grains of sand, his fingers lean,
   Pointing to the shore; a true amphibian he
   Swims into his crystal mind, and no traces
      Can he leave on the stream. Orange against green
      His robe is signal of transcendentality:
You and he are warnings to those who see
Nothing beyond the myriad cells which form
Our universes. And around us the droplets swarm
Of tiny flashes of power, gone like smoke.
But your power lies in rite and heart:
Rock, diamond, tree of life, oak,
Silent happy suffering witness of our world:
Empty and apart, and not apart.

Secular Ideologies:
A First Anatomy

Secular Ideologies versus Traditional Religions

The relation of the secular ideologies to traditional religions
is complex, overlapping, partly hostile. There is the question too of how they relate in function and spirit as
compared with the older, more deep-rooted spiritual traditions. For though it would be too simple to say that the
ideologies are in effect modern religions, there is undoubtedly much in the analysis of religion which applies to them
too. They are analogues to religion. Tillich said quasi-
religions, but that is too suggestive of a kind of fraud or
failure, as though they were religions manqué. For the
present, it is best to look at them as secular ideologies, but
to note that they occur along a spectrum another part of
which is occupied by the traditional religions. For they
mobilize deep sentiments and often demand great sacrifices;
they give a sense of identity and purpose; they propound a
theory of the world, a placement of men's lives in action
and feeling.

How best should we categorize these worldviews and
schemes of living? Maybe it is best to look very briefly at
the history of the last two centuries or so. It is a stunning
thought that it is less than two hundred years since the
French Revolution, and yet what sea changes have we seen
since then! Liberal legislation, mass armies, tricolours,
national flags and symbols, laissez faire capitalism, the rise

of the old machine age, the unification of Germany, Italy; the romantic age and the forging of national sentiment; the new industrial state, the flowering of liberal democracy, the Great Wars, the Soviet Revolution, the struggles for colonial independence . . . And the new science: evolution, relativity, quantum physics, the Big Bang, the nuclear age, the dawn of the silicon era, genetic engineering. The changes have been immense, shaking, disturbing, liberating. We have seen the glories of affluence succeed upon the darkness of depression; and we have seen both the renewal of Russia and the Gulag Archipelago. We have seen great glories and great horrors, and most devastatingly among men's massacres of men, the insane, unintelligible, monstrous Holocaust. So much, then, have we seen, and in much of it we have seen ideas as engines of change: liberal economics, the Protestant spirit, the Keynesian solution, socialism, nationalism, racism, humanism. It is to these mental engines of change and of identity formation that our gaze is now directed.

The French Revolution and 'The National Assumption'

The French Revolution, by restructuring French society and making possible a new mobilization of citizens' energies, had a double effect on other European countries. The amazing path of Napoleonic conquests helped to reshape France's satellites somewhat according to the French model and thus prepared the ground for the emergence of a powerful middle class; but at the same time, the very fact of conquest by French arms helped, especially in Germany, to arouse, by contrast, German national sentiments. The national movement in Greece, followed by the struggles for Italian and German unification, foreshadowed the eventual prevalence of 'the national assumption', that is that the state and the nation should in principle coincide, and that nations were entitled to independent existence. That principle was at the fore at the Treaty of Versailles, which succeeded in reshaping Eastern Europe out of the ruins, primarily, of the Austro-Hungarian Empire. Indeed the extraordinary thing about the Hapsburg rule was how long it managed to last, given that by the latter half of the 19th century the processes of the formation of national consciousness were well advanced among the subject countries of Eastern Europe and the Balkans. We shall later look in more detail at this question of nation-building. But it was assisted by the new industrial age, which not only demanded larger units to work with, than the old feudal jigsaw, but also encouraged new concentrations of manpower and resources in the state itself. Imperialism also, in a sense, exported nationalism in the Victorian and Edwardian ages. For briefly one could define the imperial idea as this – that the imperial nation has some kind of right or destiny to rule over other peoples. Those peoples themselves may not be self-conscious particularly; but this self-consciousness is undoubtedly stimulated by the humiliation of being conquered, and it is natural for the rising educated classes of the conquered peoples to borrow from the imperial country's milieu the theory of nationalism, that is the theory that a people nationally has a right to its own sovereign state.

The Theory of the Nation State

The nation state was in many ways a modernizing force. The fact that for many peoples, the differential was the language led to an immense revival and flowering of literature, and in turn this had its effects on schooling – now penetrating downwards and more widely to the lower classes, preparing them for a role in the growing industrial state. Also, because the main agents of national renaissance and political revival were middle class, nationalism was frequently tied in with forms of constitution which were

Secular Ideologies: A First Anatomy 211

adapted to the capitalist wave. But the relation to traditional religion was more variegated. The liberal ideal was that of toleration; and the Napoleonic era had seen the emancipation of European Jewry, bringing a great efflorescence of Jewish culture within the fabric of modern national culture. But sometimes religion itself has been one of the defining characteristics of a nation in its own selfconsciousness: thus, for instance, Ireland, by and large speaking the same language, if more extravagantly, than the English oppressor; but rooted in a different faith. Again, in Romania and Poland, Orthodoxy and Catholicism respectively have combined with language in nurturing the national past and keeping alive its hope for the future. But often liberalism found itself in conflict with religious tradition, partly because of the authoritiarian pretensions of the Church, and notably in Catholic countries, which have often nurtured a good deal of anti-clericalism (in the Italy of the Risorgimento; in France; in Spain). In general, we may say this: that the nation state has to choose not only independence but a further theory on how to run itself. It has, that is, to choose some kind of ideology and bureaucratic-economic structure. The ideology itself may be curiously mixed or even split-souled, as in contemporary Romania, which nurtures both Marxism and the Church. So with regard to nations, we have to look not just to nationalism, but to a further layer of ideology on top of that. We have a double decker ideological superstructure: at one level there is the nationalist assumption and its expression in this particularity, in other words *our* patriotism (whoever we may be: Americans, Scots, Poles, Yugoslavs, Indians, New Zealanders, Turks, Chinese); and at another level, there is our way of life – social democracy, Marxism, etc. There may even, in effect, be three layers: thus Britain, in the imperial age, could be described as expressing a complex national identity at one level; it was organized according to (roughly) the principles of emerging liberal democracy; and yet it also possessed an imperial ideology sometimes indeed in conflict with the democratic ideal (though the two could be somewhat harmonized through a paternalistic doctrine that subject peoples could be suitably nurtured and raised to such a condition that they too could benefit from liberal ideas and practices).

Nationalism and Chauvinism

In general, then, we need a cross-classification between particular nationalisms, built according to the general theory of 'the national assumption', and the political and other ideologies which were used in the structure of the nation state. Before, however, turning to these ideologies briefly, it is as well to say something about a particular form of nationalism which may be described as chauvinistic, and which found its most extreme expression in Nazism. There may be a nation such as the Finns who really do not have any particular ambition to conquer anyone else, and if they do have territorial ambitions these are the modest ones of trying to get back that great part of Karelia which the Soviets took after the Winter War and got again in the peace settlement at the end of World War II. The Finns are primarily concerned with independence; they are not given to chauvinism; it would, in any case, be highly unrealistic, for the badger does not try to overrun the bear. This kind of basically defensive nationalism is very widely acceptable in today's world, and unless a nation does something quite horrific internally, the general view is that it is wrong to interfere; some even then doubt the wisdom of such interference. Nyerere got much criticism over his ridding Uganda of Amin, and the Vietnamese were likewise upbraided for overrunning much of Kampuchea, despite the vast slaughter of the senseless Pol Pot and Khieu Sampan era. But, by contrast with this defensive nationalism, there has, of course, been a fairly rampant national chauvinism, where nations, in effect, aspire to empire, and feel they have some kind of right to conquer or humiliate other peoples. The most acute and paranoid form of this doctrine was, of course, Nazism, and what made it particularly repellent and dangerous was its explicit theory that Jews and Slavs were inferiors, the former to be finally massacred, the latter to be killed at will and used as slaves. But, of course, what fuelled Nazism above all was the humiliation and insecurity inflicted on Germany by Versailles and by the Depression. But to make the war of revenge and conquest fully credible to the faithful, nationalism had to be built up into a racist theory – or, as I shall prefer to call it, an ethnicist theory.

Ethnicism and Oppression

I use the term 'ethnicist' because in a way the expression 'racism' or 'racialism' is misleading in drawing a distinction between oppression or humiliation based upon race and oppression or humiliation which is based upon other marks of ethnic identity. Thus, Palestinians may regard themselves as being oppressed by Jewish Israelis, though technically they are supposed to belong to the same race. Animosities between Kurds and Iraqis are no different in principle from hatreds existing in Southern Africa between blacks and whites. The fact is that where ethnic groups occupy the same territory, in the modern world of nation states, the oppression by the majority of the ethnic minority is the rule rather than the exception; or at least considerable tensions between the communities exist. The Han Chinese oppress Tibetans; the Protestants have oppressed Catholics in Northern Ireland; the Basques feel oppressed by the Spanish; the Turkish minority in Cyprus felt itself threatened by the Greek-speaking majority; the Christians and Muslims of the Lebanon have been engaged in civil war; the Kurds have long and intermittently been in revolt; the Han Chinese in Vietnam are under threat; the smaller ethnic groups in Kampuchea were oppressed by the Khmer Rouge; the Chinese in Indonesia have been under attack . . . Ethnicism may be defined as the oppression of, or tendency to humiliate, another ethnic group. The oppressed themselves typically respond with hatred, which motivates attempts to assert rights, or to take revenge on the oppressor. Such ethnic hatred is very widespread in the world. Moreover, the trajectories of cruelty are long, since cruelties are remembered at the mother's knee, in the marrow of the family and clan, in the very bones of the community. It is hard to forgive. Armenians still recall the terrible Turkish massacre; Irish memories run long and deep; the Holocaust is burned deep into Jewish memory; why, schoolboys still remember in Scotland the massacre of Glencoe – can a Macdonald boy decently play with a Campbell? I remember the question quite seriously from my childhood by neighbouring children. And the iron of the slave's shackles still rust away and stain the souls of their black descendants. It is a memory of cruelty and – worse – humiliation. So, we must remember that though the face of the world may shift with great speed through technological change, the trajectories of memory are much slower. Those who travel by jet still harbour the same feelings and resentments as their grandfathers of the days of the sailing ship and the horse. The outer shells of life have altered greatly, but the burning passions smoulder on long fuses. We shall later have to go more deeply into the question of why insiders can treat outsiders so cruelly and callously. Briefly, it is a bit like the ethnicism of the Nazis: the others are seen as not fully human, as semi-persons, and so not to be accorded the same rights and love as one's own folk. It is wonderful what moral blindness can be induced in humans once a category is invented which makes divisions between us and them.

The Development of Totalitarianism

One feature of Nazism which gave it a strangely modern stamp for all its atavism was that it was a totalitarian regime, that is, that ultimately the distinction between private and public life was dissolved, since the Party demanded absolute loyalty to the Fuehrer and commitment to the values of the Third Reich. The apparatus of the state police, the concentration camp, the informer, skilful propganda, strict censorship, party rituals to cement solidarity and a whole range of other rites and performatives to make the presence of the Party all-pervasive – these measures made it contrast sharply with the older liberal and social democratic ideals. The sadness of the Weimar Republic was that these goals were under secret or open attack from too many quarters – the army high command, the President, the Communists and the brawling brownshirts. But it is the Marxist countries which have produced the most stable type of totalitarianism. And, whereas in Nazi Germany the capitalist dimension of the economy was considerable, and this meant a certain devolution of economic power, in socialist countries the whole economy is bureaucratically concentrated in the hands of the state. This makes it possible for the state to enforce certain kinds of rapid social change. But such centralization of power actually reinforces tendencies to nationalism: for the definition of the boundaries of a socialist state remain national in character, and for all the talk of international solidarity, 'the people' in practice is bound to mean a particular people (Poles, Hungarians, Chinese, etc.). However, the international character of Marxist ideology does mean that nationalism itself can acquire, under the aegis of Marxism, an imperial posture. The justification for the domination of the Soviet Union by the Greater Russians is that there must be a unified socialist state; while it is in the name of internationalism that the satellite states of Eastern Europe are kept in check by troops and economic intergration into the Soviet Union.

Marxism and National Identity

Because of this interplay between Marxism and the sense of national identity, it is often unwise to treat Marxism as though its internationalism is overriding. The weakness of Western and particularly American foreign policy in the decades after World War II lay in seeing Marxism as a threatening and monolithic ideology, neglecting the fact, more apparent even to the dimmest Presidential adviser today, that Vietnam, China, Korea, the USSR, Yugoslavia, Romania, Albania, Cuba, Angola have differing styles of Marxism, adapted to the goals of national independence and national substance. But of course the leaders of such nations see the way forward to a reassertion of identity through a form of social reconstruction. Societies threatened with collapse or dependency by war and Western incursions and exploitation can often only gather the hard strength to struggle for liberation from outside influence or oppression through internal reconstruction. Such a drastic inner social change is rather like being converted: society is born again. Yet, though it is born again, a new people, it still is identical with the old people. National identity persists through the painful purgation of a social revolution. This centralization and discipline, the imposition of new norms upon the people and the reshaping of the economy toward greater independence constitute the attractions of Marxism in the Third World. But the upheaval is great. For one thing, traditional religion is identified with the bad past and has to be purged.

Marxism and a New Identity

Further, Marxism has the attraction, from the national

point of view, of promising modernization and a scientific approach to economic and social problems while at the same time providing a historical theory which can justify constructive hatred for the imperialist Western world. In other words, modernization can be imported in order to cope with the problems posed by the West itself, both in its imperial and exploitative aspect and in its aspect as generator of modern industrial and technological powers; but this is not a matter of slavishly adopting foreign values, because Marxism is itself in violent opposition to the traditional values of the West. Moreover, adaptive Marxism can be indigenized, as in the case of Maoism. Constructive hatred is important as a mechanism for generating pride in the face of damaging humiliations. So: discipline; social reconstruction; a theory of history; a blueprint for revolution and war against the oppressor; a promise of modernization; a way of imposing a new centralization upon a nation; an anti-Western ideology – such are the attractions of Marxism in the non-European world. And to some extent the same analysis applies to the Russian Empire itself: tsarism overthrown, a new Soviet man born, an analogue to the old sacral kingship created in the Kremlin. In brief, it is important to see the growth of Marxism in terms of the restoration of national identity. I shall be later pursuing this theme in somewhat greater depth by analysing the nature of Maoism.

Social Democracy in the West

Social democracy as an alternative general ideology to Marxism has a predominantly capitalist structure, but heavily modified by socialist and welfare measures through which the state intervenes in the direction of a more equal society and the protection of the relatively poor against the possible harshness of the system. Even in America, the least socialist of Western democracies, the Roosevelt era injected a strong dose of welfare measures into the fabric of American capitalism; and the social and environmental legislation which has grown since World War II has helped to promote better opportunities and to modify the effects of capitalism. So, America too has its own kind of mixed economy. But highly important to social democracy is the freedom of opinion, toleration of differing religions and outlooks, protection of the rights of the individual: in brief, a respect for individuals, combined with an open society. The personalism of such a system is, up to a point, enhanced by the consumer orientation of modern semi-capitalist societies. A strong strand of scientific humanism runs through social democratic thinking; so that though such societies are indeed tolerant of traditional religions, the technocratic assumptions upon which they are run tend to be those of scientific humanism and utilitarianism. One of the strongest elements in such societies is that they do more easily nurture scientific thinking and enterprise, because of their openness: education is intended to breed enquiry and criticism, and free speculation and debate is of the essence of the scientific approach. It may be that a totalitarian society can permit enclaves of such freedom; but the tensions between censorship and science, between ideological conformism and scientific thought are very considerable. Thus despite the pretensions of Marxism to be scientific, it is in practice inimical to the spirit of scientific enquiry. It is no coincidence that so large a proportion of Nobel Prize winners in science come from the United States.

The Conditions of Social Democracy

But the conditions for the achievement of a social democratic society are hard ones. Thus, a partial suspension of citizens' constitutional rights has occurred in Northern Ireland, precisely because personal freedom, social justice and an open society cannot be worked together effectively in a deeply divided community, erupting into sporadic violence. In fact, the easiest background for such democracy is where the vast majority of the population belongs to the same ethnic group. Thus, though Czechoslovakia before World War II was democratic, it was imperfectly so in that German speakers and some other groups did not genuinely have equal rights with the Czechs and Moravians. It might be countered that the USA incorporates many ethnic groups. But this is a partial illusion. The formation of the American nation involved rites of passage, past the Statue of Liberty, through the high schools, on the baseball and football fields, in the universal use of English: rites which transformed the old ethnic groups into the new American citizens. The immigrants were (rightly) deprived of most of their old culture in order to take on a new one. Such a thing is possible in a great liberal nation founded largely on immigration. The melting pot produced a relatively homogeneous population. Thus, sometimes Americans misunderstand the situation of ethnic minorities elsewhere, which would bitterly resist a melting pot in their own case, as it would amount to a kind of aggrandizement on the part of the majority ethnic group.

There is little doubt that special arrangements – typically of a federal kind – need to be made in nations which comprise more than one ethnic group. Thus, not unnaturally, the Republic of India has since independence rearranged itself into mainly linguistic states, while certain understandings, caste groupings, special rights for the Harijans and so forth keep something of a balance between the various religious and social groups within the incredible mosaic of Indian society. Moreover, as 20th century history has indicated, it is hard to preserve the openness of society and devotion to individual rights – ideas largely the product of 19th century bourgeois political thinking – when a large section of the population is socially deprived and alienated.

Thus, for the Marxist, liberalism is a sham because it is tangential to social justice: but the fact is that the two ideals are quite compatible, and have to be achieved if social democracy is to work. There is a point where the need of bread overrides all thoughts of critical enquiry and *habeas corpus*. But, as events have also shown, without the critical, open society there may remain forms of exploitation which are enforced by military and police power, as riotous workers in Poland, East Germany and Romania have found out. In a planetary context it is likewise ominous if the democratic nations of the North treat the Third World countries to the South largely as a kind of external proletariat and peasantry, allowing them to suffer in deep poverty and despair. For that way leads to extreme action, and new social tyrannies. In the long term it is better to adapt the Keynesian techniques to the Third World – enhance its purchasing power in order to also stimulate the economies of the North.

The Analysis of the Nation State

Thus, of all the secular forces which have run like fire through the 20th century, it has been the drive to nationalism which has been the most widespread. It is thus important to analyse it. And in so doing we come to some very basic facts about human nature. For what has happened is that the nation state has become the predominant grouping of which modern men are conscious, and it is the one which demands the most overriding loyalty. Thus one can look at it in terms of the licence to kill. Among Albanian clans, even today, the clan is the group that can kill. Vendettas are frequent, for it is reasonable and indeed often a duty to kill on behalf of the clan group. In feudal times the lord was someone to whom one was bound by great oaths and for whom one would fight. Or again, in the Scottish Highlands until the 18th century, warfare between the clans was accepted practice (but not by the government in London, for it was a challenge to its own rights to monopolize force and killing). In modern days we regard clan killings, tribal warfare, Mafia operations and the like as somewhat primitive and basically unacceptable in 'decent society'. But our decent society now is the nation state, and it, if it wishes will command us to kill, as a duty. Warfare against other nation states is on the whole taken for granted as a possibility. So, in various stages of history we can look to differing significant groups, which have a kind of ultimate hold over the individual. Residually, we may think of the family as such a group; but that is false. Strong as the bonds of blood may be, they only in the most residual way allow me the right to kill on behalf of my family; that is in certain situations of self defence. But the nation would expect me, perhaps, to betray my brother if he were to be working against the state. So, the nation state now has become the 'ultimate' group. And not only does the state demand my obedience in the matter of killing or suffering death myself. It also imposes upon me taxes, partly to finance the glory of the nation and its defences.

Warfare as a Sacrament

I have placed emphasis on the matter of killing because warfare itself is one of the great sacraments of mankind. Warfare is much more than killing or being killed: it transforms men, baptizes them with fire, leads them to the highest sacrifice, gives the nation a sense of its own destiny. It aims at victory, and the aggrandizement of national substance. The defeat of the enemy marks too a significant change both in him and us. Warfare ends up with the performative: the acknowledgement by the others that we have won. But, above all, in causing and suffering death, warfare feeds the national glory. That men should lay down their lives for their country adds to the sacred substance of the country. These are meaningful deaths. And for many modern nations, the way to national independence and liberty was through battles, revolution, warfare, blood. Consider: the Greeks, who fought with dash against the Turks; the Italians, via the glories of the Risorgimento and Garibaldi; the struggles in South America of Bolivar and Martin; the battles which preceded Polish independence and followed it, after World War II; the guerrilla struggles of Tito and the creation of modern Yugoslavia; the Long March and the Chinese Revolution; the bitter struggle of Algeria against France; the warfare in South Yemen; the long long struggle of Ho Chi Minh and his successors; the battle for Bangladesh to break away from greater Pakistan; the still unsuccessful warfare of the persistent Kurds; the various wars to establish Israel on a firm foothold in the land; the Cuban revolution; the Sandinista fight for a new Nicaragua. And those wars which cemented patriotism: as with the Russians in 1812 and in the Civil War and intervention, not to mention the Great Patriotic War against the Germans; the warfare for Finnish independence and above all the cruel and glorious Winter War of 1939–1940; the Revolutionary War in America; the two World Wars for Britain, France and even Germany itself. Thus, it is not surprising that for many people the charged events of their history are decisive battles – Blood River for the Boers; Trafalgar, Waterloo, Clive's campaigns, etc., for the British; the victory on the Isonzo for the Italians and before that the battles that Garialdi fought; and so on. Children are often taught through battles. So, in brief, war has a kind of sacramental significance in enhancing the substance of the nation and conferring solemnity and a sense of glory upon the nation's children.

What Constitutes a Nation?

But it is at first sight a puzzle to know what it is that

constitutes a nation. Sometimes we seem to have a state with scarcely a definable people; and when we do come to definitions they seem to vary widely. Thus it may be to do with a language; or it may have to do with a religion; or maybe some kind of cultural tradition. It always involves a territory. So, let us just begin with that, for the land of a people itself has symbolic significance, and a kind of sacredness. In today's world a people without a land cannot become a nation, so for instance the Gypsies cannot now easily maintain their lifestyle, for they are increasingly expected to conform to the ways of the majority population, and so get sucked into the bureaucratic procedures of the modern state. This was also the painful predicament of the Jews of the European diaspora during the rise of nationalism: assimilation was one path; but it was natural to cry out for a land – hence Zionism and the return to Israel. The land most typically has a double significance. For, first of all, it is the space to which the people have a right, where they are at home. And it is also the scene of past deeds, and has its own characteristics which may impart a sense of warmth and beauty to the national heritage. Thus, the Scot not only looks to Scotland as his home, but also boasts of its beauties – the Highlands, the islands, the lochs, the ageless mountains, the bonny banks of Doone. Beautiful these are in themselves and also they are haunted by the ghosts of many a past heroic and significant deed! The territory is something over which the nation has control: and if any soldiers of a foreign power cross the frontier it is a kind of sacrilege: an invasion, which must be met by counterforce. It is a kind of outrage to the people invaded: they rally to defend their sacred soil. Sometimes it is supposed that *homo sapiens* is essentially a territorial animal, that he likes to have a piece of territory and to keep others out. But for vast numbers of men in distant generations and even for some men even now, life is a walkabout, nomadic, wandering from place to place. The sacred space of the tent or the cave is merely transitory, to be shifted onwards as times may require. It is most clearly among *modern* men that there is a feeling of popular sovereignity over a block of land, a country. Spatiality thus is a cultural phenomenon. So it is that the word for a nation is country. One dies for one's country. The territoriality of men is greatly amplified by the modern sense of the nation. Men are tied by bonds of affection and possession to their country. It provides the material base and the physical milieu for the life of the nation. It provides too a potent source of conflict when two quite distinct groups mingle on the same land.

Another Mark of a Nation

But in addition to the land as a mark or sign of the nation, a people is defined by some other mark: by, for instance, a linguistic heritage, or by a religion setting them up as different from their neighbours, and by some consciousness of the historic past and how it is that the members of the group come to belong to it. Consider first the manner in which descent occurs. It is, of course, a biological matter, but only in part so. When a baby emerges from the womb it might be possible, as sometimes happens, to leave it on a doorstep. This is to take no responsibility for it – in essence not to acknowledge it. But most typically, of course, the baby is welcomed into the family, and through such welcome and all the performatives which are used in connection with its arrival, the baby is acknowledged as 'one of us'. It would be very hard indeed for the child later to repudiate this cultural descent. It takes strong performative action to effectively repudiate the family and one's forebears. So, more broadly in the nation state, the new child is acknowledged as citizen, as part of the fabric of the people. And again it is hard, often impossible later on for him to effectively repudiate his heritage. So, joining a group, even in so natural a way as by being born among it,

involves performative acts. The national group partly
defines itself by descent, since it is through a chain of
acknowledged descent that the present group, however
defined, came to be. The young person moreover is
inducted into the values of the group, which means his
taking on the mark of the group. This is where the use of
language as the major mark makes things so easy: for the
baby learns the language painlessly and with every advance
in his grasp of the tongue he embeds himself more deeply
into the national group. Descent, territory, a mark or
marks: these factors are what give coherence to the national
idea. But *consciousness* of these things is important, and this
is in part a performative matter too. For I do not just hear
about descent and the ancestors in the history which has
given rise to the group. I also endorse that history and
celebrate it too, if I am a loyal citizen.

History, Nationhood and Symbols

As I tried to show earlier, the fashioning of history in the
19th century has itself been a means toward creating
national self-consciousness, so that history had, so to say,
the function of myth. As myth it guides the celebration of
the value-laden past which enhances the group's substance;
and it also provides a kind of charter for the group itself, for
'if anyone asks for our credentials, we shall tell them that
this is how our nation came to be'. History fuses descent
into the mark, for it tells of the ancestors: it tells how our
ancestors already had the distinguishing characteristic of
the nation in some way. But not only this. A nation has
heroes and prophets other than those of power and bat-
tlefield. The rise of modern nationalism has seen a great
flowering of national culture. Verdi in Italy, Dvorak and
Smetana in Czechoslovakia, Chopin and Paderewski in
Poland, Sibelius in Finland, Grieg in Norway, Beethoven
and Wagner in Germany, Berlioz in France, Rimsky-

Korsakov and Glazunov in Russia . . . So we might go on. Poets and writers, artists and architects also try to catch and express the national spirit. A nation bedecks itself with the garnishings of the romantic state: the opera house, the museums, the theatres, the university, the academy and so forth. In the 20th century the symbols of modernity are the air line and steel plant. In all these ways the substance of the nation is shaped and enhanced. And because international competition gives a convenient opportunity to manifest pride, the sports contests and the stadiums provide further occasions of patriotism: new manifestations of a secular religion. As for more formal rites: every nation now is expected to have its badge of identity, its flag; and the running up of the flag and the saluting of it constitute ways in which members pay tribute to the collective. Every nation has its anthem in which the nation's substance is celebrated. The head of state condenses in suitable pomp the glory and solemnity of the nation. The military parade is an exhibition of power designed to give the citizens a sense of machismo and security and to impress outsiders.

The Structure of National Substance

In all this, the nation is more than the sum of its citizens, for it includes the land, and it includes the substance of the group as condensed and organized, such that the nation can enter into men's consciousness as a kind of 'thing' which simultaneously transcends them, for it lays great demands upon them, and in which they, in some manner, participate. Each person's efforts and tributes to the state enhance the substance of the nation; and also, the more the nation has glory, the more the individual feels raised by it. What citizen did not rejoice when the War ended in Europe, and Britain found itself victorious? What Indian did not feel larger in his soul when an atomic device was exploded, adding machismo to the nation? What Japanese does not feel a quiet pride as he notes how the GNP has risen again this year? What Egyptian did not feel enlarged at the stealthy Yom Kippur crossing of the Suez Canal? Sometimes it may seem to us quite pathetic that human beings should find pride in such things. But a person rarely can fall back totally on his own resources. His place in the world, his security and substance – these he derives in great measure from the groups to which he belongs; and as we have seen, in the modern world the nation state is overwhelmingly the most solemn and ultimate group in which he participates. And, as we have seen, there is a kind of analogue to the religious idea of sacramental participation. For the nation, as I have said, is a kind of 'thing' which is both other than the individual and yet something too of which he is a part. The cult of personality, the *Fuehrerprinzip*, – these are ways in which the nation is incarnated in a single person. Those who adulate him also indirectly enhance their own substance, for the more effective and ideal the leader is the stronger is the nation.

'We' or 'Ushood'

We may add to these considerations a more general analysis of what it is to belong to a group. Or to put matters another way: How do we get in the position to say 'We'? It is remarkable how little attention has been paid in philosophy to the first person plural: it is as though since Descartes, if not from earlier on, there has been an obsession with the lone ego. Thus, there has been posed the formidable problem of how knowledge is built upon the basis of the individual's experience – as if the fabric of human knowledge were not well known to be a communal effort. While Buber wrote his famous *I and Thou*, we perhaps ought to turn our attention to *Us and Them*. How, then, do we say 'we'? What is, to coin a word, ushood (as opposed to themhood and youhood)? I think if a group forms itself, for instance to undertake some project – perhaps it is a group forming itself into an action committee – a certain performative transaction takes place, namely that the persons involved mutually acknowledge each other as one of us. Is this not circular, for it makes use of the notion of *us*, which is what we were trying to explain? Well, not quite: for I was trying to bring out what may be called the subjectivity of the group. What constitutes a group is not just that there are several or many people conjoined together in an organization, but they perceive themselves as acting from within towards the outside, that is, they perceive themselves, being members of the group, as us. One role of the first person is to serve as subject for expressed intentions. In the plural there is a presupposition of a mutually acknowledged joint project. We may look at this through the example of what happens when someone joins the group, however casually formed. A group of us are on our way to a film; we bump into John. If we say 'Would you care to come with us?' this is the smoothest and most explicit way in which he is invited in, and becomes if he accepts, one of us in this transitory group. He does not become one of us by proximity, but by a mutual agreement. In general, ushood, then, is a matter of a performative act, and it is indeed in an important sense a performative construct. Give the group any degree of permanence and it acquires its own substance. For instance, a family has this. A person, of course, might be ashamed of his family, because of its low degree or the unpleasant configuration of its substance (its members are perhaps poor and slothful). But it takes strong acts of distancing, itself a kind of symbolic act, if the taint of the substance is not to come down to the individual.

The notion of the nation as a kind of 'thing' is reinforced by the fact that those who may be ashamed of the nation's actions can say that it is the fault of the leaders who betray the true interests of the nation. They can thus appeal from actual national behaviour to the ideal. It is thus a function of a head of state (for example) to incarnate the essence of the nation in a way that attracts loyalty, even if there may be conflicts at the lower level between the government and its critics. Perhaps the most extreme and clear expression of this notion of the essence is found in the Japanese conception of the *kokutai*. In general, though, despite the possibilities of criticism, the national group, like any long-standing group, does demand a certain loyalty. This is where the figure of the traitor comes in for especial opprobrium. The enemies of the nation are expected to act against our interests; but people feel that, for one bound from birth onwards by performative ties to the nation, to act against it deserves the most extreme punishment.

The National Assumption and Others' Rights

Though modern nationalism has tended to occur within the 'national assumption', that is the notion that all nations should in principle be self-governing, there is built into it a tendency toward what I have called ethnicism. For other peoples can easily be considered by the patriot to be inferior, especially because the nation state finds the presence of minority groups within the territory of the country hard to deal with, given the nature of the patriotic myth. Moreover, since the nation generates very solemn duties of solidarity and self-sacrifice, because it is the ultimate group in so much of the modern world, its members are bound together in ways that imply that members of other nations have very slight rights. Thus, though the citizen of one country does not think it right to kill (meaning, right to kill a member of society, primarily one's own nation), he will have no compunction about killing citizens of another country as soon as the state calls on him to do this. Nevertheless, it is part of what I have called 'the national assumption' that national groups have equal rights to independence, and given this outlook there is nothing intrinsic to nationalism that it should be rapacious or aggrandizing.

Indeed, the national assumption seems to have a consequence: that living cultural traditions have a continued right to existence, for it is they are the stuff of national groups. Moreover, it suggests that special arrangements have to be made in countries where there unavoidably remains a minority cultural or national group – unavoidably, in that it it not easy in a lot of cases to disentangle populations which mingle, or where there are pockets of nationality 'A' within the area dominated by nationality 'B'. The Balkans notoriously have been the scene of such intermingling and untidinesses. In such a situation the federal idea, or the strong application of autonomy arrangements, must be the humane solution to the recurrent problem that within a patriotic nation state the minority will feel that it is likely to be oppressed and overruled about many of the things which it holds important for its existence – e.g. regarding the education of its children. This is where democracy as it is often practised in the West is no guarantee of minority rights, for the notion that power should be wielded by that party which gains a majority of the votes tends to mean, in a divided country, that majority and minority are defined nationally and culturally and consequently that the minority group will be liable to be oppressed by the 'patriotic' majority. This is a vitally important observation, for it touches on another matter to which we shall be paying heed later, namely the conditions for openness and criticism in a free society. Security of outlook seems to be one such condition, and this is not easily gained in divided societies.

The Nation as a Daily Sacrament

So far we have noted that nationalism is something which provides a new matrix of group identity. Ernest Renan referred to the nation as a daily plebiscite, but it might be better to say that it is a daily sacrament. Its citizens are woven together by the strong threads of rituals – the very speaking of the same language, the performative character of upbringing within the nation, the shape of values imparted through education, the more explicit rites of the nation through its anthem and flag, the sense of belonging and pride celebrated through football matches and Olympiads, the solemn demands of war, the remembrance of the sufferings of the past and their sad but glory-giving celebration, the feel for the ancestors, the general willingness to join one's country's armed forces, the expectation that to die for one's nation is a great and glorious thing. Such consciousness is acknowledgement of a particular and solemn ushood, in which we individuals merge together in solidarity, and are conscious of the nation both as something which is out there and as something in which each one of us participates. But it is not just that we owe great services to the nation: we also feel that it owes something to us, and in the age of the welfare state the nation becomes a universal provider for its children. Full-scale socialism with its centralized bureaucracy may add to a sense of close solidarity. In all this we may see the typical nation as a country whose population is held together by a particular consciousness of belonging in virtue of some mark such as the common language and of a mythic history which is charged with values relevant to the identity of the nation. The nation has its 'objective' side – the land and the people, etc.; but it also has its 'subjective' component, namely the consciousness of the people that they belong together as a nation – and this consciousness is not a matter of knowing something or believing: it is not just a kind of descriptive consciousness, for it is strongly performative in that the sense that 'we belong together' is itself shot through with performatives, such as mutual acknowledgements. The nation, in the last resort, is a performative construct, created performatively out of materials supplied by land, genes and the past. It is, in this sense, a daily sacrament.

The Problem of Nation Building

The sacramental, collectivist sense of nationhood can seem artificial in that the 'national assumption' has sometimes been applied, and especially in the transition from colonial rule, to groups which have very little in the way of homogeneity or inner meaningful relationship. This is notoriously so in much of black Africa where new nations are heir to colonial boundaries which cut across ethnic groupings and where, in any event, the mosaic of ethnicity is so highly complex that it is relatively rare to find a group, such as the Somalis, forming the primary base for a whole people. There may be dominant tribal formations, such as the Buganda and the Kikuyu, but this already suggests problems in that smaller groups may fear an unjust dominance by their rather big brothers. Thus, in such countries the problem is that there is a State, but is there yet a nation? By devices such as one party rule and the creation of some suitable history, a sense of identity can be slowly born: often the future must be brought in to redress the thinness of the remembered past. At any rate, the prime activity of the modern world is nation building: in black Africa, in the Caribbean, in some areas in Asia – for instance Singapore, born of the Empire and the entrepreneur, sternly guided in welfare and prosperity by the skillful Lee Kwan Yew (thinking too that washing machines can spin away the charms of Mao Zedong). But a price in such mosaic and mingled countries has to be paid: the centrifugal forces being so deep and strong, the regime usually has to have a strong dose of authority, or simply the terror of arms. Thus, the conditions here for the emergence of more open societies are not altogether propitious. But more of that anon.

A Balance Sheet on the National Assumption

If one were to draw up a balance sheet of the national idea, we might think it to have the following shape. On the one hand, nationalism has given birth to ethnicist or racist tendencies often and has proved to be markedly hard and cruel indeed to those groups who do not have a territorial home – the Jews, insofar as in Europe and elsewhere they could not lay claim to a distinctive territorial base (other than Israel itself, part offspring of Zionism); and the Gypsies. But though aggressive nationalism has and is a cruel thing, the general 'national assumption', if worked out in a defensive way, has much merit. For the nation state is an agent of forms of modernity which are benign. Thus, only something on the scale of the state, one of whose properties is the ability to collect taxes, can create the educational and welfare network which has come to be a part of the fabric of social justice in the modern age. For the most part it is necessary for the State too to subsidize many cultural and sporting activities which add grace to the lives of citizens. Moreover, the State, by its being, enforces inner peace; even if, by wielding the same powers, it can also create inner terrors. Modern communications make it easy for citizens to identify with a larger whole than the clan, and the State, if properly conducted, can give people a satisying sense of security and substance, proud to belong. Even so, there remains for most nations a willingness to engage in machismo, often expressed in the manufacture or purchase of many weapons; while the modern bureaucratic nation state itself can bring into being new forms of exploitation: the power of party and bureaucracy can divert great resources into the fattening of the elite under the pretext of increasing the substance and welfare of the people. Nor has the modern nation learned widely the lesson of federalism, that it is important for minority groups to have substantial rights even where necessarily they lie outside of the cultural stream of the group which forms the main basis of the nation. It is ironically often the case that nations which themselves are highly sensitive to their own rights and the importance in their case of the national assumption, become fiercely resistant to the rights of others lying athwart their boundaries. The case of the Kurds is perhaps the clearest. The Ayatollah Khomeini, great protagonist of Persian nationalism in the name of brotherly Islam, thinks that the Kurds are unbrotherly in resisting the majority, of whom they are afraid and from whom they demand rights. They become the enemies of God in Islamic Iran. The Kurds are equally mistrusted by the Iraqis, who parade their Arab socialism, but at the expense of this great minority (who, alas, also can threaten some oil fields). The Kurds do not get too much sympathy from the Turks or the Soviets. They are a people with a land, but the land is in the grasp of others. In brief, one may regard the nation state as a virtually inevitable development in the modern world. But it is a mixed blessing. Moreover, the very sanctity of its demands, its solemnity in demand for loyalty and sacrifice can combine with other tendencies in the world, towards collectivism and facile consumerism, which mean that individuals can be crushed and washed away in the great floods of ethnic and social sentiment.

The Rights of Individuals within the Collective

Thus, one of the deep questions which we have to pose to this great national passion is how the individual's rights and personality are to be protected. The question of the individual and, for that matter, of lesser groups than that of the nation is not made easier by the fatal merging of differing senses of freedom. The excitement of the cry of *uhuru* or of the 'liberation' of countries from the yoke of the Nazis at the end of World War II – such a cry signifies that we can get rid of one kind of oppression. But it in no way follows that individuals or lesser groups will, as a result of that, have any greater freedom. The contrary may well be the case. From the angle of pride and self-esteem perhaps the cruelty of one's own kind is better than the superior benevolence of the alien. Yet how many individuals thus can get sacrificed to the Moloch of independence? The problem is as to how the two freedoms are to be created together. And this, in an important way, relates to the problem of the conditions for the establishment of the open society, to which we shall be returning.

The Nation and the Open Society

The participatory character of the nation as a sacramental being and its existence too 'out there', in the mind of those who belong (and also in the mind of their enemies) give the nation an uncanny resemblance to Christ: both 'out there' and a Person in whose substance the individual can take a share. The nation too is like a vine: and when the nation essence gets to be incarnated in a Leader, the national essence is given a personal symbolization. But the sacramental nation can, of course, be betrayed by the actual State which controls it and is supposed to express it. Thus, the transcendental character (in a way) of the nation does give it a power of fuelling loyal criticism or even loyal revolution. This is where the revolution itself comes to be seen as a kind of rite of passage of the nation, shedding its old incarnation and taking on a new identity, yet still within the pattern of an ongoing substance which is identified with the hidden national essence. But here again, we often find a conflict between differing ideals, the collectivist and the individualist. For the engine of revolutionary change in the modern world is social injustice. The most attractive theory of revolution available is Marxist, for it simultaneously cries brotherhood and blood.

It marries the thirst for justice with the Kalashnikov. But revolutionary change which deals with the problem of social deprivation, as in Cuba, can also bring about the totalitarian state in which the rights of the individual are so strictly shrunken. If the liberal is often naive about the tragic bitterness of the shanty-towns of the Third World, the socialist revolutionary is often naive about the black effects of the apparatus of power which he constructs on the ruins of the old order. Sadly, men find it very difficult to think about ideals which have more than one condition for their realization. Both social justice and freedom for the individual: this demand turns out to be too complicated for many minds.

I should add too: not just freedom for the individual, but also some freedom for groups within the greater group – in other words a degree of pluralism in society: this also may prove to be of vital importance. For often the ideologies go with a certain love of homogeneity. Thus, for many liberal rationalists, older traditions or religious affiliations are not rational and should be dissolved by the acids of rational modernity. For the Marxist, typically the older traditions, because they represent forms of exploitation, should be swept away.

A Conclusion on Nationalism

In this chapter I have analysed nationalism in the modern world and related it somewhat to the prevalent northern ideologies of Marxism and social democracy. I have not yet directly brought it into confrontation with the transcendental worldviews which we have been analyzing in the first part of the book. But already we may perceive hints of how they might be related. For it is doubtful whether religion can be whole-hearted in its acceptance of the national ideal, however strongly it may have entered into the fabric of the nation upon which the State is predicated. It is a grave weakness of modern Christianity, for example, that, because it has – to a great extent in the protestant countries itself – been organized upon the 'national assumption', it has lost some of its power to criticize the State and the nation. Likewise, modern Buddhism has not been too effective in resisting the forces of nationalism. If belief in the Transcendent cannot give one a base for criticism of the cruelties and excesses of the world, must not prophecy fail?

8

The Chinese Experience in the Modern World

China and India Compared

The Russian Revolution was a kind of thunder in the modern world. But in certain ways the Chinese Revolution has been more significant, for it has demonstrated a new path for Asia, in extraordinary counterpoise to the fabulous Japanese experiment. It saw the destruction, it seems, of old Confucius; but it also saw very clearly the way that under Mao Marx himself was transformed. Socialism with a Chinese face has some important lessons about how a great people has coped with the tragic dislocations of the late imperial era. As we learn lessons from the Chinese past, and from such personages as Hung Hsiu-chüan, Sun Yat-sen and Mao Zedong, we may come to learn how the old transcendental religions may be related to the new and aggressive values of Mao Zedong thought.

It may, by way of a preliminary, be interesting to compare the fate of India in its struggle against the West and its adaptation to modernity and the fate of China. These two very different civilizations, related however by Buddhism, experienced somewhat differing styles of Western incursion. It may be that China was on the brink of being occupied by the Western powers plus Japan, had it not been for the interruption of World War I, with its weakening of imperial poise and its issuance in Versailles' not altogether consistent commitment to the 'national assumption'. But the fact is that China did not become a colonial dependency, except in those fragments of extra-territorial concessions along the coast which were conduits for the economic penetration of the hinterland. Thus China did not to the same degree undergo the re-structuring which the British conquest of India brought about. Moreover, India had already experienced invasion and dominance by the Mughals: the Hindu majority had adapted somewhat to that (for them) rather depressing experience; and the substition of the Raj was not to the same intensity as unwelcome therefore as it might have been. The Hindu educated class, itself an expression of adaptation to the new conditions of life, was able to forge, in due course, a new ideology, what I call the Modern Hindu Ideology, which blended motifs from traditional religion with more modern notions of democratic pluralism and Indian nationalism. Very roughly, this ideology can be summed up as saying that all religions point to the same truth, and that the genius of Hinduism is that it has typically embraced this unity in plurality.

Thus India has pioneered a toleration, which can combine traditional spiritual values with those of modern democracy and social reform. The twin political symbols of this ideology in the period of the struggle against the British were Nehru and Gandhi, the one standing for modernity, liberalism, economic dynamism; the other standing for tradition, peace, spiritual struggle and social justice. There was already apparent a tension visible in this alliance between the dhoti-clad Gujerati lawyer and the impeccable Kashmiri Brahmin. But at any rate Indian nationalism was given new dignity by the pluralistic ideology. Also, history was in a way kind to India, for the debilitating effects of two wars and the coming to power of the Labour Government in 1945 made it possible for independence to be achieved without armed struggle, but rather on the basis of earlier non-violent protest. The British had neither the capacity nor the will to fight against Indian independence. Thus the New Hindu Ideology was able satisfactorily to shape the Indian state; and though the partition was a terrible wound and a tragic disappointment to Gandhi, it made it easier to found the Republic on the values of Nehru and Gandhi. It also showed something about Islam – that this faith could not easily accommodate itself to the embracing pluralism preached by Hindus: for Islam does not have any wider theory of toleration than that which applies to the peoples of the Book, the Christians and Jews. It thus turned out that the Republic as a secular State drew on the mainly Hindu ideology I have outlined; and it was one which drew on deep resources of religious tradition and combined with them the democratic and other social values of the English-speaking West. It was in a sense a Hindu view of life, but given a Western dressing.

The case of China was a kind of mirror image of this. For Mao adopted a Western ideology, namely Marxism, but bent it in Chinese directions. The reasons why China could not draw on its own deep resources, as India did, are complex and instructive. In order to see why it was so we need also to go back to the 19th century and the wounding and debilitating effects of the new interplay between Western and Chinese power and cultures.

The Disintegration of the Old China

It was above all the Opium War from 1839 to 1842 which both symbolically and in reality shook China: it signalled the humiliation which the proud Chinese empire had to suffer at the hands of the barbarian invaders who though clearly (to Chinese) inferior in civilization yet could command resources of energy and armament greater than those of China itself. The energy had in great measure to do with commerce. And commerce was as yet unbalanced. While many Chinese exports were of use to the West, access to the

Chinese market was highly restricted, partly by the system which confined Europeans to factories or trading posts where business was to be done with named Chinese traders and groups. The trade imbalance could be beautifully cured by giving the British the right to sell freely in China, and in particular to sell opium, a valued product of its South Asian Empire. This basically was the motivation of the war, in which the Manchu emperor's forces were easily overcome by a force of some 25 warships and 10,000 infantry.

Part of the weakness of the Empire indeed was the Manchu character of the dynasty, still regarded as foreign, and still stirring memories of its brutal treatment of the rebellion in South China. But perhaps there was something much deeper about the crisis, which was not to be resolved for over a hundred years. That deeper problem consisted of the very success of the longstanding Chinese imperial arrangement: the Chinese bureaucracy was not altogether at fault in thinking smugly that its culture was superior. What was a weakness though was that such a sense of superiority led to lack of self-criticism: and worse, the Confucian ethos did little to make Chinese minds appreciative of the true significance of Western science and technology, beginning to emerge spectacularly from within the pores of the surging industrial revolution. The issue was to be posed in a living way in 1905 with the abolition of the old imperial civil service examination: what, seriously, was going to take the place of Confucianism as the guiding philosophy of a modernized elite?

The Taiping Rebellion

A symptom of the crisis of China's soul, and of its economic condition too, stricken with inefficient administration, rising populations and food shortages (classical conditions in the China of old for peasant rebellions), was the Taiping rebellion, under the shrewd shaman Hung. It is of profound interest because in so many ways it foreshadowed the later revolution of Mao; and we can learn something from its ultimate lack of success as to the way Marxism catered for the needs of a damaged and debilitated China. Of that, we shall see more anon.

The Rebellion, or perhaps we should call it a Revolution, in view of its drastic character in changing the social and political order (except of course that it turned out to be a failure), had in its bloodstream a strange mingling of cells – modernizing on the one hand and socially revolutionary; charismatic, visionary, religious on the other. The movement preached radical land reform, in effect a programme of collectives, equal rights for women, who were given access both to the civil service and to the army; consequently the binding of feet, prostitution, the sale of girls and other humiliations of the female were to be forbidden, and rape punished by death; monogamy was to be the norm of marriage; strict prohibition of alcohol, tobacco and the cursed opium; language was to be reformed; and older, idolatrous religion was to be attacked. Because of the Christian character of Hung's prophetic call, or at least as he saw it, the Ten Commandments were imposed as law. Many of these reforms were part of the programme of the Communists a century later.

One thinks of Chu Deh the great Maoist general, pacing the decks of a river steamer, conquering the opium addiction; one thinks of the new literary language of the people's literature in Red China; one looks onwards to the waving fields of grain of which Mao wrote sentimentally in one of his poems, after a visit to his native village, where now the collective rules where once the landlords milked the fields. Yet at the back of Hung's strange call to action there stands not some reasoned out philosophy, not some long intellectual pondering of China's crisis, not some careful economic or other analysis. What lay behind it all was a vision. And a vision, strangely, with something of a Christian content. It was thus by a strange injection of an alien faith that the enthusiasts of the Great Kingdom of Heavenly Peace were fired. It is worth while looking back on these circumstances.

The Life of Hung

Hung was born in January 1814 and was of a poor Hakka farming family. The Hakka were seen in South China as 'guest workers', foreigners, speaking their own dialect, far from those of South China, and were tough, rebellious, often doing despised work, egalitarian, fierce. Hung's brilliance as a boy led his family to make great sacrifices to give him an education, but though he was a fine pupil at school he repeatedly and humiliatingly began to fail the more advanced examinations that might have paved his way into the civil service and the ranks of the Confucian gentry. His failure in 1837 precipitated a crisis in which he lay in bed for forty days, in a kind of mixture of coma and frenzy. After he had got better he related that in the course of this crisis he had had a visionary experience, a kind of dream in which he had gone up into heaven and there had seen an old man clad in a black robe and bearing a golden sword. The old man gave him the sword and told him that he should use it to 'kill the demons'. Also there he encountered a younger man who gave him further instruction in how to destroy the demons. But what demons? Confucius was, in Hung's dream, sent for and was humiliated and whipped in his presence for his sin in not including in his books the true doctrine. But what true doctrine? Confucius was not, however, banished from heaven. The old man meanwhile gave Hung certain great titles, the most important of which was that of Heavenly King. So much, then for Hung's later account of this strange experience.

But another half dozen years were to pass, while Hung eked out a living by village school-teaching, before anything more explosive was to happen. That was brought on by the rediscovery of a small book which Hung had got several years before in the streets of Canton from a white preacher and his Chinese assistant. A cousin of Hung's borrowed the book, read it and drew its strange contents to Hung's attention. This was in 1843, shortly after China's humiliation in the Opium War and the Treaty of Nanking. The book was a set of Christian tracts and biblical excerpts, put together by a convert called Liang A-fa. It preached basic Christian truths – the creation of the world, the saving work of Christ, the equality of all nations, races and persons under God, the coming of the Holy Spirit, the sacrament of baptism, the need for moral reform. The work staggered Hung, not only for its message but because it seemed to provide the key to the interpretation of his old vision. The demons were the idols: clearly Hung had a mission to smash idolatry. He embarked on this as soon as he had begun preaching and had made a handful of converts. The old man was the Father, the younger one the Son. Hung himself was a kind of adjunct or younger brother of the Son. Though for a number of years one might look on Hung as a kind of evangelical preacher rather than revolutionary, events unwound in such a manner as to turn him and his followers into a rebel force.

The Taiping Collapse

It is not here necessary to trace out the great convulsion which led the Taipings into very spectacular conquests and the setting up of their capital in Nanking, nor to catalogue the disasters which led to their defeat in 1864, after Nanking was taken on July 19 of that year. But in the first part of their revolution, from 1851 to 1856 there is little doubt that something approaching a social reconstruction

was effected over large areas of South and Central China.
Their vigorous iconoclasm brought a decline in traditional
religion, a new asceticism through the abolition of gambl-
ing, opium smoking, etc., and the cessation of slavery and
prostitution. If land reform lagged, nevertheless a new
atmosphere of brotherly equality was generated, and a
feeling of proud independence. International equality
meant no discrimination against the foreigner; but it also
meant that the ordinary Chinese could hold their heads
high. But in the latter part of their rule, factionalism led to
paranoia in the leadership, and an increased decadence and
luxury which alienated the peasant following. The new
leadership began to display some of the worst and silliest
attitudes of the old regime. Moreover, the anti-Confucian
drive of the ideology only alienated the literati: so the
Taipings came to rely, dangerously, on their army, and not
on the warm support of the classes whom they had earlier
claimed to liberate from Manchu oppression. But despite
their collapse in the end and the follies of their rule, the
Taipings did leave an imprint on China: South-Central
China could scarce be the same again, for the wars had
caused up to twenty million deaths. But there were those
who lived on to remember the old slogans 'Down with the
Manchu devils', and 'Land to the tillers', and to prize the
way they had struggled truly for national independence,
against the opium and the arrogance of those who were
beginning to subvert the Chinese nation from without.
Moreover, the Taipings would live on in the memories of
the Reds, for it has long for them been a puzzling matter, to
relate their own great revolution to that strange harbinger
of the Great Kingdom of Heavenly Peace and the strange
vision of its shamanistic Emperor, Hung Hsiu-Ch'uan?

Ideology and Rebellion

One lesson was the great power which an ideology could

impart to the otherwise rather anarchic forces of peasant rebellion. It was, so to say, the mind which could change a restless cat into a purposeful tiger. But yet the Taiping ideology had a weakness at the mental level, and this was in part because it stemmed from vision, and in part because it flowed from evangelical Protestantism. For the trouble with the latter is that it has a disconnected ideology, and presents a biblical drama and a myth of salvation which bears with it no wider intellectual meaning. Thus for the Confucian intellectual there could be little that was attractive in Hung's religious teaching; the more so as Hung was so strongly given to the smashing of temple images and the shrines through which traditional China had kept in contact with its ancestors. While a century later Marxism provided an alternative set of ideas which the intellectual could master and apply, Hung's preaching was scarcely in the true sense educated: it was too visionary, too violent to give a coherent (not to say modern) view of the world in a time of doubt and disintegration. The intellectual is important in these matters because a new social order itself needs to be administered, and whatever happens to the older education, a new form has to be brought in capable of mobilizing the minds of those experts society still requires and of bringing up a new generation of cadres. One could add too, that Hung was as much out of touch with science, or maybe even more out of touch, than were the old Confucian elite.

What had to be seen was that beyond the ships riding at anchor in the Pearl River, and the new guns which now the armies of China were beginning to buy, and beyond (strange to say) the passionate missionaries there lay a civilization which held within itself some new and explosive styles of knowledge. As the Japanese were to see with extraordinary clarity, the menace of the West lay not so much in its grey ships and shells as in the whole implication of modern knowledge and know-how which lay in the deep hinterland (or hinterocean) behind the visible effects of the foreign devils in the East itself. Could old and new be synthesized? But what unforeseen changes would need to be made? The Opium War and the Taiping Revolution posed the question with a bright clarity. The West, blundering and greedily, though also with a strange missionary idealism, had put a stunning, torturing question to the soul of China. How was the soul of China to respond?

Confucianism and the Challenge to China

Let us revert for a moment to the comparison with India. India could make a response partly because it was able to reach deeply into its own ancient resources in order to begin fashioning a meaningful response to the West. The Indian elite could marry subtle spiritual philosophy to modern science; they could bend the institutions of the foreigner to the needs of India itself. But where were the resources deep in the soul of China? Well, one could easily enough point to the ways in which Chinese philosophy shows rationality and a concern for penetrating the realities within the harmony of the cosmos. Or at least one can now so point, due to the heroic labours of Joseph Needham. There was nothing intrinsically inimical to science in the old picture of the Tao or even in the Confucian ethic. But the Confucian religion was another matter. By this I do not so much mean the cult of ancestors which has tended to get tied in to the Confucian ethic; nor even so much the Neo-Confucian ideology which was so limpid and compelling a counterpoise to the subtleties of Buddhism. Rather I refer to the fact that Confucianism was much more than a system of ideas and rites: it was the soul of the bureaucracy precisely because it was through the Classics that the aspirant mandarin had his mind deeply formed. It was by knowing these by heart and in nuance that the ambitious young man could pass into the gentry (unlike poor Hung, whose compensation it was to be a crazed Emperor in the southern capital, Nanking). It was by mastering the ethos of Master K'ung that the ruling class gained its certification. It was by following the ideal of the scholar that he would then live out his life: not just an administrator but also a lover of ancient beauties; not only a general but a writer of poems; not only a man set over others, but given (in principle) to the grave courtesies which for the best of Confucians governed the intercourse between human beings. And in looking to the Emperor, who himself paid heed to the mandate of Heaven, the bureaucrats looked to a symbol of harmony between heaven and earth. It was a religion of no great passion, of course; and it need not be framed in a set of dogmas. It was centered more on the rituals of correct behaviour, both towards others and towards Heaven. It was an ethos surrounded by a peculiar gravity. It was fine in its way. But it was hierarchical; and through that too it became embedded in a form of feudalism which in its rural injustices could so persistently spark rebellions among the desperate and the landless poor. It could also be corrupted where the old more stoical Chinese values were overlaid by the pressures of inflation and the disloyalties occasioned by a foreign rule. The priesthood of this grave religion were the bureaucrats themselves. It was a religion of mandarins above all. And it was precisely the structure of the imperial civil service which was challenged by the incursions of the red devils. It was precisely the continued usefulness of the old classics, which had held an Empire together for over two thousand years, that the new technologies and science of the West were to call in doubt.

Confucianism and Performatives

It is a pity in some ways that the old Confucianism was due to be buried by the forces of the 19th-century history. Or perhaps, more accurately, it is a pity that it is no longer used as a resource in modern China. It is clear that as a total system it is dead, and as a living way of giving meaning and direction to an imperial administration it is no longer relevant. Confucianism as a religion has, one suspects, no future. But it does not follow from this that it cannot teach us much: just as there is no real future in Neoplatonism, and folk now are not going to revive Orphism or go back to being Aristotelians – but it in no way follows from all this that we cannot learn from those old masters. Our Western classical heritage still remains as a resource, if not as a living tradition. It is in this sense that Confucianism can be a resource today, and not only for the Chinese but also for the whole wide world, as we adopt one another's ancestors in the converging planetary culture of today. Perhaps Confucianism has the most important message to give to us in the modern world if we are truly to understand the rights and meanings of the individual. Let me expand.

The Confucian outlook is counterpoised to that of the old legalists. For the legalist school the Confucian emphasis upon virtue was dangerous as a political doctrine; for the mandate of heaven theory which made true succession turn on virtue was too unstable. For legalism law backed by power was vital. But the Confucian position was basically that the ruler, and more generally any person in his dealings with others, ought to use the minimum of force in trying to achieve correct results. It is through sincere, goodhearted, correctness of behaviour that men and women are moved to good conduct. The Confucian ethos is in the last resort a doctrine of how to move men to good ceremonial. If that is, we can translate that wondrous word *li* by 'ceremonial' ('rites', 'manners', 'good form', 'propriety' – none of the words quite fit). One way of looking at this in modern terms is to see *li* as the right use of performatives. It is through the magic of words and gestures that we influence one another. Consider love: it is not the case that when a man says 'I love you' to a woman he is simply reporting a feeling he has. He may or may not have such a feeling – let us hope for her sake that he has and that thus he is sincere. He is not, then, reporting, but he is expressing love: he is hoping to communicate his feeling to her, to make her feel that she is loved. Thus his words are doing something. The whole language of love is of this sort. Likewise it is through courtesy and concerned language that we convey reverence to one another. Thus when we talk of the sanctity of the individual what we have in mind is that he is to be treated in a certain way. He is to be treated with respect, and his privacy is not to be outraged. He is not to be humiliated. Indeed we overlook the gestural, symbolic, performative aspect of relations between human beings if we look upon their welfare crudely and simply through a calculus of pleasure and pain. For pleasures and pains come in context. Thus when a mother gives something to her child she may do it because she knows that the gift will cause the child pleasure; but the giving itself is more than this because it is expressive of her love and helps to make him feel that he is truly wanted in the world: that he is important. For the most part too the horrors of torture are not just about the pain which makes men writhe: they are about the very writhing, the humiliation which the torturer inflicts on his victim. Why else would he do it? He is not interested in moving pink flesh in itself: it is because here in front of him is a human being within his power, on whom he can inflict that horror which makes his eyes plead and plead. Thus the torturer feels himself aggrandized. It is of course unfortunate that so often men feel better when they humiliate their fellows.

Confucianism as a Resource

Now it may be that traditional Confucianism's actual performatives were, in some respects, wrongly based, in that they implied a class system in society, while the duty of filial piety may have been taken to too great an extreme. Nevertheless, the doctrine of *li* (backed by virtues such as human-heartedness or benevolence, and a sense of duty, etc.) was in part a theory of how we can so far as possible interact with one another in an ordered way without the use of force. The magic of the performative is a substitute for the cruder measures of power. By placing the rite, the performative, at the centre of the worldview the Confucians have something of profound importance to say to us. This has too often been obscured by the fact that we are puzzled (in the West) by Confucius' rather quaint concern for old forms of ritual and music. How could such an archaic view of education be relevant to us today? Moreover, in providing the basis for a rather conservative social order Confucianism often seems to modern men as 'reactionary', unprogressive; and in any event quite out of date because the society it helped to prop up has inexorably disappeared, washed over by the great red tide of Communism, obliterated; and scarcely vigorous in the secular post-Confucian societies of the Chinese diaspora and cultural fringe. Where is the mandate of heaven in Singapore? How important are the old rites in South Korea? How can the old feudalism still sound its old supposed harmonies in Taiwan? Surely the Confucianists are men of yesteryear.

But, as I have said, Confucius can still function for us as a vital resource. And it is here that we need to take seriously the thought that the performative, the rite, the courtesy, the gesture – these are embedded in our nature. We are not beings who can communicate ethical values any other way than by gesture. If I bind up your wounds, you who have been beaten up and are laying by the wayside, it is of course to staunch your pain, to relieve suffering: but it is out of a recognition that you are a person whose life and pleasures are to be respected. My action is a token of reverence. It follows from this that operationally the

sacredness of the individual means that the individual is such
that he is to be treated with reverence, and there is no other
way to do this save through gestures, through performative
utterances? I cannot show reverence abstractly but only
through a kind of ritual behaviour. It is well for bureaucrats
to remember this: what does it benefit people if the State's
handouts are doled forth with an ill grace? The whole logic
of the handout is that the community cares for those who
are unable to earn their living, because they too have worth
as human beings and as members of society. But the ill
grace alienates, and makes the person feel a degree of
humiliation. (But rough men say: why should he be treated
so well considering he gets all that money for doing nothing
while I have to work my guts out to earn my money? To
which one is tempted to reply: And so you look on money
as a kind of symbol of worth? That is indeed one way to
consider it, but note how money now becomes loaded
symbolically, a paper performative.) In brief, then, the
sacredness of the individual means that he ought to be
treated in a certain way, with sincere performatives of
respect. In a sense then personhood is a performative
construct. But where is its root? For the old Confucianists *li*
itself grew out of nature, of the interplay between heaven
and earth: it was part of the fabric of the cosmos. But is it?
To that we need in due course to return.

The Maoists were well aware of the importance of *li* in
human affairs. They turned Confucius upon his head, by
using the rites of humiliation – the dunce's cap and the like,
the struggle session and so forth – as a means of disciplining
and punishing the people's enemies. The Cultural Revolution itself was also an anti-Confucian movement, in that it
emphasized the importance of young people, not the old.
The older gestures of respect were gone, and an older
structure of society was being swept away not by crude
power but by the revolutionary rituals of a new age.

Chinese Options: Buddhism

But it is time to return to the 19th century. In fact, because Confucianism was embedded in the structures of the old Empire and because it was the ideology of a ruling class which could not adapt itself to the modern age, Confucianism, for all its virtues, could hardly by itself prove to be a structure for incorporating a new vision of China. One of the major problems indeed of the period was that the so-called three religions of China were for differing reasons hardly suited to the new tasks of construction being imposed willy-nilly on the Chinese by the challenge of the West. Thus though one can point in the modern period to a certain revival of Buddhism – summed up most clearly perhaps in the life and thought of T'ai-hsü (1890-1947). He might be said to have tried to bring together three main motifs: the notion that the religion of China should be the Mahayana (Confucianism and Taoism being reckoned as part of the fabric of Chinese culture, without representing rival ideologies to the overarching Buddhism which he preached); the dynamization of Buddhism through concern with social welfare and reform; and the revival of international Buddhist exchange. Such Buddhist ecumenism, if we may so call it, to some extent was at variance with his more immediately Chinese and nationalist concerns. His teachings, though vigorous and high minded, did not altogether seem right to many of his fellow Buddhists, who feared that social activism might rob the monastery of its power as a place of training in detachment and meditation. For many it was better to think of the Pure Land as a heavenly rather than an earthly place. T'ai-hsü's new Buddhist eschatology was thus at variance with the strong tradition of Buddhist other-worldliness. Little did the Buddhists of the inter-war period realize that soon enough social activism would be roughly forced upon them by the Communist regime after it came into power – for it made the monks pérform agricultural and light industrial jobs. But in any case perhaps T'ai-hsü's vision was not one which could seriously work: for one thing China did not have a convincing tradition of Buddhism as state religion and it was not well adapted to be the ideology of a new bureaucratic and managerial class. Though it was much more consonant in many respects with Western science than was much of the Christianity which was preached in China, Buddhism lacked a kind of material ruthlessness: and this may have been necessary in the days of China's dislocations if it were ever to reconstruct itself and stand up to the vast pressures of the capitalist powers so eager for its markets. Indeed it may well be to the credit of Buddhism that it has such deep reservations about power. But this itself meant that it was not in a strong position to function as an ideology of a renewed China.

Chinese Options: Taoism

Taoism could hardly, either, prove any kind of salvation. Its ancient ideas were a wonderful blend of the panenhenic and quiet anarchism; and they had done much to give a new flavour and vitality to Chinese Buddhism. The *Tao-teh-ching* remains a deep and beautiful anthology which can lighten our attitudes to the universe and life around us. But popular Taoism as it had developed in parallel with Buddhism was too much entangled in magic and in folk religion to provide the impetus of Chinese revival. It is true that the old anarchic motif had in more modern times expressed itself through Taoist-oriented secret societies: and these were potentially a contributing stream to the river of revolution. But Taoism in general did not provide in modern times a coherent ideology: and in any event it lived a kind of symbiosis with the other great traditions and might not be able to maintain any true vitality in a changed and in particular a modernized environment. For the

Chinese situation was such that only through the mobilizing of society and through changes in attitudes occasioned by the needs of survival in the world of modern knowledge could China gain a new form of independence in the face of the Western powers. Thus, in brief, there were serious problems about China's traditions as resources for the reshaping of China. It is therefore perhaps no coincidence that the Taipings should have had a partly Christian origin, or that two powerful leaders of the later period, Sun Yatsen and Chiang Kai-shek were both Christians.

The Question of Social Democracy

The events which saw the crumbling of the Empire in 1911 and the establishment of a Republic did not bring in their train conditions which were conducive of a social democratic regime. The reasons were various. First, there was hardly any length of time for a new order to settle down. In the first instance the attempt of Yüan Shih-k'ai to make himself into a new Emperor created turbulence. Then it was not long before China began to disintegrate into the War Lord Period. Sun Yat-sen himself, before his death, became disillusioned with the gyrations of the democratic politicians.

Moreover the Kuomintang party took a tilt towards Moscow. The fact was that democratic institutions presupposed a more stable and homogenous middle class than could be found in China; they also presupposed a method of alleviating the increasing distress of rural China, for instance through effective livelihood. The post-revolutionary period saw the disintegration of the old civil service, so that often officials themselves became parties to the higher banditry which was tearing China apart. Also, it was doubtful whether the building of a new China would be possible without a stronger sense of history and destiny than the Kuomintang theorists possessed. Earlier, there had been the admittedly somewhat fanciful utopianism of the reforming K'ang Yu-wei, who at least consciously tried to wed the past to a democratic future: it is true that his picture of Confucius as a reformer, and his view of the relativism of ethics in the context of the evolution of human institutions, alienated him from Confucian traditionalists; but at least he tried to give a rationale for a new democratic order which made sense of it in relation to the past. But to a great extent the men who came to control the Kuomintang were too pragmatically orientated to be able to shape up a new order. Further, Chiang Kai-shek, in the late twenties and early thirties when he was faced with the twin menace of the Japanese encroachments and the guerrilla war being developed by the Communists preferred to deal first with the internal menace rather than the external threat. In so doing he came increasingly into alliance with China's capitalists, and over-reliant upon the Western powers at whom nationalistically his party had long sniped.

The Attraction of Marxism

The attraction of Marxism, for young men such as Mao when he came to study it during his first years in Peking, was that it provided a key to China's history. Given that key, thoughts of the right actions to be undertaken could form. Indeed, it might be thought that Marxist analysis often oversimplifies history, and in Mao's later thinking commonly a kind of schematism was introduced, analysing the major and minor factors, and the major and minor contradictions, in a given historical situation or social reality. But it can be argued that a degree of schematism is valuable, even if it may distort things. The main reason is that without schematism there is only a blur, and a blur is as much a distortion as – more of a distortion than – a schematism. Moreover, the purpose of understanding ongoing human affairs is (for Mao at least) that thereby they can be altered. Theory and practice go together, both before and after understanding. Before, because it is by action that one gets a clearer grasp of the situation in which one is acting: after, because it is by understanding that future action is guided. Applying his theory of knowledge to recent Chinese history, Mao wrote in his *On Practice*:

> Similarly with the Chinese people's knowledge of imperialism. The first stage was one of superficial, perceptual knowledge, as shown in the indiscriminate anti-foreign struggles of the Movement of the Taiping Heavenly Kingdom, the Yi Ho Tuan Movement and so on. It was only in the second stage that the Chinese people reached the stage of rational knowledge, saw the internal and external contradictions of imperialism and saw the essential truth that imperialism has allied itself with China's comprador and feudal classes to oppress and exploit the great masses of the Chinese people. This knowledge began about the time of the May 4th Movement of 1919.

In this last Mao was referring to the storm of protest which was aroused when the news of the provisions of the Versailles Treaty reached China and which was known as the Cultural Revolution (the name being used as part of the title of the Great Proletarian Cultural Revolution which Mao instigated nearly fifty years later). The shameful treatment of China, by allowing Japan to take over the German concessions in Shantung, was a sign that the Western powers were really indifferent to the fate of the China which was trying to reconstruct herself at the end of the first and puzzling period of the Republic.

Neither the West nor Japan particularly wanted a strong China. The slide into chaos there might be advantageous from various points of view.

So, for Mao, there was a kind of leap of knowledge which took place in the very indignation of 1919: but it was not blind indignation, but a dawning of a deeper knowledge of the inner nature of capitalism and of imperialism. To some degree Mao was echoing some themes of Neo-Confucianism, of the solidity of theory and practice, but in a quite new key. For one thing, Marxism generated a theory of struggle and contradiction which was hardly in consonance with older Chinese ideas of harmony. For Mao the continuance of struggle was important and exhilarating. For him such struggles extended indefinitely into the future even through the era of communism. For it was through the continual discernment of newer and higher forms of contradiction that knowledge and action progressed. No one can understand Mao's later views on the Cultural Revolution who does not see that he not only believed in continuous revolution, in the manner of Trotsky, but more deeply, saw the whole process of change and of knowledge (which go hand in hand) as without any limit, a long spiralling upwards through higher forms; but never to reach some absolute resting place. Part of his reason for thinking this was that while the way in which knowledge comes to be is dialectical, it continually throws up rational knowledge which becomes out of date as social and other conditions change: it has to be re-corrected in order to be brought into closer harmony with reality; but though such harmony, a kind of ultimate monism in which the practical and theoretical sides of life are brought into a unity, is something which we may have as an idea guiding us in our struggles, in fact the nature of existence is replete with contradictions: and these will tend to drive a wedge between a given formulation of human knowledge and the reality which it purports to be about.

Mao and History

Mao's theory of history and of human struggle was itself an extension of his espousal as a youth of Darwinism. But for him the sight of nature red in tooth and claw was not offputting, for he relished the way in which, through struggle, higher forms of life could be born. This is in keeping too with his fascination with, and great skill at, war. One of the advantages which Mao's Marxism had was that it could serve not only as an ideology of social reconstruction but also as an ideology of armed struggle against imperialism. One could hardly expect such a doctrine to grow out of the old Confucianism; and it was inconceivable as an extension of Great Vehicle metaphysics or the philosophy of old Taoism. As we shall see there were ways in which Maoism had a kind of functional analogy to the older ideologies; but as far as its content was concerned it was radically opposed to them (though Mao partly for family reasons had some sort of sympathy for Buddhism).

One cannot say that Mao's theory of perpetual struggle was in basic conflict with earlier Marxism; still, it had a special practical meaning which meant that Mao tried to build in a kind of criticism into the society which he had helped to fashion. There were contradictory tendencies in Mao here, as was brought out in his theory of democratic centralism. He found the anarchistic flavour of some of the old Taoist secret societies attractive; and to some extent his populism suggested that as far as possible the people should be given a wide degree of spontaneous action. Indeed, his theory of war was one which implied a blend between central control and independent action. This was intrinsic to the guerrilla methods which he evolved so effectively in the struggle against the Japanese. But he never fully solved the problem of how to combine the discipline of a single Party organization and the anarchism of his youth. The Cultural Revolution did not, after all, lead to very constructive forms of criticism and social experimentation. Still it remains an important motif in Mao's thinking, and one which might in the future be exploited by those who wish to see a more open society in China.

Mao's Voluntarism and Adaptation of Marxism

A feature of Mao's outlook, his so-called voluntarism, is something which does take him further away from mainstream Marxism. For Mao came to put such a strong emphasis upon the power of the will in overcoming obstacles that into his cult, especially during the period of the Cultural Revolution, there came to be blended a strange mixture of faith and an ascetic ethic. The stress upon the will goes back to Mao's early days – his fanaticism for instance about personal fitness was an example of the way he saw the mind subordinating the physical to its purposes. But of course his voluntarism must be seen in the context of the struggle between the self and the outer social and physical reality: by driving forward in the given direction, on the basis of Marxist theory, one will discover whether the world 'gives' or hits back. If it hits back, error is thus removed and one goes on to formulate a new way of going at the problem. If it gives, then this in itself shows the truth of the idea governing one's drive. So it is in this way that the will shapes the world. Mao was especially self-confident in the powers of effort and analysis combined; and some of the later excesses of the period of the Cultural Revolution go back to a certain hubris. But this Titanism is important in relation to traditional Marxism. For it was by a double thought change that Mao shaped the doctrine to the needs of China from the thirties onward. One part of that change was to forget the dogma that the revolution is tied to the proletariat: for China was short of industrialization and of a widespread working class. The vast sea of the Chinese population was peasant. And for Mao therefore the revolution must stir that sea. Second, because of the situation of China at the mercy of foreign capitalism, Mao was able to take a favourable view of the national bourgeoisie (as distinguished from the comprador class who were agents of external imperialism). The adaptation of the programme of revolution to the Chinese situation was, of course, accompanied by the fashioning of methods of guerrilla and civil war which in due course brought Mao to power, not by some lightning *coup d'état* as in the case of Lenin, but by a fairly prolonged struggle enjoying a considerable degree of rural support. The very blankness of the alternatives in the post-war period, for Chiang had no bent towards the democratic constitutionalism which at one time had been the main thrust of the Kuomintang programme, and the fact that intellectuals had been often badly treated in this period, meant that Mao was able to draw on a certain amount of sympathy and wide acquiescence among the ranks of intellectuals and of professional people.

A Kind of Spiritual Materialism

Mao's voluntarism, his theory of contradictions, his faith in science (as he understood it), his belief in an unlimited upward struggle – these, of course, all existed within the framework of a kind of materialism. But it would be wrong to think that for Mao matter was just a kind of physical force or thing: the fact that within it there pulsed contradictions gave it a strange dynamism; while in the pragmatic application of the idea of the material transformation of society and of nature, material objects came to have, as for other Marxists, a kind of symbolic value. 'Socialism plus electrification': there is a hint of the symbol-power of matter already in this. Power stations and dams, new patterns of irrigation, the fine crops of the new era, the plants making ball bearings or cars or transistors, the artisan's bowls – such material entities exist as signs of a new life, and they glow with the haloes of the new age. Thus in the new China the most mundane achievements are celebrated, either as successes or as cases of collectivist altruism. A strong work ethic is preached which makes the transformation of matter itself into a new kind of sacrament. It is not so much that *laborare est orare*: rather that true prayer is work. Pigs, then, wear haloes, and an almost religious sanctity was ascribed to the heroisms of labour. Consider a passage from the *People's Daily* which translates Mao's voluntarism into popular piety. It concerns a truck driver.

> He got the engine running, put his toe on the accelerator while keeping the heel over the brake pedal, so that if he fainted or died he would automatically stop the lorry. Eyes blazing, he battled through the raging storm along the rugged muddy mountain road. Not only his shirt, but his arms and the steering wheel were splattered with blood. It was not the engine, but sheer will-power geared to the invincible thought of Mao Tse-tung that kept the lorry moving forward, up and down six slopes, across two streams, and round eight sharp bends. Liu Chih-chun finally reached a production team, where he fainted away as soon as he was given first aid.

Matter and Symbols

The fact that Marxism espouses a special kind of symbolic materialism, in which matter's substance becomes something which in itself can have value, in that matter transformed by human endeavour becomes itself a sign of social change and a means to the good life, should not surprise us. For it is a commonplace of human life that up to a certain degree material objects are seen not as things in themselves but as having special meaning. What we call a vulgar materialist is one often who uses the material objects at his command to signalize grandeur: he wishes, in effect, to be judged by the goods which he has at his disposal and consumes. Material possessions have a powerful symbolic value, for they show something of the substance of the individual who possesses them: that is why conversely those who renounce the world do not so much give up the world (for how in a sense could they?), as renounce the good things which men of the world typically think to be of value. The monk, in having few possessions, wishes to show that he is more concerned with the Transcendent than with the things of this life. Often those objects which symbolize power become particularly prized. Thus the cult of the great motorbike, roaring under black leather into the speedy distance, is a symbol of power, sheer power, and thus of liberation from the plodding restrictions of humdrum existence. But in the modern world especially, it is not enough for the bike to be a symbol of power in some fancy way: it has actually got to have the power. Its engine must be of grand, violent capacity as measured by the literal measurements of the trade. Thus what is real may have symbolic value, but on condition that it really is as it is claimed to be. A certain realism and love of literal actualities is thus part of the fabric of the symbolism. This is the symbolism of the actual, and it is a kind of materialism in so far as it sees primary value in the material, and in what can be measured materially. It may also be accompanied by a down-to-earth attitude which is critical of fancy and unproved ideas: a kind of bluff honesty of the visible deflating the pomps of the spiritual, and reducing pretensions by bringing on them the scrutiny of an empirical eye. Marxism tends to generate a systematic, somewhat evangelical, version of such attitudes.

Mao and Science

Part of the system, of course, is the notion that the new order which the revolution brings into being will be, or already is, based upon science and technological modernity. It is true that in China the lack of trained doctors required the expedient of the 'barefoot doctors'; while also there was interest in reaching back into the old scientific tradition – for instance through the use of acupuncture. But basically Mao conceived of his new world as scientific and he thought, of course, of his own Marxism as being scientific. The conquest of nature, the social struggle (beginning with the class struggle) and the advancement of a scientific outlook – these formed the trinity of his programme. But in various respects he failed to understand the nature of science. Indeed there is, in general, some severe conflict between the practice of Marxism and the conditions for the flourishing of the scientific enquiry. This is so important an observation that it is worth trying to spell out clearly what lies behind it and what its consequences are.

First, modern science has developed its own tradition and momentum. It is a tradition which has had as one of its principal modern bases the university as created in Western Europe and America in the 19th century: a milieu which was considered to be favourable to research (itself in its modern form a creation of the 19th century), partly because of the academic freedom which was supposed to inhere in the institutions and persons therein. This was a liberal idea, and a product of the liberalism of a bourgeois era. And despite a great deal of flabbiness in the universities, the liberal concept was a sound one, in that part of the fabric of science is its critical temper: and it is above all in a liberal milieu that mutual criticism can flourish. Where strong impositions of conformity are made by society or by the State, then the liberal spirit necessarily withers, or goes at best into hiding. It is interesting that the Chinese Academy of Sciences was in fact protected during the Cultural Revolution and beyond, so that top scientists had a privileged insulation from social criticism denied to other senior academics at this time. This is a technique in other Marxists societies: to keep key scientists in a rather cocooned state, with plenty of the good things of life, at least by comparison with their fellows.

Second, it is part of the modern conception of the scientific establishment that science is an international activity and so needs the free exchange of people and ideas. Basically, science has now become planetary. It so happens that countries which are in the midst of social upheaval may feel it highly important to seal themselves off; and it is an irony that no greater tribute can be paid to the power of ideas than the lengths to which censorship and information starvation are practised in such states. But, of course, if permission for travel, correspondence and other exchanges are themselves controlled by a bureaucracy (and a police force) then decisions about what are and what are not valid theories may ultimately be in the hands of State functionaries who are not themselves scientists. And an extreme case of this was the espousal by Stalin of the theories of Lysenko: a case, incidentally, where a mark in Lysenko's favour seemed to be that his ideas fitted in better with Marxism than the prevalent Neo-Darwinianism.

Science and Criticism

But clearly the core of the conflict between Marxism and science lies in the matter of criticism. For Marxism itself comes to function in socialist societies as itself a set of dogmas which might be harmless enough did they not claim to be scientific. It is part of the power of the Marxist myth that it is scientific. For, again, a certain symbolism of the real comes into play: what is generated by science is real, actual, in principle powerful; and it is the modern magic. So, Marxism, in claiming the virtues of this magic, can set its face dogmatically in the direction of science, and so discourage some ideas and encourage others, but for ideological rather than for truly scientific reasons. Further, the whole attitude one finds in Marxist circles to bourgeois achievements rather deplorably overlooks the fact that it has above all been in the milieu of the liberal bourgeois society that most science and most social criticism including Marxism itself has been generated. So, then, the core of the problem lies in the problem of criticism and of openness. So, we need to dig into the conditions of criticism and openness. It is obviously not just because Marxist states are socialist that they are authoritarian and – indeed – for the most part totalitarian. It rather seems to be so because Marxism itself provides an ideology which can justify totalitarianism, and can give rulers that dangerous mixture of idealism and absolute power. In the anarchic conditions of modern China, it is to be argued that, after all, there was no real alternative apart from chaos to a relatively ruthless central government, and one of the attractions therefore of Mao's ideology was that it provided this sense of orderliness from the centre, together with some concession to popular methods and a dedication to the social services by the party to the masses. But as events since the death of Mao have shown, this centralism and high degree of thought control are not quite stable. Given that some of the primary problems of order and feeding have been solved, in itself a very remarkable and almost sacred achievement (for think of the miseries that the new China replaced), the move onwards to a technologically more sophisticated society has needed a loosening of the mental bonds, and a greater degree of openness to the other world than the Mao of the Cultural Revolution was able and willing to allow. Indeed, in the modern planet, all forms of totalitarianism are increasingly liable to be unstable, and will thus have a tendency to become a bit liberalized; and this in turn will create an impetus towards greater internal freedom. Let us reflect briefly on the reasons for all this.

Freedom and the Global System

First, the planet as an economic system is becoming more and more interconnected. Thus the oil crisis of 1979 has not been sealed off from the countries of Eastern Europe. Such integration will involve an increased thirst for the means of trade: for instance, the garnering of hard currencies through tourism. Travel, even the restricted kind that constitutes most tourism, is itself a means for the transmission of ideas. Second, radio and television communication is not to be stopped very easily at national boundaries; and this is another breach in the totalitarian system of the censorship and control of information (and misinformation: for alas, so much of the so-called news which is doled out there is lies). Third, a degree of individualism is almost irresistible as an ideal. That is to say, the regimentation of the totalitarian state is not altogether very welcome to people; and while folk may make great sacrifices in a period of crisis and in the struggle against tangible enemies, it is hard to maintain such a spirit in calmer times. By definition, the success of the revolution brings those calmer times, when dams are built, floods no longer sweep down, the rice grows well, and people, though poor, have adequate clothes and shelter. It is then that the unease may start. Individualism is a form of freedom, and it may, for that matter, not be altogether devoid of social outreach, in that the family may come to dominate concerns, rather than the wider society. Thus a transition to the era of 'socialism with a human face' is to be expected. Very often the ideal of a new generation is that of socialism (whose moral qualities they would still much respect), but with a liberal interpretation. In this way there is a convergence towards the social democratic outlook.

Mao and Nationalism

But for all the problems that are coming to haunt the new China in the last part of the 20th century, nothing can take away from Mao and his associates the staggering achievement of a united China, strong enough to stand up to other great powers, and a formidable force in East Asia. That new China had, as we have seen, to be built not only through forceful action, but through an ideology. For China, of the options open to it, virtually only Marxism could fulfil the role of a chart with which to make the journey to independence and social reconstruction. In a way, it was fortunate for the Maoists that the Japanese were rampant in China in the main period of the guerrilla struggle: for it meant that Maoism could clearly present itself in a nationalist context, as a force fighting against the foreign invader, the cruellest, in a way, of all the imperialists. Moreover, though Maoism was a Western ideology adapted to the situation of China, its foreignness was moderated by the way in which, it came to fulfil some of the functions, by analogy, that the old 'three religions of China' had performed. On the other hand, though we have analogical function, there is content reversal, as we shall observe. That is, the content of Maoism was in radical conflict as far as content goes with those three systems of belief. By content reversal, an old ethos and an old system of values is opposed, is in due course swept away; but by the analogy of function, something positive is provided to replace the old.

Mao and Confucianism

Thus the old Confucian ethic was bitterly opposed, because of its hierarchical nature and because it gave expression to the old oppressive social order. It was an ethic of feudalism, and with feudalism overthrown something new was needed. Marxism's ethic of human equality, for example the equality of women (a passionate commitment of Mao himself), could provide the central value in the new society. But furthermore, just as Confucianism had supplied a kind of religion for the ruling bureaucracy, so now Maoism provided an altruist ethic for the new governing class, the party cadres (with the added twist from Mao's anarchistic soul, that the ethic should be purified by struggle, and hence the Cultural Revolution to stir the sluggard party itself). At any rate Maoism could be the belief system of a new, equal-seeming, hard-working mandarinate of the people. But the content is reversed: there is no hierarchy of heaven and earth: and instead of heaven, Mao presents the mandate of the people (when he writes poetically of heaven in his poems he really means the Chinese people). The idealism of Wang Yang-ming's Neo-Confucian philosophy is replaced by the pragmatic materialism of the new era. Thus Confucius falls in the new China: but a new system of the *li* of manners is born. Incidentally, the Chinese Communists were well aware of the performative character of individual dignity: the parade in the dunce's cap and other humiliations were potent ritual means of destroying egos. Suicide was not infrequent. For in the new China the new *li* was one of party rectitude, social service, uttering the right slogans, conforming to the party line, participating in mass demonstrations.

Mao and Buddhism

Buddhism, for many in the old China, was a faith of the masses, potent in expressing and mobilizing human hopes and fears in the ongoing troubles of this world. Its devotionalism was not something to be encouraged in the hard-headed era of material progress. The chatter of a Pure Land was to be replaced. But Chinese Communism has projected itself as a mass faith too. The apparatus of the Little Red Book, the pictures ubiquitous of Mao, the processions, the quotations and so on – these projected into the new society some of the attitudes of older faith. The new China in the future was itself a more tangible substitute for the Pure Land. So instead of the symbolisms of the other world, there is the symbolic materialism of this. Instead of the idealism of Yogacara there is Marxian materialism. Instead of an historical karma, there are the analyses of history provided by the historical dialectic. So, both as a system of ideas and as a system of popular practices, Buddhism is swept away: but its function as a devotional faith is taken over by the new cult of Mao. And yet we can wonder how far Marxism truly deals with the angst of life, that suffering which (Buddhism insists) is woven into the very fabric of this life. Do the future factories make present sorrows meaningful?

Mao and Taoism

The magical side of Taoism reflected the feeling of ordinary people that spiritual power should be relevant somehow to their material concerns. The anarchistic aspect was a means of mobilizing popular discontents. In the new China the old magic is washed away in the whole new task of educating the masses in simple science. The new era is one where truly the magic works, for it is scientific Marxism mobilized for the welfare of society. The mobilization of the masses is part of Mao's whole doctrine of democratic centralism. But the old Taoist idea that somehow we should find peace through non-action and harmonization with nature is brusquely rejected. It is through struggle, the dialectic, contradictions, that progress occurs: and if theory and practice, truth and nature, may come increasingly to coincide in the onward progression of society, this is far from the quiet monism of Lao-tze.

Echoes of the Old China

We may see then ways in which echoes and contrasts from the old China gave Chinese meaning to the new philosophy. It is clear from history since 1949 that the revolution essentially is Chinese, and almost imperial in its practice.

Tibet has been thoroughly brought under Peking's control and colonized by many Han Chinese. The Soviet Union has been kept at arm's length, suspected of old Russian-style ambitions at domination. Vietnam has been given sharp lessons to remind it that it should strictly fall within the Chinese rather than the Soviet sphere of influence. Thus has the new China reasserted an old strength. Though lip service is paid to the internationalism of the Marxist movement, basically China does not seem much interested in world revolution; but more in the expression and maintenance of China's national interests.

Revolution as a Rite of Passage

It is virtually inevitable that Marxism should fall thus into national moulds. The international solidarity of the working class does not mean much psychologically, and World War I demonstrated that the socialists of different countries would, when it came to the bitter and glorious exigencies of patriotic war, fight against one another, as also did Christians. In practice and emotionally, the 'people' and 'the masses' come to be identified with the working class and favoured elements of a particular nation or ethnic group. It is the adjective which comes before 'people' which comes to give shape to the socialist enterprise. And as we have noted before, the very centralization implied in bureaucratic socialism helps to foster a kind of national solidarity. Moreover, the revolutionary character of the new foundation of a nation, as with the Russian Revolution of 1917, the Chinese of 1949 and so on, is a kind of rite of passage, a casting off of the old (weak, exploited, divided, not truly patriotic Adam) and the taking of the new Adam (the heroic, the socialist, the brave, new Adam). The revolution, as we have seen, is like an individual's conversion experience. A fresh start can be made because the person is born again: so too is the nation born again. The bloody sacrifices of the revolutionary epoch add to the new substance of a suffering but yet triumphant people. In the case of China, the truly marvellous events of the epochal Long March provide a fabulous myth for the foundation of the new order. The immense suffering and heroism also signifies a kind of pilgrimage out of the old China and into the new. It was a kind of modern day Exodus. In such ways Marxism, by its socialism and by its sense of ritual transformation through revolution, is a suitable ideology for the re-founding of nations. It is because of that that it has proved so successful in the modern world. And where in the Third World, where there are corrupt and torturing regimes often under the sway of capitalist interests (seen as greedy forces from the callous white Northern hemisphere), can men hold high their heads, unless they can love their hateful countries by taking a draft on the future? The revolution promises a purgation, and brings in the future brightnesses to outweigh the crazed darknesses of the past. Thus Cuba and Nicaragua, Angola and Mozambique.

The New Taipings

The Chinese experience, then, in the modern world is one in which, in the historic circumstances of the breaking asunder of the old empire, the live option turned out to be a form of Marxism. It was Mao's genius that he came to formulate a yellow Marxism and that he could so excellently follow his own ideas in practice by being the foremost leader and warrior in the long process of battling both against the Japanese and the Kuomintang. His was a new vision of the material world, pulsing with inner contradictions, giving those who were conscious of the true analysis of history the opportunity to transform both a whole people and a whole land. By the glowing transformations of matter in commune and factory, new and beautiful characters could be written upon the blank page of the peasant's mind. And yet, times – as Mao always knew – change. The new China begins to enter a new phase, less certainly; for it was Mao's Marxism which gave meaning and expression to a revolutionary national struggle which is now past. The twice born China has grown older: and now the insistent requirements of progress and military strength demand a deeper use of technology and science: which in turn means an opening to the West; which in turn threatens to let new ideas and forces into the Chinese mind. But the principal achievement of the ideology of Mao has been to give direction to one of the greatest movements in history, and to solve those problems which Hung Hsu-ch'uan could not resolve.

> Mao was the mad Hung again.
>
> The Taiping rebellion, however,
> Was no blood-solution. Never
> Would China repair the gray-green willow
> And the characters on the scrolls
> Till it swam against the red-devil salt billow
> With strong arms.
> The souls
> In Hunan were bitter and rice-blown
> But Mao vowed he was not alone
> In the grassland and ice
> And in the caves of Yenan,
> And on that great day in Peking.

9

Secular Ideology, Religion and Science

The Question of Pluralism

As we have seen, nationalism, which, is a major expression of the quest for group identity, has proved so dominant that the ideologies themselves have come to be instruments of it. But nationalism though externally plural in its bent (for is it not the thesis ultimately that each nation should have its own land and State?), can impose a harsh internal solidarity. So we have the tension between outer plurality and inner conformity. Thus the person finds himself caught in this tension. In so far as he is a social being his substance is enlarged by national freedom and grandeur. But in so far as he is an individual, the demands of society can be inhibiting. For instance in Romania the cost of a limited external independence (the primary achievement of President Ceauşescu) is tight internal surveillance. The national hero is aglow when he looks outwards to the steppes, but is grey and inhibiting when he turns his gaze inward towards the printing presses and the mines. In some degree the tension is overcome in the liberal democracies. For if the ideology of freedom of the individual is the rationale for external policy, then national freedom, meaning freedom from outer control becomes easily compatible with personal freedom. Yet in fact the tensions remain, of various kinds.

For one thing the liberal democracies can become, have

often become, externally oppressive. Thus Britain practised a kind of liberalism at home and an Empire abroad.
The United States since World War II has often supported
dictatorships and fierce military governments in the supposed struggle for freedom, chiefly because they are against
the Soviet bloc. My enemy's enemy becomes my friend:
but at the cost of bringing the very ideology which justifies
the anti-Soviet struggle into disrepute.

For another thing, liberal democracy has not been known
to exist except within the context of capitalism – even if in
the most advanced liberal democracies a strong injection of
socialism is a common way of moderating some of the
internal effects of capitalism – and capitalism can externally
prove oppressive. Thus many of the experiences of the
Third World turn upon the way in which plantations, tea
gardens, bauxite mining, trading concessions and so forth
have served the interests of the more successful capitalist
countries and companies. Suspicion of multinationals
partly reflects this experience. After all, economic domination is something which diminishes national pride, and
poverty is something which inhibits good government. It is
thus not at all surprising that Marxism should prove
attractive to movements of national liberation in the Third
World. Poverty itself can amplify the demands of group
pride rather than individual dignity.

Third, liberal democracy, suffused too with capitalist
consumerism, can tend towards a negation of pluralism, by
a paradox. Because liberalism points to individual rights,
because social identity is relatively irrelevant to consumer
power, because in a technical and bureaucratic society
individuals become moveable and standard units – for such
reasons there is a tendency in many liberal democracies to
overlook the pluralism of cultures present within them.
The pressures on the minority is towards conformity with
the majority. This itself creates tensions when social and
cultural divisions are the substratum for the exercise of 'one

man one vote'. The tyranny of the majority can be oppressive.

Briefly, the problems of pluralism can be seen to be reflected in the tensions between insiders and outsiders, between group identity and individual identity and between openness and tradition. Implicitly too we have raised among these tensions the question of the relationship of science to the ideologies and to the traditions. For liberal democracy usually is seen as a matrix for scientific, artistic and technological creativity of a new order, transcending the great civilizations of the past. This is part of what its myth of modernity is all about.

But openness and scientific and artistic searching imply a kind of deep restlessness: the critical and innovative spirit. And that can produce tensions. People find security in older ways, older thoughts. Scientific and artistic experiment chimes in with social experimentation, and the latter is disturbing, even destructive. Questions of truth and happiness are thus intermingled. This is where it is necessary for us to evaluate that partial philosophic underpinning of liberal democracy and of modern economics: utilitarianism. Do we live in a utilitarian civilization, here in the northern West?

Utilitarianism and Beyond

The potency of utilitarianism as an underlying theory of modern life in the West arises partly because it blends a kind of calculus with the selection of the individual as the basic unit. It arises partly too of course from the fact that it appeals to an intelligible criterion – the maximizing of happiness, the minimizing of suffering – with which to judge policy. Its individualism brings with it a feeling of personal freedom. The calculus gives it a way of expressing technical economic imperatives, and an outlook geared towards profitable prosperity. If there have been dark tragedies in capitalism between Adam and Smith and Keynes, yet also there have been phenomenal successes – enough to stamp our Western civilization as utilitarian. Its stress on happiness gives it the style of measurable pragmatism. Human happiness should not be sacrificed to distant utopias nor to imposed dogmas.

But it has serious problems, the most severe of which is that it has been less than adequately reflective about the very concept of happiness which lies at its heart. As we shall see, once we question this concept and interrogate it, we find that utilitarianism has to be severely modified and has in a sense to be transcended. Moreover, its individualism can operate through an unreal social atomism. In fact the individual is herself a social product in great measure. We can quarrel over percentages of intelligence for instance – how much acquired, how much genetic? – and this is but a narrow instance of the more general observation that the person is a multiplication of a genetic body (and soul) by social experience. The human atoms have a genetic history and a social configuration. They are not discrete atoms any more. Sociology itself is a kind of reaction against such atomism.

Not only is happiness something which requires complex analysis, as suffering too, so that the hedonistic calculus of early utilitarianism is largely wide of the mark as an attempt to understand what it is to promote happiness; but also happiness and suffering are not 'given' but themselves capable of being criticized. There are questions thus of the structure of happiness as a concept and as a factor of human life; and there are questions too about the evaluation of models of happiness. I shall proceed to look at these two sides of the question separately.

Utilitarianism and Objects of Happiness

The analysis of the concepts of happiness and unhappiness

has much to do with public policy. Too often utilitarianism has been seen primarily as an ethical theory. But it is more perspicuously understood as a theory of politics, a way of looking at public policy and social change. But let us begin with the limitations of hedonism, for through that path it may be possible to see the 'public' nature of utilitarianism.

The symbolic character of personal communication, proceeding by outer gesture, by the smile, the sneer, the flowers, the whip, the golden handshake, the prison slopping out, means that a utilitarianism, which looks just to pain and pleasure, in the most ordinary and literal meanings of these terms, is wide of the mark. For though it is true that I may eat lobster because I get pleasure from the taste, and make love because it is even more intensely pleasurable, these activities occur in context, and the tendency of the human being is to transform these activities to a higher symbolic level. Thus the love-making can express genuine love, a kind of mad and gentle prizing of the other person for her own sake, in her very particularities of eye and body, of colour and language, of style and mind. Eating lobster is not just sucking flesh in a corner: it is part of a dining occasion, which is another symbolic and gestural event – dining in the company of . . ., dining conspicuously . . ., dining in relation to the ocean and its fruits . . . Lobster not only tickles my palate: it increases, insouciantly, my substance.

This is not to deny the pure pleasures and pains. But though sometimes the symbolic aspects may be secondary, the fact is that pleasures and pains typically have a wider meaning and a symbolic transformation. Or to use other language: they have a spiritual significance too. All this constitutes a severe limitation upon the hedonistic way of interpreting utilitarianism. Moreover, much of happiness and unhappiness is not directly related to pleasure and pain in the literal sense. Joy at my child's smile and sorrow at a friend's misfortune are related to objects outside of me, and they are not sensations.

It is thus not possible to treat happiness and unhappiness in isolation from the rites and achievements, the symbols and institutions, the personal relationships and social circumstances, which are the foci and expressions of happiness and unhappiness. That is, to simplify, happiness is *about* something or *because of* something. Thus it is that the promotion of happiness and diminishing of unhappiness proceed by a kind of indirectness – creating the conditions which tend to produce the foci of happiness and to diminish the foci of unhappiness. Thus if a certain sort of marriage law tends to produce much suffering, the utilitarian seeks a new shape of marriage institution. For such reasons, utilitarianism necessarily entangles itself with public policy, since it is the latter which is the expression of human ways of trying to produce the circumstances of welfare. So utilitarianism has to do with conditions and contexts, in recognition of the fact that human life is drenched in the symbolic and the performative. Pleasures and pains themselves get taken up into that spiritual transformation which is typical of all the elements of our social and personal existence.

As a sign of all this, pleasures and pains are short-lived, though fortunately they can be repeated: but happiness is dispositional, at least in some of its central applications. To be a happy person is to be in a certain dispositional state: and you cannot be happily married for two minutes.

The fact that unhappiness and happiness are much bound up with the performative and symbolic aspects of existence means that public policy too has to be. Thus economics and politics concern the spiritual side of life, a point which is often alas neglected. (In this connection one should also note how spiritual or mental factors enter into economic development: resources often are secondary, or even in some cases largely irrelevant.) Let us see this through an instance.

In a modern welfare state the unemployed person does

not starve. It is a fine thing that the workless are at least sheltered from destitution. But it does not follow that we can look at worklessness just in monetary or narrowly economic terms. For one thing, young people are taken elaborately through the school system by a society which sees education as fitting the young for what is called 'life' and in particular for work. Schools make citizens and citizens are expected to work. But when a young person after a childhood full of the sound of wages and comparisons come into the market and finds that there is no work for him, doors closing, heads shaking, notice boards deserted, is he not virtually bound to see this as sadly meaningful? Society somehow dumbly is saying to him: 'You are not needed: you are not wanted'. What does this do to his self-esteem? Especially of course if the young fellow is black is the state of worklessness fraught with messages: 'Predominantly white society does not need you, a black'. It is natural to boost substance with the symbolisms of revenge and violence. The destruction of property is itself a meaningful act, a way of showing power, of diminishing the system which diminishes me. The root of bitterness is the desire to harm those symbolically who harm us. Symbolically: of course this means 'really', 'actually'. In the modern materialistic seeming world the destruction of actual pieces of matter, of things owned and prized by society, is what has a most powerful spiritual significance.

So utilitarianism has to be sensitive to context and meaning. We might for brevity's sake call such a utilitarianism 'symbolic utilitarianism'. One could do worse than say that public policy should be directed to diminishing indignities and promoting the dignity of human beings: a kind of (shall we say?) dignitarianism.

Utilitarianism and the Critique of Happiness

In addition to the symbolic contextual and dispositional

aspects of happiness and unhappiness, there is a question of evaluation. Because of the spiritual transformation of our material pursuits and satisfactions, there is always in principle room for criticism: always space so to say for challenging the ideals of happiness and of personal dignity which exist in our society. Thus the question of wherein happiness lies is most typically a critical or evaluative question: Wherein is *true* happiness? Conversely there are differing ways of looking at suffering and pain.

A way of seeing this is to consider the foci of happiness or satisfaction. Thus a person is typically happy to achieve what he considers to be some important goal: happy, for instance, to be promoted, or at getting the proverbial dreamhouse, or at becoming a father. But the happiness is in principle proportional to the importance of the objects achieved. But the question of importance relates to a scale of values. And what at one phase of life or from one perspective may seem important may turn out to seem unimportant at another time or from another angle. New visions can destroy old perceptions. New glories can cause old charms to fade. And here rather explicitly we are in the realm of value and feeling.

It is of course typical of the transcendental traditions that they call 'this world' into question. They subject our happiness to a critique from on high. This is distinct from ethical criticism, which can also be a major feature of traditional religion, notably through the figure of the prophet, who imparts a special moral dynamism to belief in the divine. Calls for love and justice are important: but distinct from them are the glimpses of a new world – either this old world made new in the transfiguring vision of the seer, or a transcendental realm of supreme worth and bliss. Such new visions of the world are themselves the basis of another view of happiness: just as too we can see in artistic and musical creativity ways of directing the human spirit to fresh perceptions of life in and beyond the cosmos. Thus religion itself functions as a slant on welfare, a way of seeing the nature of true satisfaction. This is how religious experience creates an interface with the world of our more ordinary feelings of joy and sorrow. The practice of the presence of God, the perception of the great jewel net of Indra: already such ways of looking give an extra dimension to the symbolic transformation of existence which is part of the whole fabric of human life.

Thus though it is in accord with human dignity and with the general principles of utilitarianism that people should be free so far as possible to determine their own goals and so their own evaluations of happiness, it is bound to be the case that the question of happiness creates ultimate questions about reality. For most people, death stands as the great question mark against received notions of welfare. It is the symbol of our ultimate questions. And here religion in open societies such as those of the modern West serves as a perspective of criticism of the shallow and ordinary ideas of welfare. It is a transcendental angle of vision, often disturbing. In other words, religion no longer functions as a dogmatic delineation of the way reality must be viewed. It has moved over from its dogmatic to its critical phase. (It of course always contained this critical motif by the very fact that it produced people whose eyes were fixed upon the transcendental.)

Social Personalism and Tradition

Utilitarianism in one direction looks to questions of happiness. In another it looks to the individual and in some senses rests upon the sanctity of the person. But as we have noted, persons are in part precipitated out of society. Thus any realistic personalism has to recognize the social dimension of the individual. Let me spell this out further, in framing a point of view which can be dubbed *social personalism.*

First, there is the elementary fact that a person is a linguistic animal – that is it is through language above all that the human individual becomes capable of thinking and of refining his expressive and in general performative behaviour. Not only does this of course give the individual powers of foresight and calculation which give him a much greater freedom and range of behaviour; but it also precipitates in human society and in the person a novel kind of freedom. The deeper unpredictability of human action stems in part from the creative powers of human beings in science, the arts, in life-style. Consider the conceptual revolutions which were sparked by the light from Einstein, Cézanne and the Buddha, not to mention many more minor but still significant luminaries. What is not yet invented or discovered cannot be predicted: and theories cannot forsee the details of their own demise.

Thus a vital component of personal capacities for freedom is social in configuration. A person though scarcely imaginative himself can yet gain illumination from others. Think of the hundreds of thousands who now have an understanding of relativity – a growth outward like the seeding of a field with poppies from a first plant, or like the creative effect of a genetic mutation. Think too of how the extraordinary new ideas of the Buddha came to spread outwards into whole civilizations. So we may say that freedom is precipitated in the individual by society – first through the existence of language and second through the communication of discoveries and new slants on things.

But although this linguistic character of an individual is a commonplace, it is less often pointed out that a person is not only a linguistic animal: by the same token he typically has a primary particular language. His mind and thoughts are based in the nuances of a particular tongue. It is naive to be so Whorffian as to think that thereby the individual's mind is squeezed into a kind of linguistic mold into which also a particular view of the world is necessarily squeezed.

It is however vital to recognize the deep way feelings and outlooks are affected by the particularities of language. A person is not just comfortable in his own language, but finds his loyalties subtly determined by it. This is a main attraction of linguistic nationalism. For this and other reasons a person is not a bare individual: both his openness and his substance are precipitated in him by language, and by a particular social and linguistic inheritance.

Thus necessarily social personalism involves a recognition, though it need not be uncritical, of the tradition in which an individual finds himself. In showing reverence for the person we are within limits treating the social tradition out of which he comes with respect. This can be regarded as the positive side, in the modern world, of the whole phenomenon of nationalism.

A consequence of social personalism is cultural pluralism and the recognition within any given society of minority rights. The very concept of a minority recognizes a grouping and some kind of tradition. Individuals are already in this very recognition not considered purely as such, but as belonging to a definable collectivity. But it should be noted that social personalism involves a severe modification or any traditionally authoritative collectivism, since the way a cultural group has to express itself within a libertarian society is restricted by the demands of liberty itself. Thus there is bound to be a tension between some traditions and the ethos of utilitarianism. Consider, for instance, how women's rights bring a modification of Islamic law in predominantly utilitarian societies (such as Britain).

Nevertheless respect for cultural pluralism implies that so far as possible society should be arranged on plural lines, that is through such arrangements as federalism, cantonalization, protective legislation for minorities and so forth. It is of the essence of the contemporary world especially outside the Marxist areas that migrations and travel produce nearly everywhere culturally and ethnically mingled populations. Perhaps we can look forward to cities with many quarters – not forced ghettos, but places of cultural centrality.

Social personalism then implies a kind of interactive pluralism. But in providing an individualistic dimension to plural societies, the personalistic outlook necessarily in some degree challenges, though it can also enrich, traditions. Thus traditions have to adapt, and this is the task, in each tradition, of a kind of hermeneutic, a method of self-interpretation in the light of a changed world. But this is only the kind of task this book itself is engaged in – for I am trying to frame a way of using the Christian and Buddhist heritages within the circumstances of modernity and of the global city.

Traditions in Interaction

Effectively, the creative use of tradition involves a kind of syncretism – the welding together of older values and the new forces released in modern society. Despite the fact that the coming together of differing cultural forces often presupposes ethnic and other collisions and hence violence and destruction, yet on the whole cultural encounters have proved extraordinarily creative. One variant is where by historical means a past is rediscovered which is brought into confrontation with the tradition as it has developed: for instance, the rediscovery of the European classical past at the time of the Reformation and the rediscovery of the biblical outlook at the time of the Reformation. The present planetary world from this point of view harbours unparelleled opportunities of mutual fecundation and challenge, since in principle all cultural traditions are in interaction with one another. But this, alas, is often counterbalanced by drives towards homogeneity and lack of receptivity. Men are naturally parochial, and parochialism is multiplied in intensity when it is given an ideological dimension, as in

Marxism and as more mildly in liberalism (when the assumption is that every society should be 'modern' and 'liberal' like us – forgetting that the conditions for social democracy are complex, and that, too there may well need to be great variants upon our conceptions of modernity and liberalism in the differing conditions of other societies). Thus at the mental level one should do something parallel to what should be done at the level of nations and divergent cultural groups. It seems unavoidable that in a world which has contained within it so many forces driving in the direction of the 'national assumption' that also internal pluralism and federalism should be recognized wherever possible and appropriate: that is, where a pure territoriality (one land, one people) cannot be achieved, as often it cannot at least rights should be accorded to minority ethnic groups, and this will often most naturally occur through the application of federal arrangements. Such internal and external pluralism seems an important ideal for the modern world, though modified of course by some other conditions – the sanctity of the individual at one end, and the desirability of binding nations together in economic and other bonds on the other. In brief: modern nationalism should be the basis for ethnic pluralism. Such ethnic pluralism itself can be reflected at the mental level: as the willingness to enter into the mind of other groups, in an empathetic manner. In other words, the methods which we employ in the sensitive exploration of religions – the marrow of the true method of comparative religion – are part of a wider human demand. And in entering the minds of others we can learn from them. In a sense every other society can be, in some degree, an illuminating critique of our own life, and lead to greater and more creative self-understanding.

The stance of what may be called interactive pluralism thus both enhances group rights and the creative use of traditions in mutual illumination and criticism. This will

work out, favourably, not just in terms of ideas but through
new experiments in living, as is evidenced, for instance, in
the growth of Buddhism in Western countries and notably
California (a great laboratory of life-styles). Interactive
pluralism also corresponds to a fact about humanity which
I have been at pains to underline in my treatment of
nationality and nationalism: that the individual finds part of
his substance through participation in the group, and that
in the modern world the most demanding and significant
group, for most folk, is the nation.

Social Personalism and the Ego

Social personalism, as I have called it, recognizes, then, the
interlocking relationship between the recognition of personal worth and the social context in which a person
perceives himself. Yet is it not possible for an individual to
attain a kind of stoical self-sufficiency? Buddhism has much
to say here. For Buddhism, in its analysis of the individual
– an analysis it must be recalled which has practical aims,
for it helps to guide a self-vision and a self-training which
will take a person along the road towards serenity and
insight – stressed the emptiness within, the absence of an
ego. The disintegration of the stream of consciousness into
the fine droplets of mingled events and the vain search for
anything permanent, save the non-dual consciousness of
the Transcendent, of nirvana, are means of deflating substance. And the fact that Buddhism sees no depth in the
sacramental process also implies a certain detachment from
those gestures and performative acts through which good
substance is conveyed. Is this not a rather desolate outlook?
We, who love to be loved and esteemed, and who seek
security among our fellows, have here no comfort. Precisely: classical Theravada is self-reliant, and the saint must
be independent. In effect he abandons all that: the persona
goes, society is at best a convenience, the substance of the

inner man dissolves. The saint is free, because he no longer need depend upon others. He is trackless, like the hippo in the swamp or like the seagull in the roadless sky. This is symbolized in the main Indian ascetic tradition to which of course Buddhism belongs by the figure of the wanderer: the monk or swami who walks from place to place begging alms, dependent on no one in particular, and above all homeless. He is a strange challenge to all the politics of the symbolic utilitarian: a man needs shelter (hence public housing), food (hence if necessary welfare payments), a sense of dignity (hence legislations about work, women, exploitations and the like). But the wanderer does not have shelter beyond the skimpiest: his food is nearly nothing: he has no home, no security in the ordinary sense. If he has dignity it is because somehow to ordinary folk he seems to have risen above the human condition, so that he is mysteriously richer than the rich, mightier than the mighty, fuller of bliss than the pleasure-seekers. He is not of course literally any of these things (save possibly having the bliss). But he has gone somehow beyond. So there is a paradoxical kind of self-fulfilment in self-emptying. You have all you want if you want nothing, and have nothing. 'I got plenty of nothin', and nothin's plenty for me,' as the Gershwin song has it.

The shaven head of the monk, the staff of the wandering recluse, even the unkempt beard of the hobo – these represent a living critique of social personalism. They seem to point to a higher solitude, and a strange self-emptying. Also, as we have seen, the self-control of the Buddhist and more generally of the ascetic yogi is directed to the ultimate purification of consciousness. And perhaps we sympathize with this, even apart from the fact that mysticism has been the heart of certain religions in that the cosmos is only known (only self-known we might think looking at the world in a more metaphysical manner) because of conscious beings: and somehow in penetrating to pure consciousness the yogi may be finding the strange essence of living existence, that which makes possible the active life in which we are aware of others and of the world about us. We may also think that the quest for consciousness-purity is a way of humility, of training in selflessness, and thus excellent in generating a calm compassion and concern for others so frequently blocked by our egocentricity and concern with aggrandizing our own substance. The self-emptying of the Buddhist path may be most excellent as moral training in the humility which the West too prizes. Nevertheless, though the egolessness of the Buddhist path is rightly the source of much admiration, it does not by itself form an ideology which is apt at explicating the sanctity of the person. And this is where we return to the problem of contemporary personalism. What lies at the basis of the fundamental rights which the individual should possess? Why should we treat the person with respect and love? Is our modern individualism after all just a hangover from the old doctrine of the immortal soul? Or do we just baldly state that men are gods, to be worshipped through rights and humaneness?

A Transcendental Logic of Personalism

It is indeed open to us to make the individual the stopping point, so to speak, of our ethical system: there has to be a first principle, and why not make it the fundamental rights of man? That man is an end in himself, never merely to be treated as a means. But still we may seek a basis. Indeed the collectivist forces of the modern world, no less powerful than the shibboleths of ancient gods, devourers of human sacrifices, are so domineering today that a deeper basis of the sacredness of the individual would be a godsend. Perhaps, indeed, literally. It is not of course necessary or likely that the majority of modern men should accept the Christian myth, in order to justify belief in the sanctity of the individual; but yet this sanctity itself has arisen historically as an outcome of Christian civilization. There is an interesting way in which a Christian outlook has a special relevance to our problem. Let me sketch how this is.

There is something compelling about the Buddhist analysis, in the sense that we do not find anything other than shifting states of mind when we look inwards. It is not as if we can detect anything intrinsically immortal in the human spirit. If there is something ultimate in the individual, which commands our reverence, it is not anything which can be established on a natural basis – beyond the fact that we have feelings and so can enter into symbolic relationships. But in the theistic worldview, the ultimacy of the human being, as having inalienable rights, is itself actually penultimate: that is the sanctity of the individual derives from divine sanctity. It is not simply a natural property (how could it be?) but something rooted outside the natural world. Thus the notion of the Beyond, of a transcendental dimension of reality, is crucial to the ethic of reverence of humanity. One does not here especially need to believe in the special creation of mankind, or in a special superself, namely the soul; but rather in the notion of a special relationship between human beings and the Transcendent: that affinity through which human beings can have experience of the Other, which transcends the world and concentrates in itself supreme value and holiness. This affinity has of course traditionally been expressed through the idea that man is made in the image of God.

The doctrine has, from the angle of the 'justification' of the sanctity of the individual, two sides to it. Thus on the one hand the ultimacy of human rights is not something which is established on the basis of anything in this world. One cannot go from the facts of this world to the ought of the sanctity of human existence. How indeed could one? Nor are the rights of the individual something which flow from some further obligation within this world. Again, how could they? Even if it can be shown, which maybe it can, that you get a more efficient state, a greater creativity in science and the arts, by respecting human rights, this is too fragile a basis: for it is open to anyone to think more experimentally, and think that it is possible that even greater creativity could be yielded by certain kinds of despotism. So on the one hand the doctrine of men's divine creatureliness does point up the transcendental nature of human rights. A human being is sacred because he or she has so to speak a foothold in the ultimate, in the supreme holy, in the eternal, and so beyond the vicissitudes of human argument.

Second, the doctrine 'places' belief in human rights in a wider picture, and this involves a sort of explanation. The placement sees human beings in relation to the whole of experience, as understood by the theist. It sees men in relationship to the whole of the cosmos, for men are created beings within the total fabric of a universe which derives its beauties, its terrors, its challenges, its dreamlike and sometimes nightmarish quality, from the Other, the mysterious Being who is both full of frightening power and massive love. This is a picture of the universe which arises in part from religious experience, as we have already argued: but it is also a picture which undergoes change in relation to the particular knowledge of the universe which is got through scientific enquiry. In other words, though it is a transcendental picture, and not itself a scientific theory or what not, it is modified by our present knowledge.

But it may be asked why this picture of the world, even if it does in some sense explain and give a basis to the sanctity of the individual should be taken seriously by those for whom the categories of theism are foreign or out of date. In order to answer this question I shall have to create a diversion. For part of the dynamic of freedom and creativity – and indeed of the evolutionary process too, if one chooses somewhat to romanticize it – comes from what in the broadest sense may be called criticism.

Criticism and Imagination

The thesis that the heart of science lies in criticism is, because of Popper, familiar. But more needs to be said about what the nature and conditions of criticism are. Moreover, though scientific enquiry may have its sources in criticism, there are ways in which the critical attitude itself is important, though in a differing style, or styles, outside science: in the arts, in politics, in the practical life. In a way, the term 'criticism' itself may be too narrow: for if one is testing out a theory for instance it is not just a matter of putting it up against various awkward experimental situations, but also quite possibly of trying to think up alternative theories. And as we know many of the great advances in science have occurred through conceptual revolutions. Here the important thing is not so much testing as imagination. In a broad sense, or in various senses, it is imagination which can be considered to be the affirmative side of criticism: the attempt to disprove a position being the negative aspect. Thus we may develop Popper by saying: falsification plus imagination. Let me illustrate how imaginative changes have brought new perspectives in areas outside science. In the visual arts perhaps the point is obvious: for consider the revolution in perception wrought by the Impressionists. But consider also how modern sculpture has been affected by the discovery (that is, discovery by the West) of 'primitive art'. The tribal eye has already been absorbed into the rounded visions of Brancusi and Moore. And as we have seen, a stimulus to imagination is the pluralism of cultures which the empathetic approach to the study of religions is one means of exploring. In ethics also imagination is a main instrument of change, and one may say advance: thus modern men for all their great cruelties are undoubtedly more aware of the suffering of animals and so are beginning to take animal rights more seriously in the West than has in the past been common. Moreover, the growth of anthropology and sociology has led to the placing of various resources at our imaginative disposal: part of a wider movement which is towards varied experiments in living. In brief, a main ingredient in creative criticism of traditions of thought or practice is, in the wide sense, imagination.

Thus one of the occasions of the liberation of the imagination is when cultures meet: when very different styles of living and thinking come into interplay with one another it can in principle provide members of each with new perspectives on the world, and a new kind of understanding of their own tradition. This is not comfortable: and is threatening sometimes. It is not surprising if for this and other reasons culture contact is often marred by misunderstanding and cruel conflict. A mixture of fear, arrogance and failure in imagination brings about fearful atrocities, as (for instance) the history of imperialism has too often shown. It can hardly be thought that the Crusades were a creative aspect of Christian-Islamic encounter, or that the sacking and burning of Buddhist centers of learning in India was an advance of any sort for the human spirit. We are left in a peculiar and uncomfortable position.

On the one hand, the pluralism of traditions is a good thing in that it provides differing ways in which the human spirit has come to terms with the world and with the social placement of the individual: on the other hand, the very pluralism which can fuel human imagination is also a combustible of mass murder and hatred. It is tempting to think it would be nice if all major differences of custom were ironed out, as though the whole world could sail past the Statue of Liberty and be processed into all-American, rational people. It is tempting to argue for a great global melting pot. But this is neither how things are (for men do not all sail past the Statue of Liberty) nor is it how they ought to be (for a homogeneous global society would lose many opportunities of the human spirit). So the question is: How can we attain to a creative rather than a destructive interplay between differing cultural forces and ideologies? There is no magical formula, of course. But this much can be said: That the inevitability of conflicts and tensions should be moderated by the demands of peace and compassion. The test is not whether tensions can be eliminated; but how they can be moderated. At the political level, the federal idea and the national idea are means of roughly assigning power to differing cultural traditions. At the social level, the attitudes of pluralism must be intensified and nourished. At the individual level, the multiplication of individualism by empathy is a major way: and it so happens that the approach and the techniques of the phenomenology of religion are vital, and a good example – which is one reason why I think that the study of religion has a noble and a central place in education. Culturally, then we have to live in the tension which are created by pluralism and change (which is a kind of pluralism in time, and which asks us not to despise the past absolutely when effecting our own, shortliving, new world); and to use those tensions creatively. This is part of what we called 'interactive pluralism'. But when we probe further into the conditions of this we come up against another severe paradox, perhaps a fatal contradiction.

Security and Pluralism

A free and critical society rests on a great degree of security. Without security, paranoia simply views dissent as a threat, to be washed out by blood and prison. It requires a reasonably self-confident society before you can get relaxed attitudes to dissent, as being itself a source of strength rather than weakness. Consider even in such relatively confident and homogeneous societies how hysterically often the student dissent of the sixties and early seventies was viewed by many folk. Yet without a certain painful edge often dissent has not the power to prize open the imagination of those in power. It is a hard thing to achieve: the balance which enables a society to involve itself continuously in the exercise of the critical imagination. Now given this fact, that we need security for criticism, it is harder even than normal to achieve interactive pluralism in a society which is itself plural. For the existence of differing groups (Muslims and Hindus, Catholics and Protestants, Turks and Greeks, blacks and whites) is itself a potent engine of paronoia. Justifiably often, since it is the habit of groups to oppress one another. Consequently, it is important that the concept of the rights of communities as well as of individuals be nourished: for it is one of the fatal weakness of certain forms of Western-style democracy to endorse the principle of one-man-one-vote in a manner which opens the way to majority tyrannies, where communities are deeply divided. At any rate, there clearly is a tension between pluralism and criticism. Thus it is no good arguing in the abstract for the open society without recognizing that certain conditions may have to be fulfilled first: order, where necessary internal federalism, enough social and economic justice to diminish explosive bitterness between rich and poor, etc. It may thus historically be necessary for some countries to go through periods and revolutions in which there is scant regard for openness before the conditions of openness are realized. Thus as we have argued there was, historically, no real alternative for China, if it was to be plucked from the devastating waters of anarchy and economic dislocation, but to undergo the Maoist revolution. Of course there are might have beens: if Western powers had been less rapacious; if the 1911 revolution had come earlier; and so on. But by the thirties there seemed to be no alternative. And it is remarkable how roughly speaking two of the conditions for a more advanced society have been realized in so short a time. But the advocate of critical pluralism does not need because of such historical 'inevitability' (actually I overstate determinism here) to condone features of the present Chinese regime which are stupid and cruel: for instance the shocking treatment of Tibet, the continuing dogmatism and so on.

Creativity and Pluralism

So I have argued that criticism and creativity in society and in the mind rest upon imagination plus falsification: and apart from the fact that a sense of security is bound up with the dignity accorded to a group's social identity, pluralism as the doctrine that differing traditions should be respected is a lively ingredient of the open world, since it fosters imagination. Thus so far as possible the meeting of cultural traditions should be turned into something creative (but it often as we note turns into bitterness). Incidentally, one may add that because of our powers of retrieving the past, within certain severe limits admittedly, the cultural debate should also take place with our planetary ancestors. Indeed, now that the frontiers of the global world have evaporated, and there is hardly anywhere left to explore, we shall not encounter new civilizations: but we can encounter dead ones, and find in them resources for the interpretation of life. (Perhaps too, following science fiction, we may have a new genre of culture fiction: CF, which brings to life in detail alternative civilizations, would thus be another way to expand the imagination.) Having said all this about the vital nature of critical pluralism in our search for greater insight into the nature of the world and of living, I can now turn back from my 'diversion' to the question of why theism should be taken seriously in the modern age.

Critical Theism and Divine Substance

We have seen ways in which the spirit of the Beyond can be in line with the critical temper of human creativity. But it is also critical in the sense that it is no longer magical. By this I mean that if we accept that belief in God does not add an extra potency to the cosmos, an extra factor so to speak to enter into cosmological calculations, then theism involves at its heart a kind of metaphysical emptiness (as we argued earlier in our delineations of the relationship between Christianity and Buddhist Emptiness). One can see this as a development, if we like, from Kant. The Divine Being has a noumenal character: lying so to speak locked for ever beyond phenomena. But there are it should be noted differing kinds of 'beyond'.

There is a story about an Englishman in Belfast who was asked by an Irishman whether he were a Protestant or a Catholic. Wishing to avoid trouble he said he was an atheist. 'Yes', responded the native, 'but are you a Protestant or a Catholic atheist?' So one might say that there are differing forms of the noumenal – three kinds. There is the numinous noumenal, the mystical noumenal and the scientific noumenal. To put it a different way: that which lies 'beyond' phenomena can lie there in three different styles of beyond. There are two forms of the transcendental beyond, and there is a form of the investigative beyond, or perhaps we should say the empirical beyond. The numinous and mystical styles are represented respectively and predominantly in theism and Buddhism: the investigative or empirical beyond might be said to be an ingredient in science.

We can look upon science itself as the product of a complex dialogue between nature and human enquiry. The scientist interrogates nature, who dumbly gives him answers, sometimes desperately disappointing, often baffling, sometimes amazingly consonant with human aesthetic judgement. But since nature herself is a construct, in that the nature of nature is delineated in a complex way by the various theories which have so far survived the processes of testing, we need the postulation of nature as 'there' to be described. This noumenal aspect of nature lies beyond the various representations of it.

Already our theories go beyond the early layers of representation which perception and 'common sense' bring to us: the fact that nature as discovered in modern physics is fluid, mathematical, impermanent in detail, relational – already such a picture of nature is suggestive of the Buddhist portraiture. Two motifs here, of interconnectedness and emptiness, are woven together out of inner experience and philosophical reflection. So we can see a kind of 'mystical' form of what is noumenal, in which there is a kind of emptiness beyond perceptions. This indeed is the goal of interior training in the Buddhist style – to attain a kind of transcendental experience of samsara and nirvana.

The theistic noumenon is somewhat different, for it lies Beyond (so to speak) nature, even that hidden unsayable aspect of nature which we postulate 'out there' beyond our representations. The Divine is figured as an Other. But that configuration of the Divine arises chiefly from the fact that numinous experience is dual, dynamic, personal: as I have remarked before, like a personalized H-bomb exploding. In experience and in sacrament it communicates personal power.

But it is, as noumenal, metaphysically empty. Its power lies in religion and in the experiences of creatures. It is thus not magical Power. If it has power, that is reflected in the phenomena. It is thus mythologically appropriate that the man-God should have emptied himself of the divine attributes, as if in any event he could import an extra dynamism from the metaphysically empty reaches of the cloud of unknowing.

But nothing I have said in any way diminishes from the

actual power of the religious and prophetic spirit, from the sacramental efficacy and visionary dynamism, of actual theism. This is where we can say that the continuing relevance of theism lies. In brief, the theism which presents itself to the contemporary world is one which in principle can be critical in temper, both about its own transcendental emptiness and about human experience seen from the commanding heights of what lies Beyond, as reflected in the experience of the Divine.

Christian Theism and the Person

Theism, because it roots men in the Transcendent, and gives those who have faith a different kind of security (participation in the divine substance and a sense therefore of the overcoming of alienation), provides a strong base for the critical evaluation of worldly ideologies. This is part of the meaning of the prophetic vocation. It is perhaps not surprising that the old prophets had an encounter with the Other: for this gave them a new and a different point of view. To some extent all those inspired by the mad otherness, in the arts and in literature, belong to the prophetic tradition, even if often in a new and secular key. But theism has a special power, born paradoxically out of its weakness (and this is why it is specially luminous that Christ should have suffered on the Cross: luminous, that is to say, by hindsight). For in looking at the world from the perspective of the Beyond the theist is nourished by his faith, his experience, his sense that nothing in this world can, ultimately, touch him. This is the power of going beyond the world.

The weakness (which is a paradox) is that in practice it can only speak through human beings: as we have seen, it is not that in addition to the vision and dynamic which the believer may discover in his sense of encounter with the Other there is some further magic power which God

exercizes and which constitutes a higher knowledge than
men's present knowledge –as though a new, spiritual,
science can be added to the other sciences, transcending it.
For transcendence as we may truly understand it means
that indeed God is beyond (and secretly within) the
material cosmos: not that he is an extra part of it. In other
words, insofar as science deals with the material cosmos,
God is beyond science: there is no science-beyond-science
of him. It is like the case of the Buddha: he is called 'god
beyond gods', but he is not a god, for he plays in quite a
different league. So theism represents a dynamic point of
departure for criticism of the secular order and for the
secular ideologies. It gives a sense of the world in which
men have in principle a transcendental umbilical, a point of
contact with what lies beyond this world. Rooted thus in
this timeless and divine nature, the human being has a
sanctity which cannot be supplied (so to speak) merely by
social conditioning. That conditioning is important in
developing the *li*, the performative gestures which salute
the dignity of human beings. But its logic lies in the
Heaven of which Confucius spoke little.

Thus sacramental theism supplies a transcendental root
of the sacred character of the human being. The reverence
which we should feel for one another is a reflection of the
awe before the Divine Being; while the dignity-bearing
performative acts which we should aim at one another
reflect the sacramental communication of divine substance.

This picture of the world gives a placement to the idea of
the sanctity of the individual. But it is not in any way a
proof of the reverential imperative. Whether we look to a
post-Christian humanism to express human rights, or to the
kind of theism I have sketched, the affirmation of human
sanctity is yet a matter of commitment, and that reveals in
still another way our essential fragility.

Faith and Uncertainty

It is not in the nature of religious or ideological truth to be absolutely perspicuous: it is in essence debatable, the tests are soft, the fruits difficult to evaluate. It is strange that ideologies and religions so often attract those of dogmatic temper: the uncertainty of faith is given a special and fanatic assurance in the strenuous repetition of credos, in the tread of the thought police, in the burning faggots of the auto-da-fé. The reason is, it seems, that because a world-view orients the individual and society to the cosmos, and to action here and now – so that issues become simultaneously cosmic and practical – it demands a kind of commitment which in turn demands a sense of assurance. The very fragility of higher truth means that it has to be asserted with almost violent conviction. To put it all in a nutshell: uncertainty perceived deep down explodes into certainty at the surface. So it is that those who criticize the main tradition of a society are often perceived as deeply menacing, subverting the very order of things. The Sorbonne riots seem to rock the whole universe; just as in old days the Christian 'atheists' made the whole Roman world unsafe (so throw them to the lions). Well, it may be that because of the structures of human nature we cannot do much about this deep disease – that passion has to be predicated on dogmatism, and commitment nourished in blinkers. But at least we can reflect that since the criteria of truth (or acceptance) of a worldview are so strange and difficult to apply, it is not reasonable to be vociferous in talk of proof or knowledge of the Transcendent.

Thus theism must share with other belief-system a certain epistemological modesty. But those who have faith in Christ should not because of this fail in passion: for it is a noble, strange, exciting vision of the cosmos which they have, and one which bids them seek in a particular direction, along a path which brings them to the conviction of the tragic dignity of men's state, and to a kind of overcoming of evil and suffering. At any rate, from the angle of theism, the nature of men is in a sense transcendental: and it is because of this, and because of the central value of love as exhibited through Christ's self-emptying, that the perspective of faith must be critical of those who treat men as social fodder. Thus theism, and in particular Christianity as I have been trying to interpret it, are not fashionable viewpoints somehow *de rigueur*. They are risky places from which to sally into the ideological marketplace. Theism is one of the many visions which have moved men and will live on in creative and one hopes peaceful combat and interplay with its rivals and friends.

The Question of Poverty

The arguments which I have deployed to suggest that there is a certain complementarity between Buddhism and Christianity, and to try to relate that perception to the critical evaluation of ideologies, point unmistakeably in a particular direction – namely a new synthesis between Western and Asian civilization. It seems to me that the ideals of social personalism, interactive pluralism, transcendental criticism and noumenal faith are congenial particularly to the Buddhist tradition, and are also a not unnatural outcome of modern liberal Christianity. Because there is here an emphasis upon tradition and the recasting of self-identity in the context of modern political and scientific change, this new synthesis escapes the flatness of ethical humanism. There is no reason why the resources of the past should not be brought to bear in forming a spiritual outlook which is critical, not dogmatic, self-emptying rather than magical, and which can appreciate both the need for identity and the demands of innovation.

But our new pluralism can easily slide into a kind of higher selfishness. The securities and the rights which can be preserved in the social democracies of the northern West are in part the outcome of prosperity and in part its cause. That prosperity has not been cleanly arrived at, however: for the economic miracles of the post-World War II period occurred in societies which continued some elements of colonial policy and the exploitation of resources among poorer nations. If problems of internal poverty in the northern world were for the most part, if not wholly, solved by new economic techniques and social policies, the problems of severe external poverty have continued in the so-called Third World.

Patterns of History

We can see the course of history as being a tangled affair of traditions and civilizations in interchange and collision. Often the exchange of ideas and of social values between cultures has flowed from war and conquest or other violences such as slavery. Greed, hatred and delusion have been woven closely into the fabric of events. But yet in other ways these interchanges and collisions have been creative: Hegel's dialectical theory represents a crude and simplified way of expressing a certain truth. We can see how the revived classical culture of the Renaissance fertilized the Christian civilization which had resulted from among things the marriage of northern European culture to the Christian values of the late Roman period. We can see how Chinese and indigenous Japanese culture fused in medieval Japan. We can admire the Sikh solution to the problem of Hindu-Muslim reconciliation. We can see how Byzantine and Slav motifs came fruitfully together in the religious culture of old Russia. And so forth. The history of the world has been a rhythm of separate development and syntheses. It is a different mode of development, much shorter in time, than that which occurred through the immensely long process of evolution. But it is a kind of evolutionary analogue. Nature has moved into history; genes have been bathed in cultural traditions; mental superstructures have transformed material and economic realities. There is also something like the survival of the fittest, in the sense that new cultural ideas come for various reasons to have great, even overwhelming power: consider the magnetism of Christianity as an ideology for the Empire and then for the emerging peoples of Northern and Eastern Europe; consider the power of Indian ideologies of kingship, Hindu and Buddhist, in South-East Asia; consider the grip which the values of technocracy and modernity have on the contemporary mind, both North and South. Ideas, so to speak, have their times: cometh the hour, cometh the idea. For varying reasons some of the older systems can no longer live, though they may still be carried in the cultural chromosomes of their succeeding systems. We have seen something of this in the older worldviews and values of China: it is even more clearly seen in the way smaller ethnic groups' beliefs have to succumb or at least transform themselves under the impact of modern values.

The Creative Struggle of Ideas

But it is not that ideas die or live by jugulars and hunting. The processes are more obscure, in intellect and heart, in the mobilization of energies, in the acceptability of insights. It is thus partly a rational struggle, partly a symbolic one, partly a moral one – this combat of ideologies: it is also very frequently a bloody one, in which ideas mobilize not just energies but armies. In this messy rhythm of development, synthesis, genocide, war, the worldviews of the world have struggled onwards: what they currently leave is that dynamic deposit of contemporary faiths. Who knows how the future may turn out, in the febrile atmosphere of the global city? But it is part of the thesis of critical pluralism which I have been advocating that creative and peaceful struggle is what should be looked for, so far as possible. This is not just a placid 'dialogue' (a world now much tinged with the sensation of kindness between religions, and praying together, and seeing, no doubt admirably, the goodness in one another's lifestyles); but a genuine struggle. For in my view (for instance) the way in which human rights have been trampled in nationalism and under Marxism is appalling, as also the horrors of the Third World slum and the starving bones of unfortunate peoples: in all this, there is contempt for human dignity, and this contempt finds its corrective, I believe, in seeing the divine light which diffuses from the Beyond into the human person. The notion of the Beyond may also – and in a Buddhist way – contribute to this struggle within the bounds of critical pluralism. I shall come to that shortly. But in the meantime let us note that the condition which is mentioned above, namely that the struggle should be creative and so far as possible peaceful, itself points to certain political values, such as toleration and federalism. Despite phases of aggressiveness in Christian history, it is hard to believe that one can deduce from the New Testament or from the main structures of Christian belief anything other than a peaceful outlook: pointing if not to pacifism at least to the minimization of violence. Thus leaving aside institutional arrangements for the settling of conflicts, one may also use this as a criterion in attempting to judge the way nations live politically.

Empathy and Two Levels of Truth

The empathy which is both part of the method of the study of religions and more generally is the way in which we come to understand one another, means that we so to speak look at the world from the point of view of others whom we encounter, whether in friendship or rivalry. It is also the basis of the moral evaluation of values: for once I understand another's values then to the degree that they are dear to him they should be respected by me. But if they are cruel, destructive values? In consistency of course I cannot prize them or respect them (though it can be that something relatively good hides behind the destructive feelings: Hitler's hatred of the Jews was a catastrophe and an outrage, but it had behind it a love of the Germany for which he had fought for four terrible years on the Western Front – and that love of Germany was not altogether bad, and could conceivably have had a more creative outlet). Still, there is a prima facie value in what others value. But it is only a provisional stance, this. It is what underlies among other things the national assumption and the federal idea – the respect for nations derives from the fact that politically national sovereignty or at least some degree of autonomy is felt, deeply, by most of the relevant people to be vital to their sense of identity, their 'being at home' in the world. But just as I may stand outside other folk's values, so the conception of God or the Ultimate stands outside both my and their values. It is a vantage point, so to speak, for criticism of worldly values, and a vantage point too for seeing them as non-ultimate. Thus though we should be in our worldly dealings committed, as I have suggested, to social personalism, it would be somehow absurd, at least from the angle of the Beyond, to shrink people into their social identities: to boil them down even to their own self-images. Thus the Buddhist conception of two levels of truth – that which is conventional, of this world, provisional, and that which is Beyond, is ineffable, is to be experienced – can be applied here: the individual is not to be lost in social relationships, however fulfilling and comforting they may be. The ethics of respect for such social values is itself provisional, since one can always point to something which lies beyond them and beyond existence in the cosmos.

The Public and the Individual Search

I may sum up the position I have outlined in this chapter. First, both Christian theism and Buddhism (for these are the major examples I have been working with) can be used as points of departure in the critique of secular ideologies – a critique that is itself part of a kind of interactive or critical pluralism in which cratively we can, in the global city, move towards a richer realization of human life: for not only science and the arts flourish through openness and imagination, but also the political and moral life. Second, however, we need to measure the conditions of openness: very often tensions of both social and political kinds need to be resolved, often in a harsh way: though the clearly preferable pattern is for pluralistic and federal ways of dealing with group identities; while social inequities too may make openness immediately hard or impossible. But the fact that a nation may have to pass through a revolutionary and dictatorial phase should not prevent us from thinking positively about future possibilities of openness. Third, part of the critique of the secular ideologies is that in the last resort social personalism – for all its recognition of the way people exist and feel their identities in a social way – makes individuals the ultimate atoms of the moral life: and the dignity of the individual is something expressed in *li* or performative action. Yet what is the basis of that *li*?

Theism assigns to the individual a transcendental worth not derived from nature but which flows, so to speak, from the Beyond. This transcendental aspect of the individual is approached in a differing and negative way in the twin Buddhist doctrines of non-self and the two level theory of truth. Fourth, we noted that the utilitarianism of modern Western political and economic thinking needs to be seen in the perspective that in fact most of men's activities are liable to symbolic transformation: and so policy has to be indirectly concerned with happiness, but more with promoting those things which men find symbolically satisfying. But of course religions and ideologies can provide different ways of viewing the world, and so differing evaluations of what we may take in a given culture to be symbolically satisfying. This is a further way in which both Christian theism and Buddhism can provide a transcendental critique of the secular.

But here we can return to the individual search. For in the above discussion I have chiefly been involved in the evaluation of public, large scale belief systems: and the validation of such a social and moral value as the sanctity of the individual. But the spiritual path also begins from within the individual, in regard to his hopes and his fear, his pains and his loves, his worries and disasters, his hope for peace. Seeing the world from the perspective of the Beyond is to see it transformed. It is this excitement, joy and sadness in living in the shining, suffering jewel net of Indra, the glad creation of the one Logos, which causes other personal values to become changed too. Thus there is a deep way and a special way in which the Transcendent offers a critique of the world, for it changes it: giving it that strange emptiness of which Buddhism speaks or that mysteriousness and echoing power of which Christian theism speaks. In the end we are indeed alone, as centres of consciousness which help to constitute separate worlds: each individual's cosmos is in a way all that there is, and yet each person knows that there are worlds which lie beyond his world. To these he reaches out in hope and love. Such hope and love can transform his world: and that ultimately is what religion is about – transforming the world.

Postscript

———————————◆———————————

Towards a New Worldview: The Pacific Mind

East and West in Complementary Existence

I have been advocating a certain outlook, based on the complementarity of Buddhism and Christianity. They are different ways of going towards the Beyond: and by dreaming of that destination – a dream stimulated by the experiences of the numinous Other and the mystical Emptiness – we find ways of providing a support for and yet also a critique of the personalism and pluralism which should govern our global world. They both indicate the provisional character of secular identities, whether framed in regard to the nation or the economic class. They provide a different perspective on the question of human identity: they can affirm a pluralistic acceptance of the social dimension of personal identity, and yet see beyond that to the emptiness of the atoms of consciousness which spray like droplets through our streaming life, and to the self-emptying power which transcends the cosmos and material identity. The one is a way that takes us through history and sacrament: the other takes us through analysis and yoga.

I believe, as I have argued, that they are complementary; and that in the long run there can be a fruitful living together of the two traditions, so formative of East and West. From this perspective, it is possible to look anew on human history, as it has converged into a single whole in the contemporary world. We need to ask ourselves how our contemporary world is related to the complex religious past. Only a partial picture has emerged here: but I have suggested that there is a possible complementarity between Eastern and Western traditions; while the notion of a creative critical pluralism helps to make sense of the relationship between the traditional theistic and secular ideologies born out of the Western world. Also, the present interpretation of both theism and Buddhism is in line with science, in the sense that what they offer does not conflict, in principle, with the scientific outlook: and provided that they remain critical, their affinity to the open imagination which is so crucial to both the sciences and the arts is a vital factor in relating ancient traditions to the modern world. Indeed, that critical outlook is partly a consequence of the way they offer visions of the world which go beyond everyday perception, and partly stems from the manner in which they view the world from the perspective of the Beyond.

The Critique of Collectivism

It may have been a necessary part of the rebellion against Victorian capitalism which was called forth by the grim effects of the first Industrial Revolution, but the doctrinaire atheism which Marxism has embraced is part of the tragedy of the new social order of the socialist part of the planet. But since it is a simple truth that men do not live by bread alone; and since too it is a simple truth that a modern society demands ultimately a degree of scientific freedom to be effective in the creation of wealth: it is easy enough to be optimistic that in the global city a greater amount of openness and a greater sensitivity to the spiritual dimension of life will spread into the social tyrannies which Marxism has helped to produce. Yet it is wise also to temper optimism with the thought of what is unknown. New instabilities in the global city, new earthquakes in the

South, new storms in the Middle East, new and more terrible national clashes are possible: and nationalism itself, national sovereignty, remains the dominating ideology, nurturing paranoia often, and driving leaders greedily to new forms of armament, not least nuclear weapons. Can we say with confidence that they will not be used? Madness and machismo are not infrequent among leaders: and international relationships are often pursued with a customary but still surprising crudity of motivation. What dreadful storms has our planet still to live through?

Here the critique from the Beyond remains vital. The secular ideologies which have proved most powerful, nationalism and Marxism in particular, have fed upon the thirst for identity and social justice. They have made great claims on the allegiance of men and have elicited such splendid heroisms, such sacrifices, such rivers of nobly spilled blood. But they have also encouraged violence and hatred. We have a deep need to take collectivism with a certain scepticism: to use skilful means to tame the beasts of collective pride and economic revenge. The love which Christ self-emptyingly symbolizes, the compassion and non-violence which the Buddha expresses – these values are of even greater importance now than they were before such terrible means of destruction reposed in the hands of hard and confused men.

Beyond Flat Secularism

But I have also tried to show that the study of religion itself has illumination in it too. It is in some ways the most crucial of the social sciences, for it casts a strong light upon the essentially symbolic character of so many human activities: not least upon the symbolisms and ritual elements in which our 'secular' existence is drenched. And in making the demand of empathy the study of religion tells us of an important method in all our dealings. We should not act towards others without making a move into their minds. It is the mutual interpenetration of cultures through empathy that the comparative study of religion offers as a major ingredient in the formation of a peaceful global city.

This exploration, then, of the complementary worlds of Buddhism and Christianity, and of religious and secular ideologies, is part of a wider quest to make sense of our new world, in which traditions are having to find themselves anew and in which the modern ideologies are beginning to look careworn. As we have emphasized, one of the many fruits born of European civilization has been the modern study of religion and politics, to which I here make a modest contribution: that study is itself part of the open heritage which is Europe and America's most astounding achievement, and which is in a sense the most eminent saving grace of Christian civilization. That civilization now has the opportunity of transcending itself, and through an interactive pluralism to form a critical basis for a global culture. If Europe is looking for its destiny, it must surely lie in a new appraisal of the connections between liberalism and the Christian past; and if America is searching for a new frontier once again, it may find it in the new meeting of East and West which the broad waters of the Pacific cannot prevent. A new sense of Atlantic and Pacific civilizations may well be part of our future, in the West. But without finding means to stimulate hope and prosperity for the impoverished South and the teeming tropic belt, there can be no stability. Social justice is one of the conditions of those dreams of a new pluralism of which I have written. Compassion thus turns out to be common sense: without dignity for the poor, and hope, the rich rot.

The Pacific Mind

We are only at the beginning of the life of the global city. What I have here tried to write about, the complementarity of Buddhism and Christianity and their relationship to the ideologies, is only one among many kinds of reflections which must arise as the cultures of the planet mingle. What vast changes will a hundred years of global travel, of television, of radio satellites, of trade, of electronic translators, of new exchanges of people bring about?

Since nationalism has been the most powerful force in modern politics, ultimately any global civilization must be pluralistic. This is a weakness of the theocratic ideologies of Islam and Marxism (not of course literally theocratic, but having the same properties as a theocracy, amplified by the techniques and institutions of the totalitarian state, to which Islam is itself inimical). The values of Hinduism and Buddhism and the modern West are more favourable to pluralism, and for this reason a new Pacific culture can find room for the pluralisms of ethnic liberation throughout the 'Third World'. Thus this new transcendental ideology, incorporating the open spirit and a sense of social personalism, seems to me to be the one best suited to the humane development of the global city. Thus can the resources of the past be used to give a sense of vision and dignity to the inhabitants of our beautiful planet. As we look across the cold North Sea we remember the cruelties of collectivism and wild nationalism. As we scan the Pacific we can remember cruelties too but the sun shines upon new waves of thought and culture. There may be born that Pacific mind which balances dynamism with non-violence, and this may prove to be the starting point for new relations between East and West and North and South. We look to a transcendental humanism, no longer magical, but both critical and enchanting.

Bibliographical Notes

CHAPTER 1
The World's Religions and Ideologies in Interaction

The Views across the Pacific and the North Sea. A beautiful and scholarly introduction to the Pacific as a cultural area in modern history is Rosélène Dousset and Étienne Taillemite *The Great Book of the Pacific* (Secaucus, NJ: Chartwell Books, 1979).

Religion and Ideology: an Ideological Distinction. For discussion of some of the issues about the relation between secular and traditional worldviews see David Martin *A General Theory of Secularization* (New York: Harper and Row, 1978), which also deals interestingly with the way deep cultural structures affect secularization. John Plamenatz *Ideology* (New York: Praegaw, 1970), I have found a useful guide to the history of the idea of ideology. The meaning of the breakdown of the religion-and-ideology distinction is explored partly in my *The Principles and Meaning of the Study of Religion* (University of Lancaster Religious Studies Department, 1970), and 'Ways of Looking: Religion, Philosophy and the Future', *Encounter*, March 1978.

The Global City. I substitute 'city' for 'village' for reasons which relate to the complexity of the planetary situation, following Marshall McLuhan *Understanding Media: The Extensions of Man* (New York: McGraw Hill, 1964) and his earlier *The Gutenberg Galaxy* (Toronto: University of Toronto Press, 1962). There is also recent sociological interest in 'globology', starting from a somewhat Marxian and economic point of view: see Albert Bergesen (ed.) *Studies of the Modern World-System* (New York: Academic Press, 1980), and Immanuel Wallerstein *The Modern World-System* (New York: Academic Press, 1976).

The Relationship of Worldviews a Matter of Flesh and Blood. I tried to expound some of the human factors of these larger relations in *The Long Search* (Boston: Little Brown, 1978; London: BBC Publications, 1978). A relevant pioneering work is Trevor Ling *Buddha, Marx and God* (New York: St Martin's Press, 1966). One example of the way some religious and ideological clashes have been worked out can be seen in William Shawcross *Sideshow: Kissinger, Nixon and the Destruction of Cambodia* (London: Fontana, 1980).

Eastern Worldviews Today. There is of course an extensive literature. Among relevant titles are such classical (but value-laden) expositions as S. Radhakrishnan's *The Hindu View of Life* (London: Allen and Unwin, 1927); surveys such as Jerrold Schecter *The New Face of the Buddha* (London: Gallancz, 1967) and Raymond Hammer *Japan's Religious Ferment* (London: SCM Press, 1960). Holmes Welch's various magisterial works on modern China are important, including *The Buddhist Revival in China* (Cambridge, Mass: Harvard University Press, 1968). On smaller Eastern faiths, two important modern approaches are W. H. McLeod *Gurū Nānak and the Sikh Tradition* (Oxford: Clarendon Press, 1968), and Padmanabh S. Jaini *The Jaina Path of Purification* (Berkeley: University of California Press, 1979).

Western Asia. Some of the underlying forces shaping recent Islamic events are described in Wilfred Cantwell Smith *Islam in Modern History* (Princeton: Princeton University Press, 1957). For modern Judaism see Joseph Blau *Modern Varieties of Judaism* (New York: Columbia University Press, 1966).

Christianity at Large. I have attempted a new look at the variations of contemporary Christianity in *The Phenomenon of Christianity* (London: Collins, 1979), published in the United States as *In Search of Christianity* (New York: Harper and Row, 1979). See also William Clebsch *Christianity in European History* (New York: Oxford University Press, 1979). My analysis of Christianity owes points to the following works: Ronald Knox *Enthusiasm* (New York: Oxford University Press, 1950); F. Ernest Stoeffler *The Rise of Evangelical Pietism* (Numen Supplement 9, Leiden: Brill, 1965); A. R. Vidler *The Church in an Age of Revolution, 1789 to the Present Day* (Baltimore: Penguin, 1971); Steven Runciman *The Orthodox Churches and the Secular State* (Auckland: Auckland University Press, 1971); Stephen Charles Neill *Christian Missions* (Baltimore: Penguin, 1965).

Each Worldview Needs a View of the Others. I explored the issues informally in *World Religions: a Dialogue* (Baltimore: Penguin, 1966) – a reprint of *A Dialogue of Religions* (London: SCM Press,

1960). See also John Carman and Donald Dawe (editors) *Christian Faith in a Religiously Plural World* (New York: Orbis, 1978); John R. Hinnells (ed.) *Comparative Religion in Education* (Newcastle-upon-Tyne: Oriel, 1970); Arnold Toynbee *Christianity among the Religions of the World* (New York: Scribner, 1957); and Emma Layman *Buddhism in America* (Chicago: Nelson-Hall, 1976). Some of the primary issues about the attempt to see a transcendental unity of all religions are discussed in my *The Yogi and the Devotee* (London: Allen and Unwin, 1968).

Buddhism and Christianity: Widespread and Mirroring.   Among writings on the relationship between Buddhism and Christianity are Henri de Lubac *Aspects of Buddhism* (New York: Sheed and Ward, 1953); Heinrich Dumoulin *Christianity meets Buddhism* (La Salle, Ill.: Open Court Publishing Co., 1974); Douglas A. Fox *Buddhism, Christianity and the Future of Religion* (Philadelphia: Westminster Press, 1972) and Winston King *Buddhism and Christianity: Some Bridges of Understanding* (Philadelphia: Westminster Press, 1962). Ahead of its time was B. H. Streeter *The Buddha and the Christ* (New York: Macmillan, 1933).

Nationalism and other Identities.   The analysis of nationalism by political scientists owes much to Karl W. Deutsch, as seen in his *Interdisciplinary Bibliography on Nationalism* (Cambridge, Mass.: Technology Press of MIT, 1956). See also Hans Kohn *Ideas of Nationalism* (London: Macmillan, 1961) and various works by Anthony D. Smith *Theories of Nationalism* (New York: Harper and Row, 1971), *Nationalism in the Twentieth Century* (New York: New York University Press, 1979), *Nationalist Movements* (New York: St Martin's Press, 1977) and *Nationalism: A Trend Report and Bibliography prepared for the International Sociological Association* (The Hague: Mouton, 1975). Important to our whole argument is the concept of civil religion: see Robert Bellah 'Civil Religion in America' in *American Civil Religion*, edited by Russell E. Richey and Donald G. Jones (New York: Harper and Row, 1974) and Phillip Hammond 'The Sociology of American Civil Religion: A Bibliographic Essay', *Sociological Analysis*, 37, No. 2, 1976. Also important is W. J. M. Mackenzie *Political Identity* (Harmondsworth: Penguin Books, 1978).

The Understanding between Worldviews and a New View of the Planet.   On the persistence of religion and its transformations works from two very different context make an interesting counterpoint: Michael Bourdeaux *Opium of the People: the Christian Religion in the USSR* (London: Mowbrays, 1977) and Jacob Needleman *New Religions* (Garden City, New York: Doubleday, 1970). See also the good discussion in Trevor Ling *Karl Marx and Religion* (London: Macmillan, 1980).

CHAPTER 2
Towards a Theory of the Configurations of Religion

Histories and Patterns.   For the history of the history of religions J. de Vries *Perspectives in the History of Religions* (Berkeley: University of California Press, 1977) could be more reflective. Fuller is Eric J. Sharpe's excellent *Comparative Religion* (New York: Scribner, 1976). See also Jacques Waardenburg's two volumes *Classical Approaches to the Study of Religion* (The Hague: Mouton, 1973 and 1974). For a briefer anatomy of the study of religion see my 'The Study of Religion' in *Encyclopedia Britannica* (1975 edition). I have been somewhat influenced in this chapter by such phenomenological and comparative works as W. Brede Kristensen *The Meaning of Religion* (The Hague: M. Nijhoff, 1960); Mircea Eliade *Patterns in Comparative Religion* (New York: Sheed and Ward, 1958), M. Eliade and J. Kitagawa (editors) *The History of Religions: Essays in Methodology* (Chicago: University of Chicago Press, 1959); Gerardus van der Leeuw *Religion in Essence and Manifestation* (New York: Harper and Row, 1963), and Victor Turner *The Ritual Process: Structure and Anti-Structure* (Chicago: Aldine, 1969). On certain aspects of related areas of enquiry I have drawn on E. E. Evans-Pritchard *Theories of Primitive Religion* (Oxford: Clarendon Press, 1961); B. Malinowski *Magic, Science and Religion and Other Essays* (Garden City, New York: Doubleday, 1970); Thomas F. O'Dea *Sociology and the Study of Religion* (New York: Basic Books, 1970) and Bryan R. Wilson (ed.) *Rationality* (Evanston, Ill.: Harper and Row, 1970).

Types and Organisms.   On the organic character of religious systems see my earliest discussion of the point in *Reasons and Faiths* (London: Routledge and Kegan Paul, 1958).

Culture, Interpretation and Intra-religious Explanation.   On the general question see Clifford Geertz *Interpretation of Cultures* (New York: Basic Books, 1973) and 'Religion as a Cultural System' in William A. Lessa and Evons Z. Vogt, editors, *Reader in Comparative Religion* (New York: Harper and Row, 1965). See also Nathan Söderblom *The Living God: Basal Forms of Personal Religion* (Boston: Beacon Press, 1962) and Joachim Wach and Joseph Kitagawa *The Comparative Study of Religion* (New York: Columbia University Press, 1958). The notion of intra-religious explanation is explored in

Ninian Smart *The Science of Religion and the Sociology of Knowledge* (Princeton; Princeton University Press, 1973).

Bracketing the Transcendent: Standing Back from God. My approach is somewhat critical of the non-neutral theoretical approach of Peter L. Berger *The Sacred Canopy* (Garden City, New York: Doubleday, 1969). For the general notion see also Edmund Husserl *Ideas* (London: Macmillan, 1969).

The Relationship of Power and Performance. For general theory see John Searle *Speech Acts: an Essay in the Philosophy of Language* (Cambridge: Cambridge University Press, 1969). Also relevant are Victor Turner *The Ritual Process* (Chicago: Aldine, 1969) and various works by Erving Goffman, notably *The Presentation of Self in Everyday Life* (Garden City, New York: Doubleday, 1959).

Ritual and Performative Acts as Paths of Power. The analogies between religious and 'secular' uses of performative power are partly explored in 'The Bounds of Religion and the Transition from the Tao to Mao' *Sri Lanka Journal of the Humanities*, vol.i, no.1 (June 1975).

The Science of Religion as an Interpreter of History. For Eliade's views on this see *The Quest: History and Meaning in Religion* (Chicago: University of Chicago Press, 1969) and *A History of Religious Ideas* (Chicago: University of Chicago Press, 1978; London: Collins, 1979). For a divergent view see my 'Beyond Eliade: the Future of Theory in Religion' *Numen*, xxv, fasc. 2, August, 1978, and 'Ways of Looking: Religion, Philosophy and the Future', *Encounter*, March 1978.

CHAPTER 3
Christianity Seen from Adam's Peak

Buddhism Ancient and Modern in Sri Lanka. An excellent account, blending text and participant observation, is Richard F. Gombrich *Precept and Practice: Traditional Buddhism in the Rural Highlands of Ceylon* (Oxford: Clarendon Press, 1971). I have commented on this in 'Precept and Theory in Sri Lanka', *Religion*, vol.III, No.1, 1973. For a brief introduction to the Theravada see Ninian Smart *Buddhism and the Death of God* (Southampton: University of Southampton, 1970). For modern history see Walpola Rahula *History of Buddhism in Ceylon* (Colombo: M. D. Gunasena, 1966) and for ancient history A. K. Warder *Indian Buddhism* (Delhi: Motilal Banarsidass, 1970).

A Question from Christianity. Part of this question is raised in a more formal way in my 'The Work of the Buddha and the Work of Christ' in S. G. F. Brandon, editor, *The Saviour God* (Manchester: Manchester University Press, 1963).

Western Civilization and the Eastern World-picture. On the divergence of cosmologies see my 'Reincarnation and Eastern Attitudes' *The Listener*, August 9, 1962; and K. N. Jayatilleke *The Message of the Buddha* (London: George Allen and Unwin, 1975).

The Cultural Effects of the Small Cosmos. A good source for cosmologies in the Western tradition is Milton K. Munitz *Theories of the Universe: from Babylonian Myth to Modern Science* (New York: Free Press, 1965).

Divine Power and Buddhist Knowledge. The best account of the early Buddhist notion of knowledge as interpreted by the Theravada, see K. N. Jayatilleke *Early Buddhist Theory of Knowledge* (London: George Allen and Unwin, 1962). Also for a different perspective, H. V. Guenther *Philosophy and Psychology in the Abhidharma* (Lucknow: Buddha Vihara, 1962).

Emptiness and Substance. David J. Kalupahana *Causality: the Central Philosophy of Buddhism* (Honolulu: University of Hawaii Press, 1975) is excellent from a more technical direction, and Frederick Streng *Emptiness: A Study in Religious Meaning* (New York: Abingdon Press, 1967) is a sophisticated religionist's explication of the religious sense of Emptiness. For a somewhat less 'negative' interpretation see T. R. V. Murti *The Central Philosophy of Buddhism* (London: Allen and Unwin, 1955).

The Meaning of Buddhist Transcendence. See *Udana*, 80-81, Khuddaka Nikāya, 1:3,8. For an account of the relationship of transcendence to consciousness see Rune Johansson *The Dynamic Psychology of Early Buddhism* (London: Curzon Press, 1979) and also his *The Psychology of Nirvāna* (London: Allen and Unwin, 1969). For the distinction between theism and Theravadin conceptions of the ultimate see Gunapala Dharmasiri *A Buddhist Critique of the Christian Concept of God* (Colombo: Lake House Investments, 1974). For what I consider to be the clearest analysis of transcendence, see my article 'Myth and Transcendence' *The Monist*, vol. 50, no. 4 (October, 1966).

Christ and the Buddha. The quotation is Thomas Aquinas *Summa Theologica* III q.16, art.6, obj. 1 and 2. For the notion of Christ's mythic defeat of evil see Gustaf Aulén *Christus Victor* (London: SPCK, 1953). As for the results of more recent reflections in myth and historicity, there is James M. Robinson *A New Quest of the Historical Jesus* (London: SCM Press, 1959). In 'The Work of the Buddha and the Work of Christ' I compare the two contexts, in S. G. F. Brandon (ed.) *The Saviour God, Comparative Studies in the Concept of Salvation* (Manchester: Manchester University Press, 1963).

Priest and Monk.   The typology is discussed in Van der Leeuw *Religion in Essence and Manifestation* (New York: Harper and Row, 1963); and elsewhere, see especially Joachim Wach *Sociology of Religion* (Chicago: University of Chicago Press, 1962). Note the evolution of monasticism in Buddhism, as described for example in Nalinaksha Dutt *Early Monastic Buddhism* (Calcutta: Oriental Book Agency, 1960).

The Existential and the Holy.   Some of the issues are discussed in my 'Beyond Eliade: The Future of Theory in Religion' *Numen*, vol. xxv, Fasc. 2 (August, 1980).

Self-help and Other-dependence.   The contrast is discussed in a theological context in my *The Yogi and the Devotee* (London: Allen and Unwin, 1968).

The Shape of Sacramental Power.   An outline of this theory is found in my *The Phenomenon of Religion* (2nd edn. London: Mowbray, 1978).

The Self and the Non-self.   A very useful clarification of relations between these ideas is formed in Lynn A. de Silva *The Problem of the Self in Buddhism and Christianity* (New York: Barnes & Noble, 1979). The question of how to interpret the Buddhist outlook is central to the discussion of mystical experience, e.g., R. C. Zaehner in his *At Sundry Times* (London: Faber and Faber, 1958) reads a Self into Buddhism. For a critique of this not uncommon Western view see my 'Interpretation and Mystical Experience' *Religious Studies* vol. 1, no. 1 (1965), and 'Mystical Experience' *Sophia*, vol. 1, no. 1 (April 1962), and the volumes *Mystics and Scholars*, edited by Harold Coward and Terence Penelhum (Waterloo, Ontario: Waterloo University Press, 1977) and Steven T. Katz *Mysticism and Philosophical Analysis* (New York: Oxford University Press, 1978).

The Drama and the Centre.   For a recent placement of drama and ritual, see T. J. Scheff *Catharsis in Healing, Ritual and Drama* (Berkeley: University of California Press, 1979). For the way history is perceived dramatically, see Reinhold Niebuhr *The Self and the Drama of History* (New York: Scribner, 1955) and my *In Search of Christianity* (New York: Harper and Row, 1979).

Rebirth and Karma.   A full discussion of the afterlife is found in John Hick *Death and Eternal Life* (New York: Harper and Row, 1977; London: Fount Paperbacks, 1979). I discuss the idea of Eastern liberation in 'Living Liberation: *jīvamukti* and *nirvāna*' in E. J. Sharpe and John Hinnells (editors) *Man and His Salvation* (Manchester: Manchester University Press, 1973), and in my *Doctrine and Argument in Indian Philosophy* (London: Allen and Unwin, 1964).

CHAPTER 4
Reflections on Buddhism and Christianity

Pattern and Accident in Religion.   Some of the theoretical issues are discussed in my *The Science of Religion and the Sociology of Knowledge* (Princeton, NJ: Princeton University Press, 1973).

The Purification of Consciousness.   For a discussion of some of the problems of mystical consciousness see Robert Gimello 'Mysticism and Meditation' in Steven T. Katz (ed.) *op. cit.*, and 'Mysticism in its Context' in Steven T. Katz (ed.) *Mysticism and Religious Traditions* (New York: Oxford University Press, 1980). However, my own view is less intellectualist than Gimello's.

The Context of the Buddha's Search.   The most recent full length biography of the Buddha is that of Trevor Ling *The Buddha: Buddhist Civilization in India and Ceylon* (London: Temple Smith, 1972). As the title suggests it is very much a contextualizing account of the founder of the religion as seen in the later texts.

Types of Religious Experience.   The theory here outlined owes something of course to Otto and Söderblom, and was first presented by me in *Reasons and Faiths: an Investigation of Religious Discourse* (London: Routledge and Kegan Paul, 1958). See also 'Problems of the Application of Western terminology to Theravada Buddhism, with special reference to the relationship between the Buddha and the Gods' *Religion*, vol. 2, no. 1 (1972), and 'Nirvana and Timelessness' in *Journal of Dharma*, vol. 1, no. 4 (July, 1976).

The Numinous in Buddhism.   A classical account of Buddhist worship and bhakti is Har Dayal *The Bodhisattva Doctrine in Buddhist Sanskrit Literature* (Delhi: Motilal Banarsidass, 1970). There is much relevant material in Mircea Eliade *Shamanism: Archaic Techniques of Ecstasy* (Princeton, NJ: Princeton University Press, 1964). See also, for the sacramental ambience of the numinous, Guiseppe Tucci *The Religions of Tibet* (Berkeley: University of California Press, 1979).

Substance and Sacrament in the Indian Tradition. I have found some of the following useful in reflecting on the diversity of the Hindu tradition Alain Daniélou *Hindu Polytheism* (Princeton NJ: Princeton University Press, 1964); Nirad C. Chaudhuri's maverick and sometimes suggestive *Hinduism* (New York: Oxford University Press, 1979); Mircea Eliade's magisterial *Yoga, Immortality and Freedom* (London: Routledge and Kegan Paul, 1958) and the also magisterial Surendranath Dasgupta's writings, especially of course his *History of Indian Philosophy* (Cambridge: Cambridge University Press, 5 vols., 1951-1955).

The Logic of Non-self. See my *Buddhism and the Death of God* (Southampton: University of Southampton, 1970), and Edward Conze *Buddhist Thought in India* (London: Allen and Unwin, 1962).

Buddhism as Pure Mysticism. This view of Theravada is found in a different form in K. N. Jayatilleke *Early Buddhist Theory of Knowledge* (London: Allen and Unwin, 1963).

The Validity and Invalidity of Religious Experience. See Steven T. Katz, *op. cit.*, (1978).

Prophetic Religion and Christ in History. For modern 'prophetic' interpretations see Hendrik Kraemer *The Christian Message in a Non-Christian World* (Grand Rapids: Kregel, 1961), and A. Van Leeuwen *Christianity in World History* (New York: Scribner, 1964).

Identity, Myth and Personalism. Some of the issues are explored in John Perry (ed.) *Personal Identity* (Berkeley: University of California Press, 1975) and in my 'Religion, Myth and Nationalism' in *The Scottish Journal of Religious Studies*, vol. 1, no. 1 (1980), and 'Creation, Persons and the Meaning of Life' in R. Ruddock (ed.) *Six Approaches to the Person* (London: Routledge and Kegan Paul, 1972).

The Mystical in Christianity. For a recent anthology see Walter Capps and Wendy Wright (editors) *Silent Fire* (New York: Harper and Row, 1978). Influential have been Evelyn Underhill's classic *Mysticism: A Study in the Nature and Development of Man's Spiritual Consciousness* (New York: E. P. Dutton, 1961); W. R. Inge's *Christian Mysticism* (New York: Meridian, 1956); F. von Hügel's *The Mystical Element in Religion as studied in St Catherine of Geona and her Friends* (London: Dent, 1909); and David Knowles' *The Nature of Mysticism* (New York: Hawthorne, 1966). Such writers were largely unaware of Indian and Far Eastern parallels and contrasts.

Emptying in Christianity. A number of recent writers have stressed kenotic forms of Christianity in relation to Buddhism. As for the general problem see Michael Pye and Robert Morgan (eds.) *The*

Cardinal Meaning: Essays in Comparative Hermeneutics, Buddhism and Christianity (The Hague, Mouton, 1973).

A Final Note on Christian Mysticism. See my 'History of Mysticism' in Paul Edwards (ed.) *The Encyclopedia of Philosophy* (New York: The Free Press, 1967).

CHAPTER 5
The Great Vehicle and the Protestant Spirit

The Logic of Devotion.   The argument is laid out also in a different form in my *The Long Search* (New York: Little Brown, 1979).

Novelty in the Great Vehicle.   See the seminal *Skilful Means: A Concept in Mahayana Buddhism* (London: Duckworth, 1978) by Michael Pye, as also his 'Assimilation and Skilful Means', *Religion*, Vol. 1, No. 2 (1971).

Two Levels of Truth. See a recent discussion: Chris Gudmunsen *Wittgenstein and Buddhism* (London: Macmillan, 1977).

Developments in Greater Vehicle Philosophy.   The writings of Edward Conze are most important, of course, especially his *Buddhist Thought in India* (London: Allen and Unwin, 1962); *Buddhist Wisdom Books* (do., 1958); *Thirty Years of Buddhist Studies* (London: Cassirer, 1967); and his various editions of the *Prajñāpāramitā* texts (London: Luzac, 1973); *Vajracchedikā* (Rome: Serie Orientale XIII, 1957); *The Large Sūtra on Perfect Wisdom* (Berkeley: University of California Press, 1975); *The Perfection of Wisdom in Eight Thousand Lines and Its Verse Summary* (Bolinas: Four Seasons Foundation, 1973); *The Prajñāpāramitā Literature* (Indo-Iranian Monographs, no. 6, The Hague: Mouton, 1960). Also important are: Étienne Lamotte *Histoire du Bouddhisme Indien* (Louvain: Publications Universitaires, 1958); A. Rawlinson *Studies in the Lotus Sutra* (2 vols., University of Lancaster Doctoral Thesis, 1972); D. T. Suzuki *Outlines of Mahayana Buddhism* (London: Allen and Unwin, 1963), and R. H. Robinson's fine *Early Madhyamika in India and China* (Madison: University of Wisconsin Gress, 1967).

Nirvana is Samsara. See J. Takakura *The Essentials of Buddhist Philosophy* (3rd edn., Honolulu: University of Hawaii Press, 1956); and D. J. Kalupahana 'Prolegomena to the Philosophy of Relations in Buddhism' *University of Ceylon Review*, 19 (1964).

The Bodhisattva. Quote from *Siksāsamuccaya* 281, in E. Conze *Buddhist Texts* (London: Cassirer, 1954) p. 132. See also I. B. Horner (tr.) *Milindapañha: Milinda's Questions* (London: Luzac, 1969).

The Three Bodies of the Buddha.   See my 'The Logos and Eastern Beliefs' *Expository Times*, 1974, and the discussion in *The Religious Experience of Mankind* (New York: Scribner, 1969).

Transformation Body of the Buddha.   A good discussion is found in Sangharakshita *Survey of Buddhism* (2nd edn. Bangalore, 1959).

Buddhas as Celestial.   See the still delightful account in Sir Charles Eliot *Hinduism and Buddhism*, vol. 2 (London: Routledge and Kegan Paul, 1954).

Buddhas: Gods and not Gods.   See the full discussion in M. M. J. Marasinghe *Gods in Early Buddhism* (University of Sri Lanka Press, 1974); and the argument in my 'Precept and Theory in Sri Lanka', *Religion*, vol. 3, no. 1 (1973).

The Unity of Buddhas and the Non-dual Experience.   See my *Reasons and Faiths*, and Raimundo Panikkar *El Silencio del Dios* (Madrid: Guadiana, 1970).

The Philosophical Argument for Unity.   See Toshihko Izutsu *Towards a Philosophy of Zen Buddhism* (Tehran: Imperial Iranian Academy of Philosophy, 1977).

The Devotional Turn.   An economical account is to be found in Trevor Ling *A History of Religion East and West* (London: Macmillan, 1968).

Belief and the Buddhas.   Relevant are D. T. Suzuki's classic investigations of the Lankāvatāra: e.g., in *Studies in the Lankāvatāra Sutra* (London: Routledge and Kegan Paul, 1930).

Buddhism and the Business of Rent-a-God.   I offer the suggestion in the spirit of serious levity displayed by my friend and colleague Edward Conze, regarding whose achievements see my obituary *The Middle Way*, vol. 54, no. 4 (February 1980) and other tributes there.

Pure Land and Martin Luther.   Quotes from: T. de Bary and others (eds.) *Sources of Japanese Tradition* (New York: Columbia University Press, 1958), p. 217, from *Tannisho* 'Collection Inspired by Concern over Heresy'; and from Spitz and Lewis *Luther's Works*, vol. 34 (Philadelphia: Muhlenberg Press, 1960), p. 337.

The Dramatization of Experience and Grace.   I work out this theme in *In Search of Christianity* (New York: Harper and Row, 1979).

The Vitality of Numinous Dependence and the Question of Validity.   See John Baillie *The Idea of Revelation in Recent Thought* (New York: Columbia University Press, 1956); also my article 'Karl Barth' in Paul Edwards (ed.) *The Encyclopedia of Philosophy*.

Self-criticism and the 19th Century.   A major philosophical appraisal is Van Harvey's *The Historian and the Believer* (New York: Macmillan, 1966). See also Claude Welch's excellent *Protestant Thought in the Nineteenth Century* (New Haven: Yale University Press, 1972) and John Macquarrie's compendious *Twentieth Century Religious Thought* (London: SCM Press, 1970).

A Comparison of Jesus and Muhammad.   W. Montgomery Watt's *Muhammad: Prophet and Statesman* (London: Oxford University Press, 1964) is very useful, as an example of modern evaluation of the evidence.

Fruits of the Critical Mind.   On demythologization see Rudolf Bultmann *Faith and Understanding* (New York: Harper and Row, 1969): the problem of experience and religious truth is explored variously. The beginnings of an interesting approach were found in Paul Tillich *Christianity and the Encounter of World Religions* (New York: Columbia University Press, 1937).

Buddhist so-called Idealism and the Problem of Representation.   The quotation is from E. Conze's article on the Mahayana in R. C. Zaehner (ed.) *Concise Encyclopedia of Living Faiths* (London: Hutchinson, 1959).

Buddhism between Idealism and Realism.   See the account of Vijñanavāda in A. K. Warder *Indian Buddhism* (Delhi: Motilal Banarsidass 1970).

The Hua-yen Variant.   the most decisive recent work is Robert Gimello *Chih-yen and the Foundations of Hua-yen: A Study in the Sinification of Buddhism* (New York: Columbia University Press, 1981). More pious, but enjoyable is Francis H. Cook *Hua-yen Buddhism: The Jewel Net of Indra* (University Park: Pennsylvania State University Press, 1977).

The Modernity of Buddhism.   Popular works making this point in a rather sophisticated way are Fritjof Capra *The Tao of Physics* (New York, Bantam Books, 1975) and Filmer S. C. Northrop *The Meeting of East and West* (New York: Macmillan, 1946).

Buddhism and Myth.   A major study is T. O. Ling *Buddhism and the Mythology of Evil* (London: Allen and Unwin, 1962).

Religion, Science and Symbolic Values.   Some of the issues I discussed in 'The Universe keeps hitting back' *Listener* October 23, 1975, and 'The Ethical Meaning of Science' *The Advancement of Science*, New Issue No. 2, September 1976.

CHAPTER 6
The Buddhist Meaning of Christianity:
The Christian Meaning of Buddhism

The Relationship between Buddhism and Christianity. Apart from the works already cited, it is useful to consider the relation between experience and the transcendent in such discussions as in my *Philosophers and Religious Truth* (2nd edn. enlarged, London: SCM Press, 1969).

Experience and the Transcendent. See John E. Smith *Experience and God* (New York: Oxford University Press, 1968) and H. D. Lewis *Our Experience of God* (London: Allen and Unwin, 1958) for a different approach from mine.

Classifying the Concept of Transcendence. For some traditional views see Josef Pieper *The Silence of St Thomas* (London: Faber & Faber, 1957); F. L. Prestige *God in Patristic Thought* (London: SPCK, 1952) and E. Gilson *God and Philosophy* (New Haven: Yale University Press, 1941).

The Transcendent and Empirical Access. For further discussion on this see my *Science of Religion and the Sociology of Knowledge* (Princeton, NJ: Princeton University Press, 1973).

The Paradox of Religious Experience. For recent, rather diverse discussions, see T. R. Miles *Religious Experience* (London: Macmillan, 1972) and my *The Philosophy of Religion* (2nd edn. New York: Oxford University Press, 1979).

The Power of Experience. This is celebrated in my already cited *The Religious Experience of Mankind* (New York: Scribner, 1969; London: Fontana, 1971).

The Existence or Non-existence of God: Does it Matter? The thought might appeal to J. N. Findlay, in relation to his celebrated Ontological disproof (which however may have a deeper existential meaning) – see A. G. N. Flew and Alisdair MacIntyre *New Essays in Philosophical Theology* (London: SCM Press, 1956).

The Need for the Focus. This terminology I use in *The Phenomenon of Religion* and *The Concept of Worship* (New York: St Martin's Press, 1972).

A Question of Priorities: Dhyāna and Bhakti. The contrast is crucial for much of religion. In the Indian context it is discussed in *The Yogi and the Devotee* (London: Allen and Unwin, 1968).

Neoplatonism and Buddhism. The quotation is from Pseudo-Dionysius *De divinis nominibus*, 1:1-2, in C. E. Rolt *On the Divine Names and Mystical Theology* (London: SPCK, 1971).

The Relation of Criticism to the Spiritual. This has been an important topic for modern Christian discussion – as in Alec Vidler (ed.) *Soundings: Essays concerning Christian Understanding* (Cambridge: Cambridge University Press, 1962).

Complementarity between Theism and the Great Vehicle. A recent nod in this direction is found in Hans Küng *Does God Exist?* (New York: Doubleday, 1980; London: Collins, 1980).

The Problem of Karma. This has been explored recently in the Indian context by David L. Gosling *The Impact of Science on Indian Society* (University of Lancaster Doctoral Thesis, 1973).

Religions and the Secular Ideologies. An interesting discussion is Trevor Ling *Buddha, Marx and God* (New York: St Martin's Press, 1979).

CHAPTER 7
Secular Ideologies: A First Anatomy

Secular Ideologies versus Traditional Religions. Influential discussions are found in Paul Tillich *Systematic Theology*, vol. 1 (Chicago: University of Chicago Press, 1973) and *What is Religion?* (New York: Harper and Row, 1969). Also see my 'Ways of Looking: Religion, Philosophy and the Future' *Encounter* (London, March 1978). And in relation to the question of the study of religion 'Towards a dialogue at the level of the science of religion: a reply to Ren Jiyu' *Ching Feng* vol. xxii, no. 4, Dec. 1979. See also Jorge Larrain *The Concept of Ideology* (London: Hutchinson, 1979).

The French Revolution and 'The National Assumption'. See for instance Eric J. Hobsbawn *Age of Revolution: 1789 to 1848* (London: Weidenfeld and Nicolson, 1962).

The Theory of the Nation State. The best survey of theories is Anthony D. Smith *Theories of Nationalism* (London: Duckworth, 1971).

Nationalism and Chauvinism. The relationship is brought out in the article 'Nationalism' by K. Deutsch in *Encyclopedia Britannica*, 1975.

Ethnicism and Oppression. See E. Franklin Frazier *Race and Culture Contacts in the Modern World* (Boston: Beacon Press,

1965), and Jaroslav Krejčí and Vitezslav Velinsky *Ethnic and Political Nations in Europe* (London: Croom Helm, 1980).

The Development of Totalitarianism.   A good general history is James Joll *Europe Since 1870: An International History* (Harmondsworth, Middlesex: Penguin Books, 1976).

Social Democracy in the West.   For a general account S. I. Benn and R. S. Peters *Social Principles and the Democratic State* (London: Allen and Unwin, 1959); and for a Popperian defence, see Bryan Magee *The New Radicalism* (New York: St Martin's Press, 1963).

The Analysis of the Nation State.   Much of the discussion here echoes my account in 'Religion, Myth and Nationalism', *Scottish Journal of Religious Studies*, Vol. 1, no. 1, (1980).

History, Nationhood and Symbols.   On the general question of the analysis of symbols, see U. Eco *A Theory of Semiotics* (Bloomington: Indiana University Press, 1976); M. Eliade *Myth and Reality* (New York: Harper and Row, 1967); Paul Ricoeur *The Symbolism of Evil* (New York: Harper and Row, 1967), Victor Turner *The Forest of Symbols* (Ithaca, New York: Cornell University Press, 1967).

The Structure of National Substance.   See also L. W. Doob *Patriotism and Nationalism: Their Psychological Foundations* (New Haven: Yale University Press, 1964) – but I prefer a performative rather than a psychological analysis.

'We' or 'Ushood'.   I follow partially Martin Buber *I and Thou* (2nd edn. New York: Scribner, 1958). See also P. Giglioli (ed.) *Language and Social Context* (Harmondsworth: Penguin Books, 1972). In regard to the notion of a 'Substantial' identity see Delmer M. Brown *Nationalism in Japan: An Introductory Historical Analysis* (Berkeley: University of California Press, 1955) and R. K. Hall (ed.) *Kokutai no Hongi, Cardinal Principles of the National Entity of Japan* (Cambridge, Mass.: Harvard University Press, 1949).

The Nation and the Open Society.   On Karl Popper, see the excellent introduction by Bryan Magee: *Karl Popper* (New York: Viking Press, 1973). Popper's most seminal political writing was, of course, *The Open Society and its Enemies*, 2 vols., 5th rev. ed. (Princeton: Princeton University Press, 1966).

CHAPTER 8
The Chinese Experience in the Modern World

China and India Compared.   For a general discussion see my 'The bounds of religion and the transition from the Tao to Mao' *Sri Lanka Journal of the Humanities*, vol. 1, no. 1 (June, 1975) and 'Maoism and Religion' in *Ching Feng*, vol. xviii, no. 4 (1975). Part of these formed the substance of a plenary address at the 13th Congress of the International Association for the History of Religions, Lancaster, 1975.

The Disintegration of the Old China.   A marvellous account of the ideas in the background of Mao's revolution is Frederick Wakeman's *History and Will: Philosophical Perspectives of Mao Tse-Tung's Thought* (Berkeley: University of California Press, 1976). This is a masterpiece in the history of ideas.

The Taiping Rebellion.   See Immanuel C. Hsu *The Rise of Modern China* (New York: Oxford University Press, 1975) and Vincent Y. Shih *The Taiping Ideology: its Sources, Interpretation and Influences* (Seattle: University of Washington Press, 1972).

The Life of Hung.   See Franz Michael and Chang Chung-li *The Taiping Rebellion: History and Documents*, 3 vols. (Seattle: University of Washington Press, 1971).

The Taiping Collapse.   Mao's own critique of the Taipings can be gleaned from *On New Democracy* and *On Practice* ((Peking: Selected Works of Mao Tse-Tung, 1953).

Ideology and Rebellion.   See the conclusions of S. Y. Teng's very full *The Taiping Rebellion and the Western Powers* (Oxford: Clarendon Press, 1971).

Confucianism and the Challenge to China.   For a general view see Wing-tsit Chan *Religious Trends in Modern China* (New York: Octagon, 1970).

Confucianism and Performatives.   I have been greatly influenced here by Herbert Fingarette's masterly *Confucius: The Secular as Sacred* (New York: Harper and Row, 1972). For a good systematic account of performatives and their relationship to theism, see Donald Evans *The Logic of Self-Involvement* (London: SCM Press, 1969).

Confucianism as a Resource.   A recent attempt to look at these aspects of Confucianism which can be abstracted and used in a wider world, eclectically, see Julia Ching *Confucianism and Christianity* (Tokyo and New York: Kōdansha International, 1977).

Chinese Options: Buddhism.   A good general survey is K. K. S. Ch'en *Buddhism in China, A Historical Survey* (Princeton: Princeton University Press, 1964). The various works of Holmes Welch are important, notably *The Buddhist Revival in China* (Cambridge, Mass.: Harvard University Press, 1964) and *The Practice of Chinese Buddhism* (1900-1950) (as above, 1967).

Chinese Options: Taoism.   Here and elsewhere the importance of Joseph Needham's work is, of course, impossible to overrate: *Science and Civilization in China* 5 volumes (Cambridge: Cambridge University Press, 1954-1970).

The Attraction of Marxism.   Quote from *Selected Works*, 1.300 'On Practice'. For a general discussion see my *Mao* (London: Collins, 1974) and Jerome Ch'en *Mao and the Chinese Revolution* (New York: Oxford University Press, 1965).

Mao and History. Apart from Frederic Wakeman's *History and Will* aforementioned, I owe a lot to Stuart R. Schram's writings, e.g., *Chairman Mao Talks to the People* (New York: Pantheon Books, 1975), *Mao Tse-tung* (New York: Simon and Schuster, 1967) and *The Political Thought of Mao Tse-tung* (New York, Praeger, 1963).

CHAPTER 9
Secular Ideology, Religion and Science

The logic of pluralism can be set forth, as in my 'Does a universal standard of values need to be higher-order? *Science and Absolute Values, ICUS Proceedings* (London, 1974).

Utilitarianism and Beyond.   Among other modern accounts of utilitarianism see Alasdair MacIntyre *A Short History of Ethics* (New York: Macmillan, 1966), J. J. C. Smart *An Outline of a System of Utilitarian Ethics* (Melbourne: Melbourne University Press, 1961) and J. J. C. Smart and Bernard Williams *Utilitarianism: For and Against* (Cambridge: Cambridge University Press, 1973). Also my own work 'Negative Utilitarianism' *Mind*, vol. 67, p. 542 (1958).

Social Personalism and Tradition.   The problem of tradition and how best to use it is posed, among other places, in Karl Popper *Conjectures and Refutations: The Growth of Scientific Knowledge* (New York: Harper and Row, 1968).

A Transcendental Logic of Personalism. The effects of differing kinds of transcendentalism on ethics can be seen from David

Little and Sumner B. Twiss *Comparative Religious Ethics* (New York: Harper and Row, 1978) and Ian T. Ramsey *Christian Ethics and Contemporary Philosophy* (New York: Macmillan, 1973). For varying views see Emmanual Mounier *Personalism* (South Bend: University of Notre Dame Press, 1970) and Martin Buber *Between Man and Man* (New York: Macmillan, 1965).

Christian Theism and the Person.   For rather different but well argued approaches see Paul I. Lehmann *Ethics in a Christian Context* (New York: Harper and Row, 1976), and C. C. J. Webb *God and Personality* (London: Allen and Unwin, 1918).

The Question of Poverty.   This has recently been explored by Willy Brandt and colleagues *North-South: a programme for survival* (London: Pan Books, 1980).

Empathy and Two Levels of Truth.   My position is not unlike that of John Dunn *The Way of All the Earth: Experiments in Truth and Religion* (London: Collins, 1978).

POSTSCRIPT:

Towards a New Worldview: The Pacific Mind

The Pacific Mind.   I hope to develop further this notion in a forthcoming book covering the various worldviews of the countries of the Pacific area.

INDEX

Index

Mystical experience; (*cont.*)
required, 113; and
transparency to the ultimate,
57
Mysticism; Buddhism pure,
122–5; in Christianity, 123,
131–3, 135–6, 192–3; Jewish,
131; and knowledge of the
cosmos, 288–9; paradox of
Eastern and Western, 104;
theistic and non-theistic, 52
myth, 11, 18, 26; and Buddhism
and Christianity, 170, 201;
and creation of identity,
129–30; and nationalism, 37.
See also history

Nagarjuna, 140
nation; building, 232; as daily
sacrament, 231–2; essence of,
228–9; and national
substance, 226–7; and
revolution, 235, 271–3, 295,
307; significance of territory
and descent, 223–5
nation state, 210–12, 220–1, 224;
agent of modernity, 233; and
ethnicism, 213–14; and
licence to kill, 220–2, 229
'national assumption', 209–10,
229–30, 233, 286, 306; and
groups in transition, 232
nationalism, 11, 29, 37, 41, 43,
89, 209, 287; and anti-
semitism, 30; and chauvinism,
213; defensive, 212;
dominating ideology, 311,
313; and ethnicism, 233–4;
and group identity, 13, 230–2;
growth and spread of 23–4,
205, 209–10, 220; and history,
201–2; Islamic, 23; linguistic,
284; and Marxism, 215; and
tension between plurality and
conformity, 274; and
transcendental world-views,
236–7
nature, noumenal aspect, 297–8
Navajo Indians, 32
Nazism, 18, 66–7, 205, 212–13,
214–15, 235
Needham, Joseph, 247
Nehru, J., 239, 240
Nembutsu, the, 154
Neoplatonism, 52, 84, 129, 132,
133, 249; and Buddhism, 195
Nepal, 36
Nestorianism, 31
Newton, Isaac, 53
nibbana, *see* nirvana
Nicaragua, 222, 272
Nichiren, 116
nirmānakāya, see Buddha,
Transformation Body
nirvana (nibbana), 49, 51, 54,
63, 71, 140, 178, 287, 298;
and doctrine of
impermanence, 83, 121;
identification with samsāra,
141–2; and transcendent in
Buddhism, 80–4; the *summum
bonum*, 83, 115–16. *See also*
emptiness, void
Nixon, Richard, 127, 196
non-self, doctrine of, 96–8,
119–20, 307
Norway, 225
noumenal, the, 297
numinous, the; and mysticism,
52, 53–4; and possession, 118;
subsidiary for Buddhism,
115–16; symbolization of, 87–8